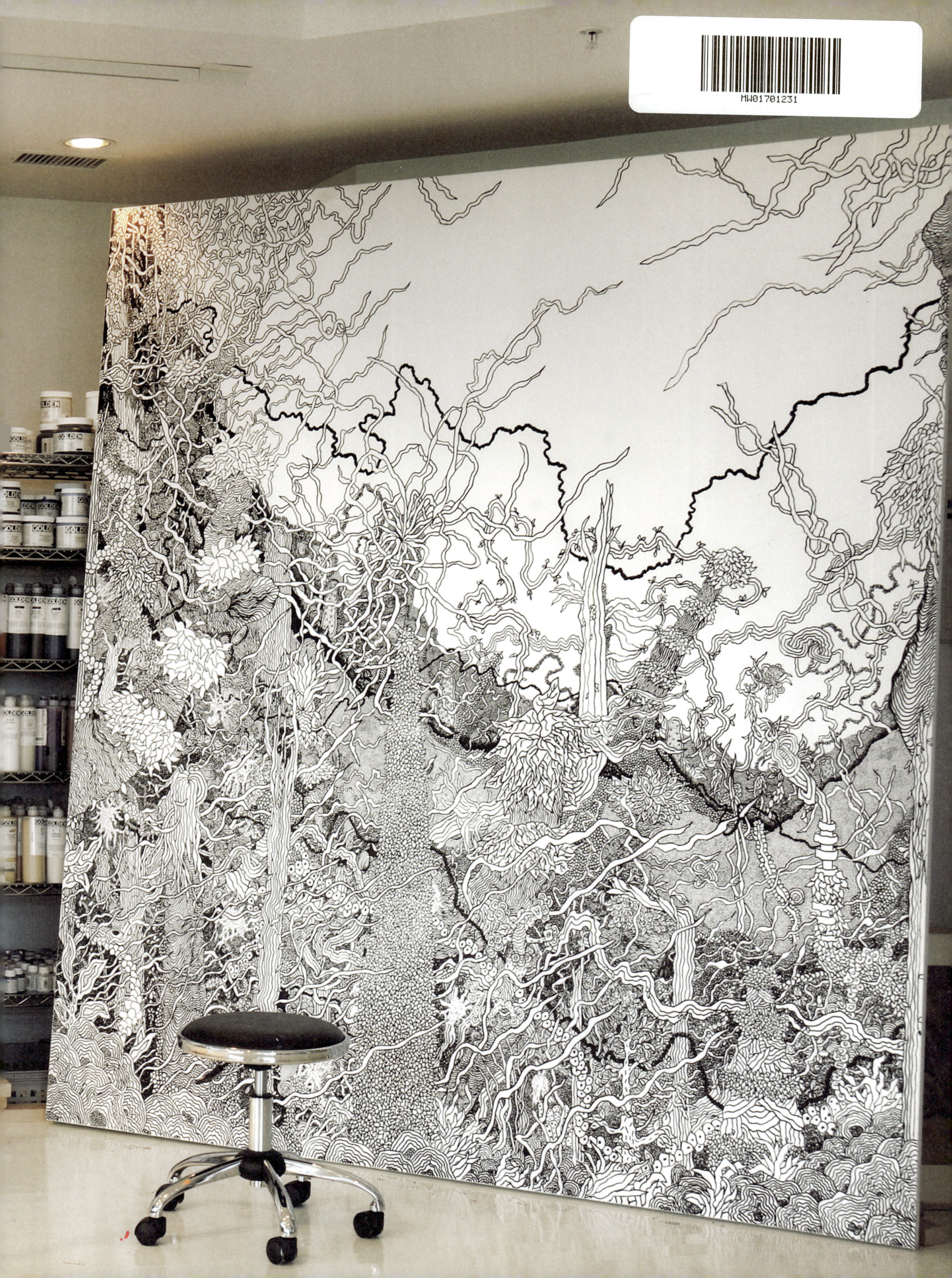
GOLDEN

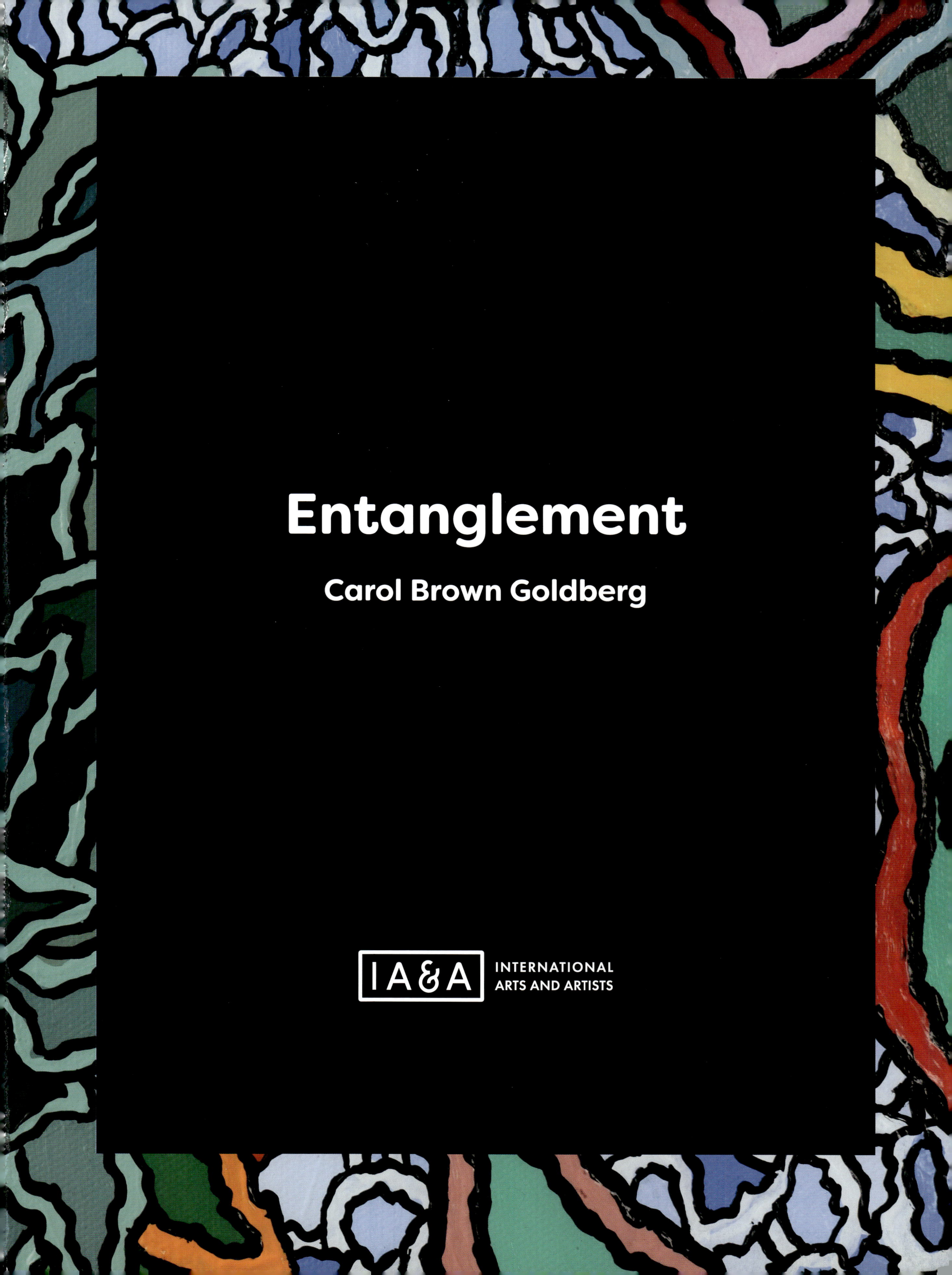

Entanglement

Carol Brown Goldberg

IA&A INTERNATIONAL ARTS AND ARTISTS

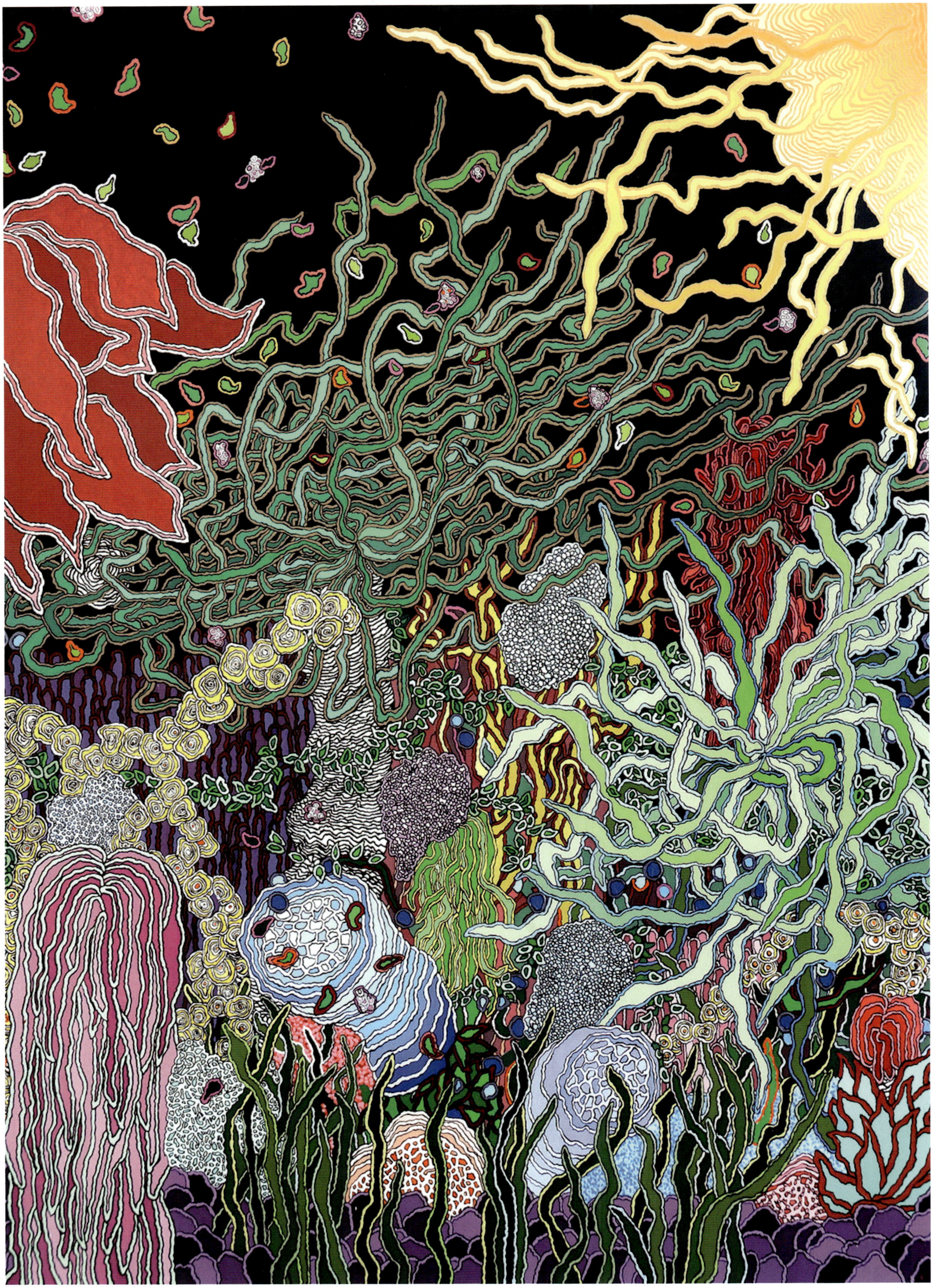

Entanglement

Carol Brown Goldberg

Entanglement emerged out of a conversation with curator Klaudio Rodriquez, about the inspiration of pen and ink on paper. We talked about the direct connection between mind and line, the spontaneous movement of pen across paper. We talked about the freedom of the hand to be instantaneously energized.

Klaudio asked... 'why not do this on canvas?'.... His suggestion was all it took to begin this series.

Published in the United States by International Arts & Artists in partnership with the American University Museum at the Katzen Arts Center.

International Arts & Artists is a nonprofit arts service organization dedicated to promoting cross-cultural understanding and exposure to the arts internationally.

Exhibition is available for tour. Contact IA&A.

9 Hillyer Court NW, Washington, DC 20008
www.artsandartists.org | 202.338.0680

Designer: Deanna Luu, IA&A Design Studio
Copy Editor: David Walker
Photographer: Gregory R. Staley
Author: Robert M. Mattison

Printed through Four Colour Print Group
2410 Frankfort Avenue
Louisville, Kentucky 40206
Printed in China

ISBN: 978-098-834-977-3
LOC: 201-893-1197

This catalogue was published in conjunction with an exhibition curated by Jack Rasmussen and organized by the American University Museum at the Katzen Arts Center, Washington, DC.

Jack Rasmussen, Director and Curator
Kristi-Anne Shaer, Associate Director

American University Museum
at the Katzen Arts Center
Washington, DC
April 3–May 27, 2018

Image Credits

Front Cover: *PM 28,* Pen and ink on paper, 29 3/4 x 22 1/2" (plate 40, page 107)

Back Cover: detail of *PM 28,* Pen and ink on paper, 29 3/4 x 22 1/2" (plate 40, page 107)

pg 1: detail of *Beverly's Garden*, 2015, Acrylic on canvas, 48 x 24" (plate 14, page 53)

pg 2: *Maggie on my Mind*, 2015, Acrylic on canvas, 79 x 58" (plate 1, page 27)

pg 8: detail of *What We Cannot Touch*, 2016, Acrylic on canvas, 72 x 36" (plate 11, page 47)

pg 25: detail of *The Garden of Uruk,* 2015, Acrylic on canvas, 48 x 24" (plate 19, page 63)

pg 89: detail of *PM 45*, 2016, Pen and ink on paper, 29 3/4 x 22 1/2" (plate 42, page 111)

pg 126: detail of *The Garden of Sumer,* 2015, Acrylic on canvas, 48 x 24" (plate 17, page 59)

Front end papers, back end papers, pg 122, and 124-125: Carol Brown Goldberg studio images courtesy of Gregory R. Staley

pg 134-135: detail of *Thank you Ad*, 2016, Acrylic on canvas, 96 x 84" (plate 4, page 33)

IA&A INTERNATIONAL ARTS AND ARTISTS

the KATZEN
AMERICAN UNIVERSITY MUSEUM
COLLEGE of ARTS & SCIENCES

Contents

Foreword

Carol Brown Goldberg's exhibition *Entanglement* offers us vivid evidence of her artmaking as the convergence of intellect, emotion, and technique. Goldberg has a remarkably edgy and inquisitive mind. Her paintings in the current exhibition—marked by images of dense, imagined foliage—are rooted in a unique interplay of tightly-packed philosophical concepts and more ethereal poetic imaginings.

In describing to me the intellectual concept of "entanglement" that fuels this body of work, Goldberg writes:

> *The idea of autonomy and interdependence is contained in Bell's Theorem of quantum entanglement with its own equation in physics... AS ABOVE SO BELOW... we are part of the universe, we are a replication of the universe... our body has billions of cells, the universe billions of stars... the micro and macro are mirror images in many ways... We are all interconnected, and the idea of consciousness among quantum particles should not surprise us. It is called 'spookiness at a distance'.*

Goldberg's love of science is already well established in her writing and art. But it would be a mistake to think the path to interpreting *Entanglement* runs solely through the field of quantum physics. Rather, as an artist, she informs these hypernatural pictures with a deep emotional connection to the experiences of her childhood. For Goldberg, the small-town Baltimore in which she grew up was a warm place—more Barry Levinson's *Liberty Heights* than John Waters' *Hairspray*. This was an environment where it seemed that everybody at least knew each other, and many were related in extended families. There was above everything a sense that people were connected—*entangled*, if you will.

In this exhibition, Goldberg uses her invented elements of nature as visual metaphors for our interconnectedness and our autonomous growth. This poetic approach seeks to resolve and reconcile two seemingly contradictory and exclusionary states of being—the solitude of the artist alone in her studio, and the interconnectivity of clans and moieties that binds us into a family, a group of friends, a community.

Entanglement is Goldberg's gift of her particularly *spooky* talent. She shows us that although we exist, work, think, and dream in our separate existences, we also are inextricably united to others.

Technically, Goldberg credits Klaudio Rodriguez, curator of the Frost Museum at Florida International University, for suggesting she try translating the spontaneity and immediacy of her small pen-and-ink works to large-scale paintings on canvas. Goldberg was able to achieve the speedy yet controlled hand-to-brain coordination required at this scale through her discovery of acrylic paint sticks. This new medium enables her to envelop us visually, drawing us deep into the work in a way that is physical and poetic:

> *I want my art to be everything and everywhere... it seems at once ordinary... just made by black lines... and extraordinary in its excess... as if I am crowding life with marks of experience with marks of people with marks of bits upon bits of information... pile ups of memory and imagined futures... my art is made inside a space where I bring the complexity of thoughts and opinions and fears and realities of existence. The work is a compression of all of art history, of all of my known history, of history of humanity... the entanglements speak to the total existence of one's life... of anyone's life...of everyone's life...*

On behalf of American University's students and friends, I want to thank Carol Brown Goldberg for sharing her art, Dr. Robert S. Mattison for his insightful catalogue essay, Dr. Nancy M. Waters for her keen eye and botanical knowledge, Michiko Okaya for her careful reading of the text, International Arts & Artists' Design Studio, and our extraordinarily talented Museum staff.

Jack Rasmussen, Director and Curator
American University Museum at the Katzen Arts Center
Washington, DC

Entanglement:

Carol Brown Goldberg's Recent Art

Dr. Robert S. Mattison

Over the past two years, Carol Brown Goldberg has created an extraordinary body of new work: the series *Entanglement*. On the one hand, these complex and stunningly beautiful paintings and drawings embody Goldberg's profound meditations on the creative process and the origins of art-making. On the other, they personify the artist's intuitive feeling for the biological world, as well as her continuing investigations of the advanced sciences of our age. These large paintings and smaller drawings propose a procreative and fecund connectedness between nature's forces and artistic activity.

The *Entanglement* works are complementary to Goldberg's paintings from 2005 to 2015, which dealt with her thoughts about the macrocosm. In them, freely painted centers and undersurfaces are overlaid with fields of radiant particles that pulsate throughout the compositions. They suggest a poetic equivalent to physicists' search for the unified field theory and "implicate order" in the universe. In *Entanglement*, Goldberg takes on the microcosm rather than the macrocosm. These new paintings and drawings embody the search for connected growth patterns in our organic world, down to its smallest and seemingly most basic level. Stylistically, Goldberg's earlier paintings were based on shimmering color and mark-making, while these more recent works rely on the growth sequences realized through drawing.

Human depictions of the mysterious and interconnected forces of nature go back to our origins. For instance, carvings on the inner walls of the Newgrange Mound in Ireland (ca. 3000–2500 BCE) show interwoven spiral motifs that could be abstracted versions of vines connecting one plant to another. Likewise, ancient Aegean artifacts such as the Kamares Ware jugs (ca. 2000–1900 BCE) feature curving, intersecting shapes seemingly derived from sea life. The jugs' swelling forms, with their bulging contours, further suggest the bountiful aquatic world. And the early medieval world featured such works as the manuscript pages of the extraordinary Lindisfarne Gospel Book (ca. 715–720), with its breathtakingly complex ornament pages depicting hybrids of animal and vegetal forms tangled in acrobatic interlaces. Such powerful belief in the fecundity of nature as both intellectual investigation and spiritual revelation is germane to Goldberg's art. In Western art history, this sensibility continued into the early Renaissance, as found in *The Hunt of the Unicorn* tapestry series (ca. 1495–1505) at the Metropolitan Museum of Art in New York.

One must also look beyond the Western world for the intricate foliate patterns that populate Goldberg's recent paintings and drawings. Near and Far Eastern art filled Goldberg's childhood home, the

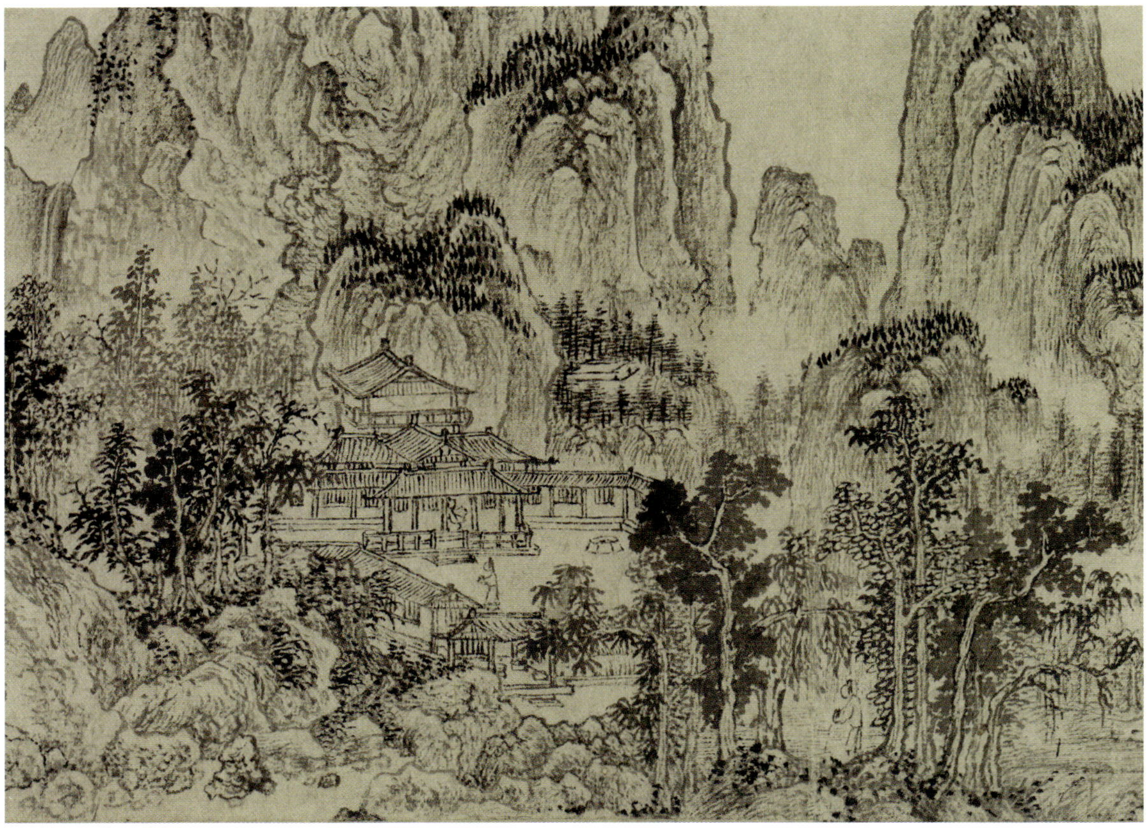

fig. 1
Zhao Yuan
Landscape in the Style of Yan Wengui and Fan Kuan
China ca. 1370
Handscroll; ink on paper
9 13/16 x 30 1/2"

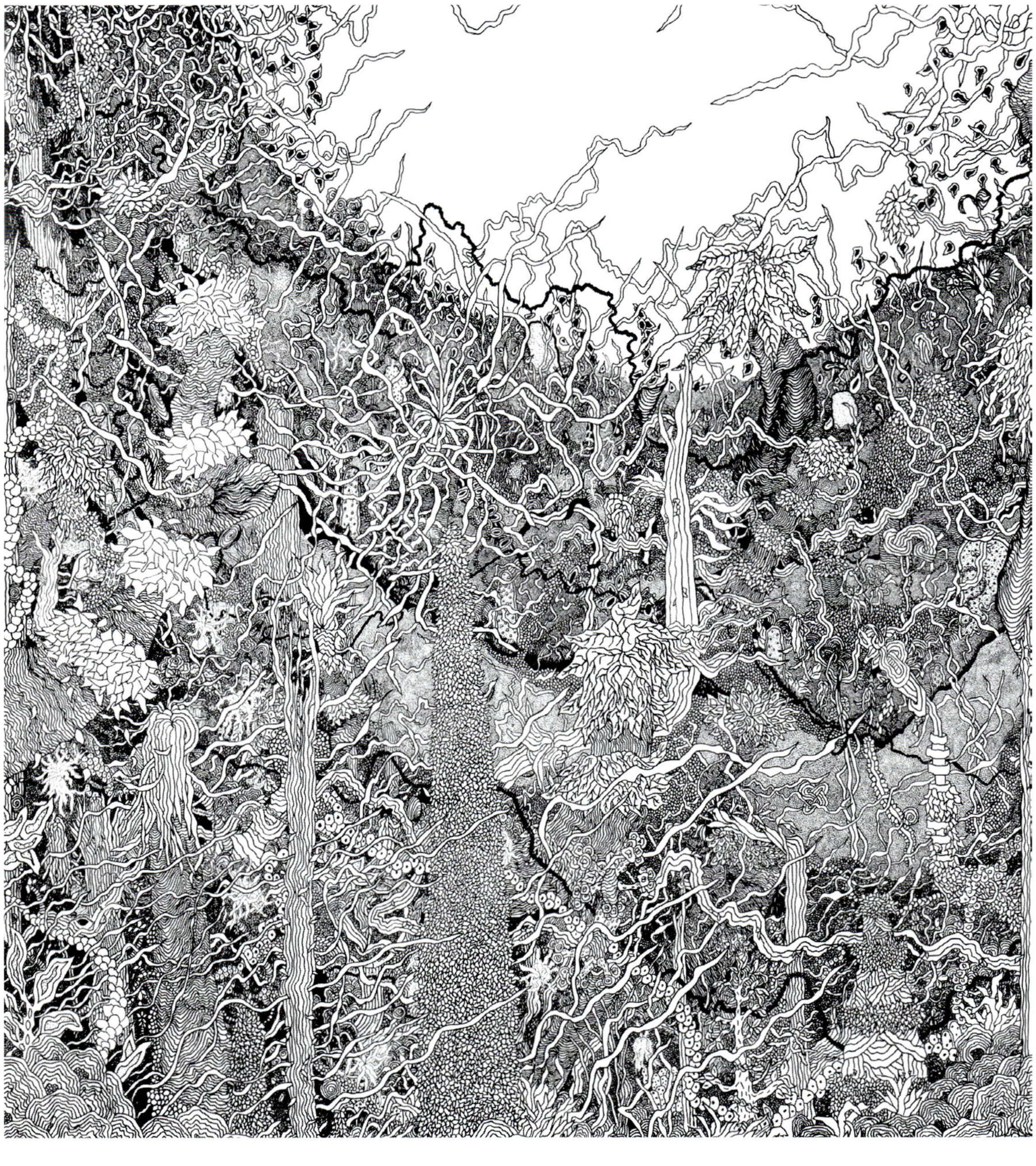

fig. 2
Carol Brown Goldberg
Thank you Franz
2016
Acrylic on canvas
96 x 84"
(plate 5, page 35)

majority of it gifts sent to her mother by an uncle who had an import/export business. In college, Goldberg spent two years studying the Chinese language, which she termed a "philosophical exercise." She spent much of her museum time during the 1980s at the Arthur M. Sackler Gallery and the Freer Gallery of Art, in her words, "looking at Far and Near Eastern art–very influenced by these works." In the Ottoman Empire, a culture in which animal and human depictions were forbidden, the blue- and turquoise-glazed tiles found in mosques and in such royal structures as the Topkapi Palace, Istanbul (1638), capture in abstract form the bounty of the organic world. *The Garden Prayer Carpet* (Iran, seventeenth century) uses intricate patterns to represent Paradise as a shady garden with rivers, dense fields of trees, and flowers. Goldberg has commented that she was particularly influenced "by the detailed flat space of Islamic art."

One major source for Islamic art was the rich and ancient traditions of China. Goldberg's *Entanglement* series draws on the remarkable developments in Chinese landscape painting of the Northern Song Dynasty (960–1127), as seen in the master Fan Kuan. Works by Fan Kuan and those in his style are often monumental compositions set forth in vertical formats. They feature dense natural forms and intricately harmonious shape relationships. Natural elements are crisply drawn, and the black-and-white compositions feature rich tonalities. *Landscape in the Style of Yan Wengui and Fan Kuan* (ca. 1370) (fig. 1) contrasts a highly detailed and imaginary landscape with empty spaces above. (Goldberg has spoken of "honoring the 'empty' space" in Chinese landscape painting.) The Song period landscape is a view of nature that includes humans but is uncorrupted by their presence. It represents no specific place, but its intricate composition, ordered despite its complexity, expresses the belief in an intelligent universe.

The Northern Song style of nature painting has a powerful heritage in Chinese art extending to the Qing Dynasty (1644–1911), as can be seen in Wang Shimin's *Landscape in the Style of Huang Gongwang* (1666). In this work, an abundance of natural forms are layered vertically, and appear to morph one into another. The brush does not pause anywhere to dwell on differentiation, but concentrates on transforming mass into movement. Goldberg's *Entanglement* works are profoundly related to the stylistic discoveries expressed in such works, as well as to their philosophical convictions about nature.

Along with her global context, Goldberg is a quintessentially American artist. Nature was essential to America's self-definition during the

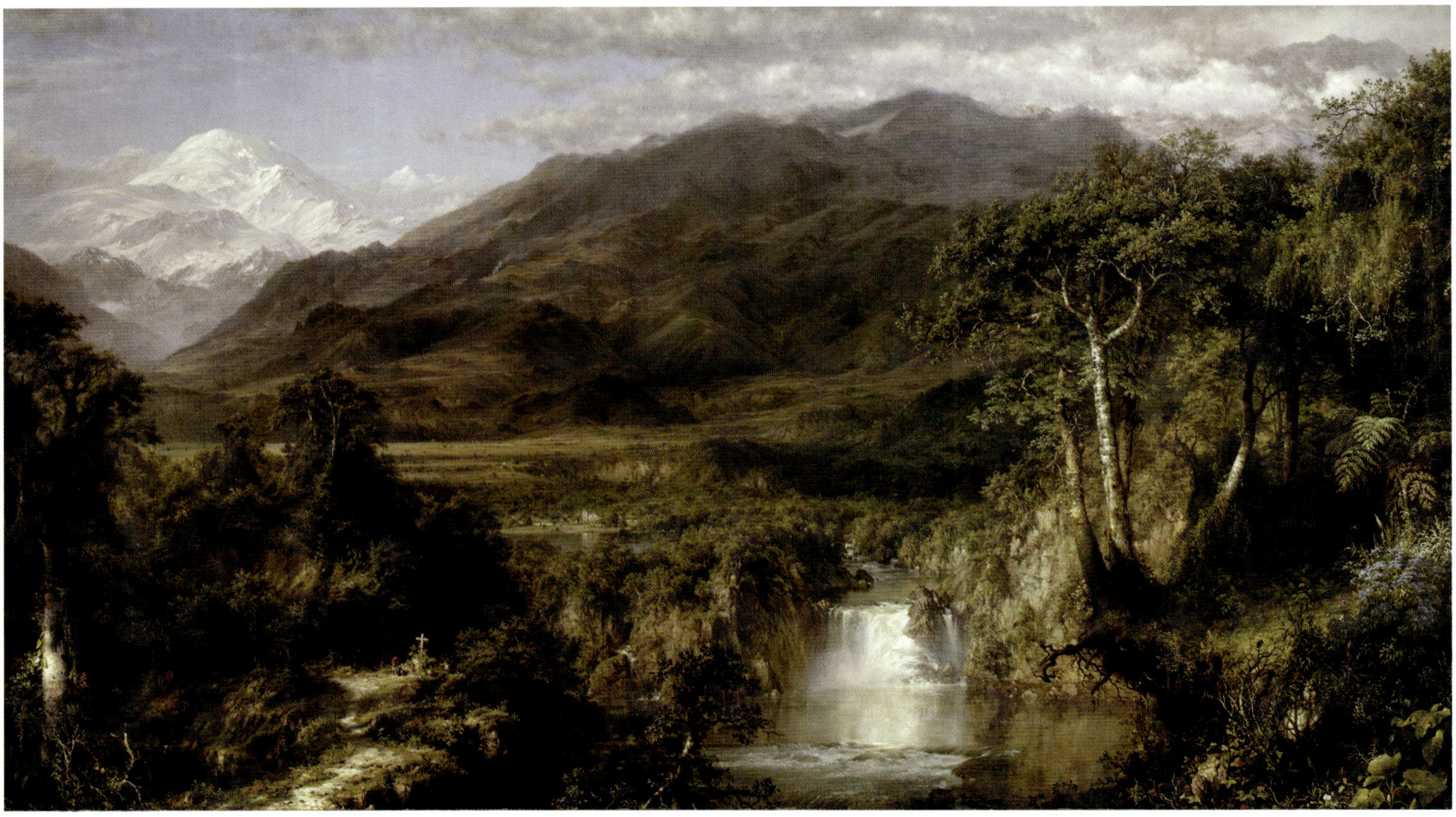

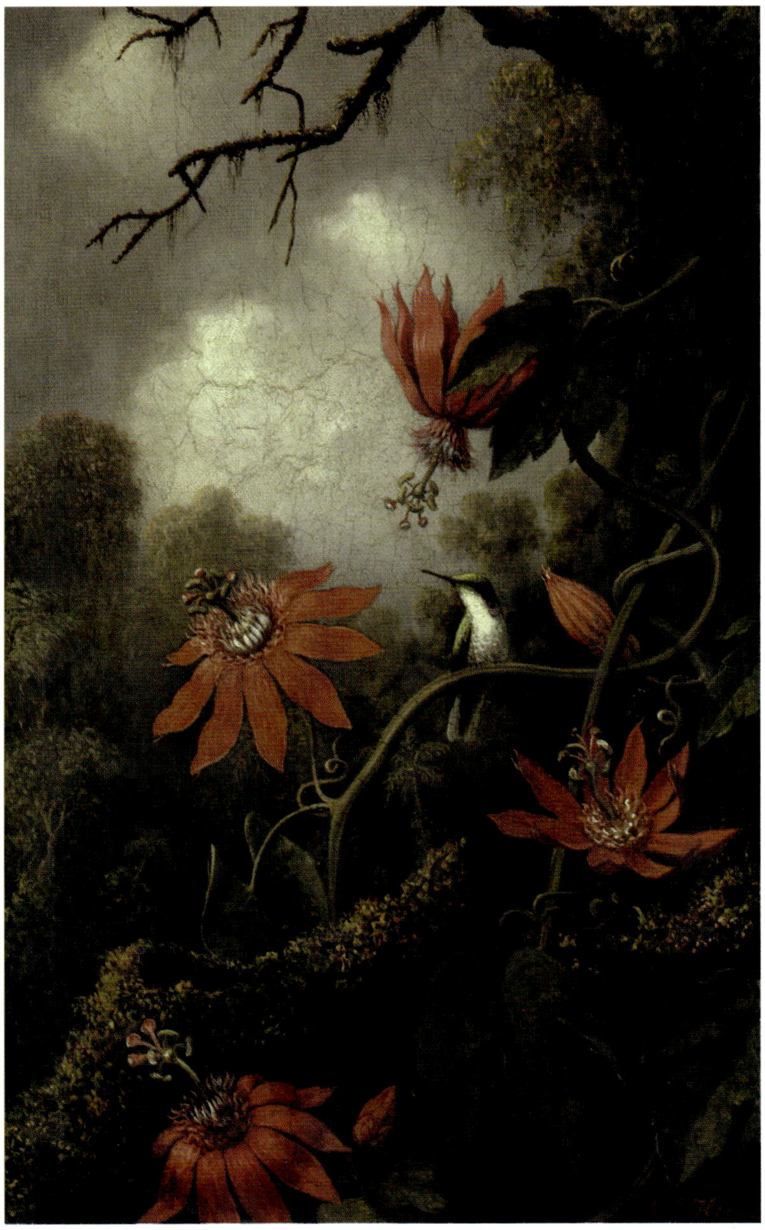

TOP fig. 3
Frederic Edwin Church
Heart of the Andes
1859
Oil on canvas
66 1/8 x 119 1/4"
Image copyright © The Metropolitan Museum of Art
Image source: Art Resource, NY

BOTTOM fig. 4
Martin Johnson Heade
Hummingbird and Passionflowers
1875-85
Oil on canvas
20 x 12"
Image copyright © The Metropolitan Museum of Art
Image source: Art Resource, NY

eighteenth and nineteenth centuries, when it was said that Europe had the history, civilizations, and the cities, while America had nature. America was called the "natural paradise" and the "new Eden." The Hudson River was sometimes referred to as the cathedral "nave" of the nation, and the country's first important group of artists was the Hudson River School of landscape painters, who in the mid-19th century painted this scenic region. It is significant that one of the greatest repositories of works by those artists is Washington, DC, Goldberg's home. The Corcoran College of Art, the institution at which Goldberg studied, housed a major collection of that art, including works by such figures as Martin Johnson Heade, Asher B. Durand, and Frederic Edwin Church.

For the Hudson River School artists, especially Church and Heade, nature was both a scientific and a spiritual experience: a dual sensibility that is intrinsic to Goldberg's art. These 19th-century American artists worked on the cusp of an age when biology, botany, and geology were advancing as sciences. At the same time, nature as a mystical entity was essential to the imagination of the age. The naturalist Alexander von Humboldt was a key figure in this dualistic approach.

Von Humboldt, who was born and educated in Prussia, came to America in the late 18th century in search of its natural wonders. Between 1799 and 1804, he explored South America, documenting his travels in his multi-volume treatise *Cosmos* (Volume I, 1845), which became a seminal book among scientists and other intelligentsia of the time. In essence, von Humboldt extrapolated his personal observations of the interactive elements of nature with detailed analyses worthy of Charles Darwin. He proposed a holistic view of the universe as a single interacting entity. But, contrary to Darwin, von Humboldt concluded that the multifaceted order of the world could only result from a "divine presence." Thus, he combined science with a spiritual understanding of the forces of nature.

Both Church and Heade were mesmerized by von Humboldt's treatise *Cosmos*, and each of them followed his journey to South America, often painting the sites described by him. Church's immense painting *Heart of the Andes* (1859, Metropolitan Museum of Art, New York) (fig. 3) sets the giant mountain range against a profusion of foliage that dominates the foreground of the work. Though rendered with accurate detail, the plant life represents four different climatic zones that do not coexist in nature. So Church's painting is at once science-based and an imaginative invention. Goldberg's paintings evoke the dense, interwoven vegetation found in this work; more significantly, they participate in the synthesis of science and free artistic inspiration that motivated Church. When completed, *The Heart of the Andes* toured America as an inspirational lesson in the grandeur of the Americas. On a more intimate level, the less imposing works of Martin Johnson Heade, such as *Hummingbird and Passionflowers* (ca. 1875–85) (fig. 4), capture the detailed wonders of the biological world.

The specific impetus for Goldberg's *Entanglement* series came from a 2015 exhibition in which she was invited to participate at The Phillips Collection, Washington, DC. The exhibition, *One on One: Carol Brown Goldberg/Henri Matisse*, was curated by Klaus Ottmann, who personally

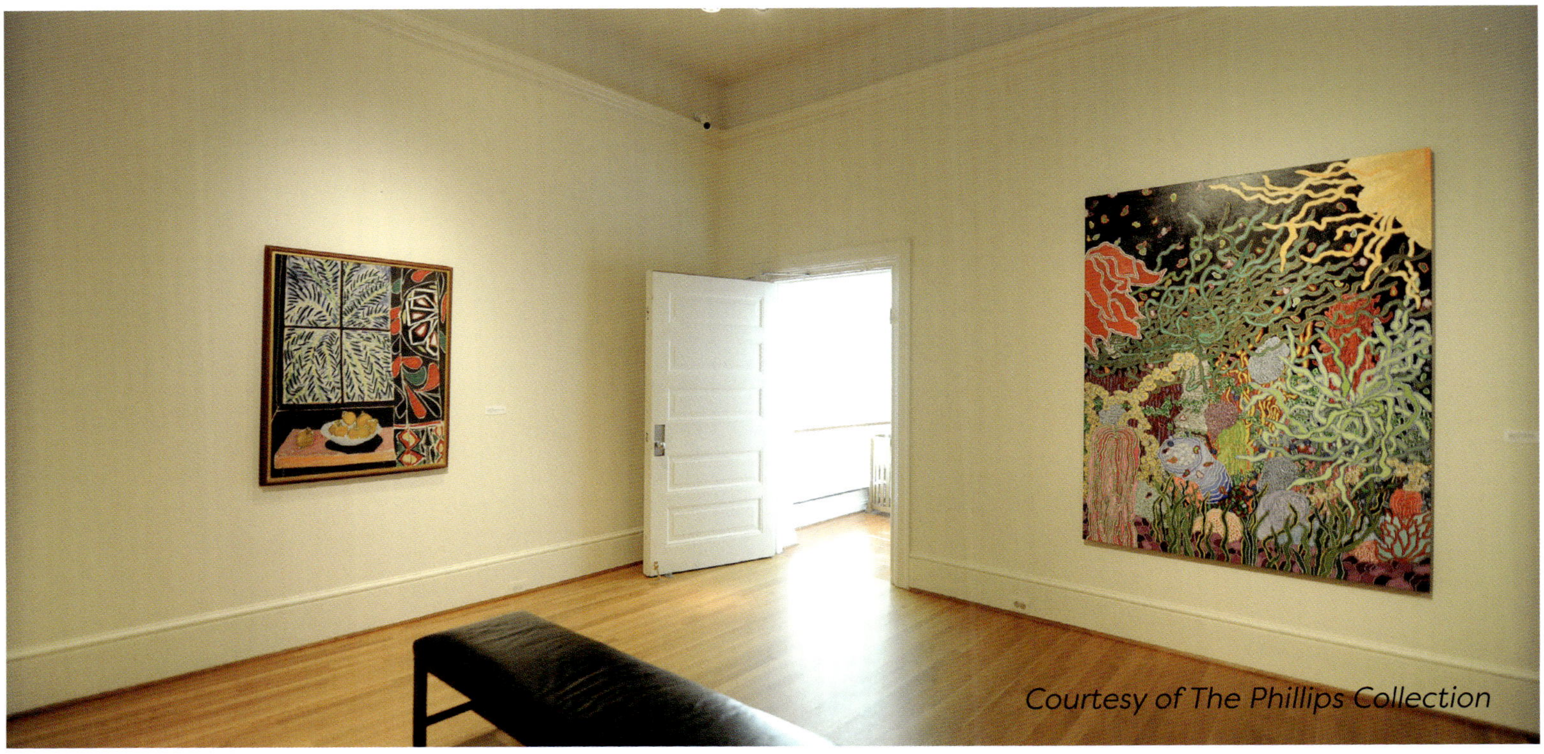

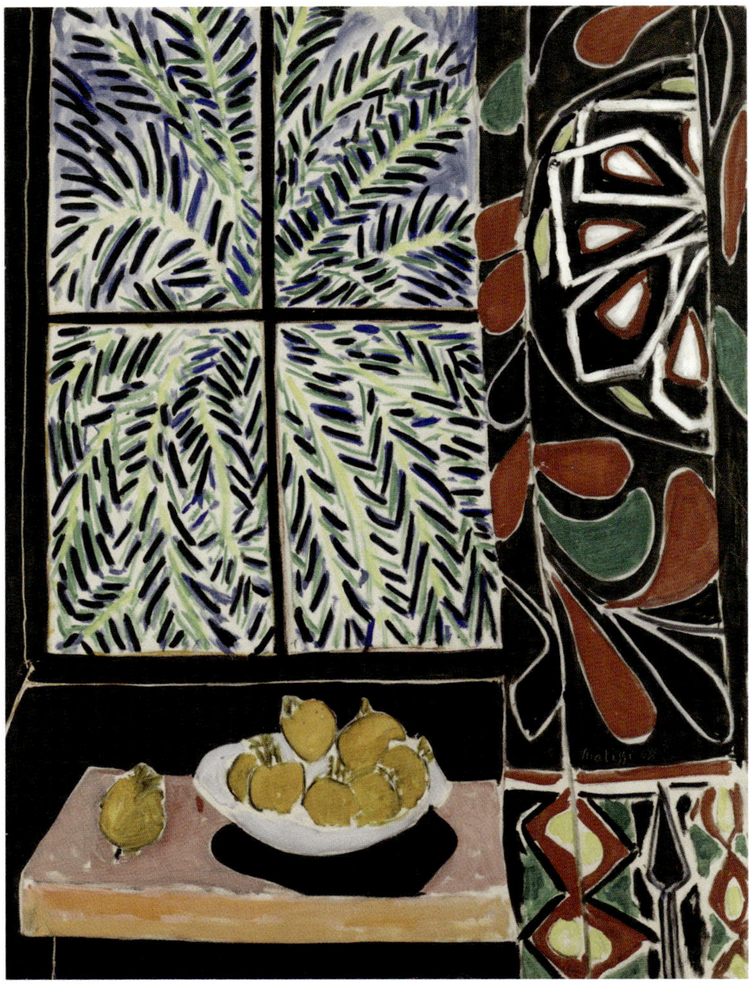

fig. 5
Henri Matisse
Interior with Egyptian Curtain
1948
Oil on canvas
45 3/4 x 35 1/8"
The Phillips Collection, Washington, DC
Acquired 1950

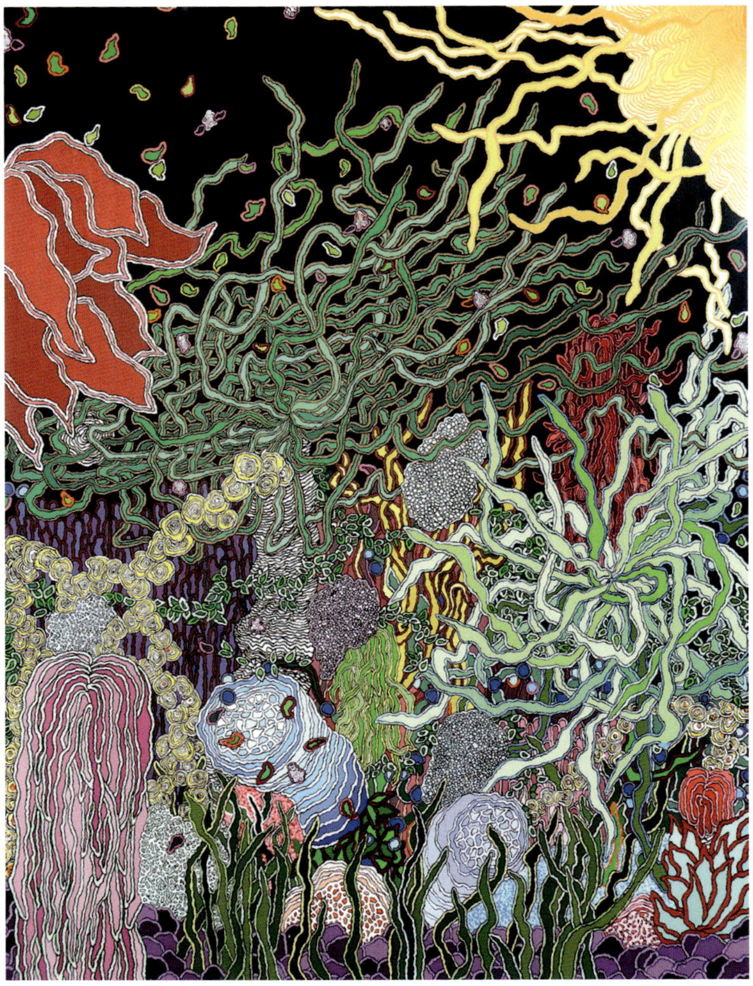

fig. 6
Carol Brown Goldberg
Maggie on my Mind
2015
Acrylic on canvas
79 x 58"
(plate 1, page 27)

chose from Goldberg's studio collection the painting *Maggie on My Mind* (2015) (fig. 6) (plate 1, page 27), as well as two complementary works on paper. Together, Goldberg and Ottmann selected an older work from The Phillips Collection to be displayed beside these choices as a counterpoint. That painting was Matisse's *Interior with Egyptian Curtain* (1948) (fig. 5), an extravagantly lush work painted by Matisse shortly after moving to the Mediterranean hill-town of Vence, where he would fashion his late masterwork *The Chapel of the Rosary*. Matisse resided next door to the chapel in the Villa Le Rêve, and his upstairs studio window looked out on the giant palm tree that features in his *Interior*.

Interior with Egyptian Curtain is a riot of rich colors and organic forms, and its freely executed brush marks recall the lushness of Matisse's post-Fauve paintings of forty years earlier. The vibrant pattern of the palm fronds particularly communicates the vitality of nature. The painting melds three of Matisse's great themes—exterior nature, still life, and decorative design (here, the Egyptian curtain)—into one sensuous experience. Goldberg has had a career-long admiration for Fauvist color and linear freedom. She has said, "I love Matisse's outlined flat colors, the combination of color and line. I definitely relate to the Fauves and also Japanese woodprints."

For *Entanglement*, Goldberg devised her own version of one of the most radical ideas in the Modernist canon, "automatism." In his 1924 *First Manifesto of Surrealism*, André Breton proposed "pure psychic automatism" as a mode for inventing a new art. Based on his interpretation of psychology, Breton intended the technique as a means of bypassing consciousness in order to tap directly into the deep creative wellsprings of the unconscious mind. In the 1920s, the technique was embraced by Max Ernst, André Masson, Roberto Matta, Joan Miró, Yves Tanguy, and other Surrealists. In her own words, Goldberg "has a deep affinity with and draws endless inspiration from the Surrealist painters and their imaginations."

Goldberg creates the *Entanglement* works in automatic modes. She has said:

> My hand is not fighting my thoughts, my brain. My hand just moves, it's not unconscious, of course. I'm still very conscious. But while I work, I'm listening to books on tape or listening to a lecture, really taking in information with one part of my brain while I'm drawing and creating with the other and making aesthetic decisions, it's like taking my pen on a journey.

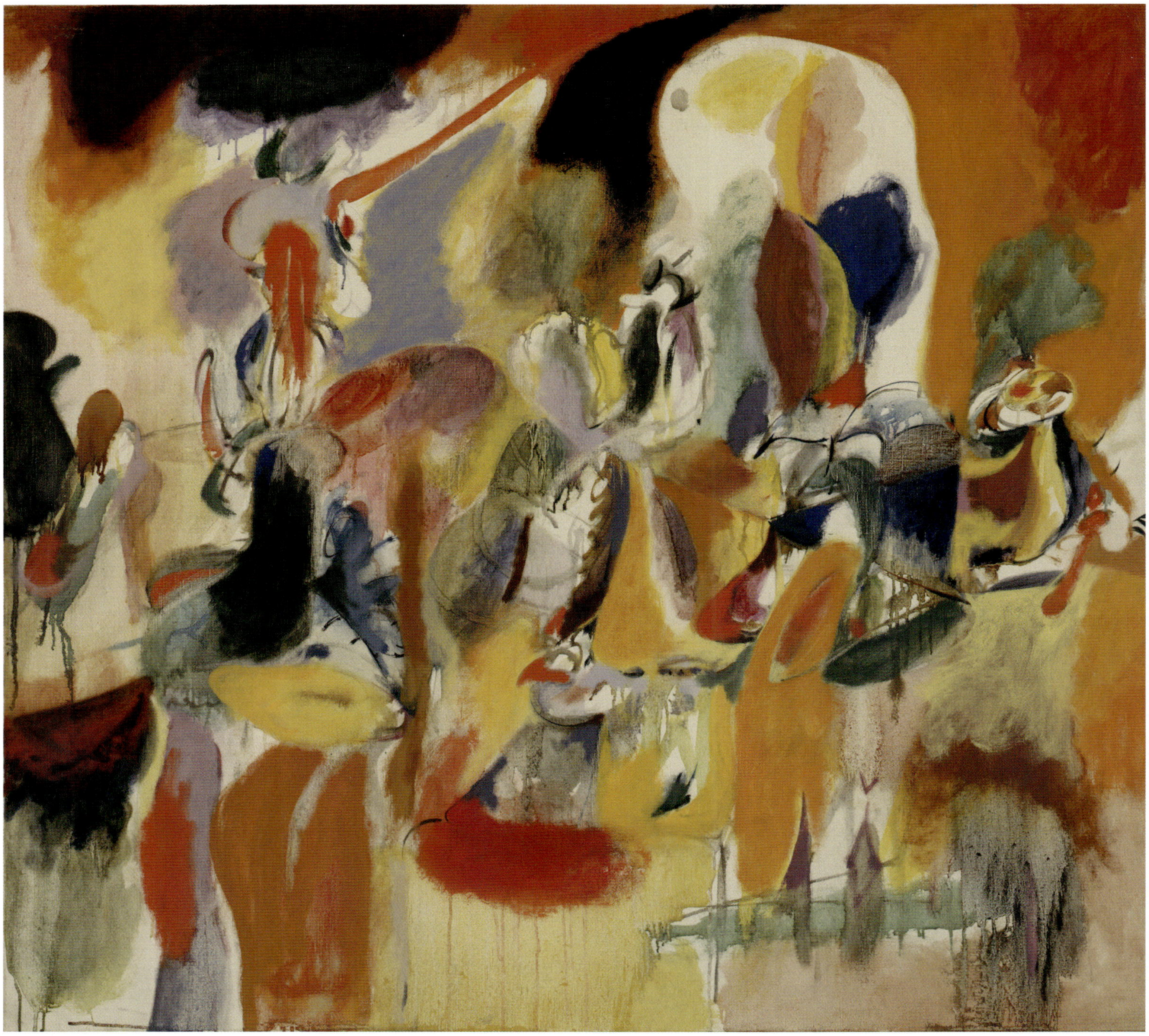

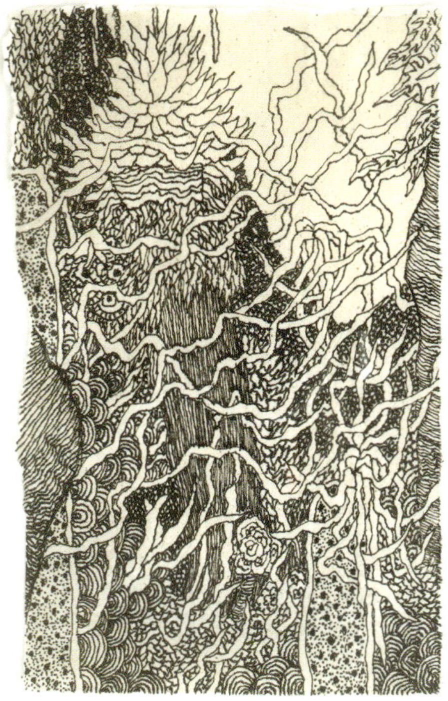

TOP fig. 7
Arshile Gorky
Water of the Flowery Mill
1944
Oil on canvas
42 1/4 x 48 3/4"
Image copyright © 2018 The Arshile Gorky Foundation / Artists Rights Society (ARS), New York
The Metropolitan Museum of Art
Image source: Art Resource, NY

BOTTOM fig. 8
Carol Brown Goldberg
Extravagant Eden 32
2016
Pen and ink on paper
8 x 5"
(plate 33, page 93)

Goldberg has also called this process "spontaneous, system-less mark-making."

While Goldberg's statement makes the process sound simple, it is actually far from it. Her works are created without the usual preliminary drawings and with no conscious pre-planning. Each pictorial decision is immediate and must be made with absolute certainty; every gesture must coordinate perfectly with already executed marks, while also anticipating a wide range of future marks. To suggest unity, a continuous rhythmic balance is maintained between the outlines of forms, and repetitions which might deaden the composition are avoided. Each shape is given characteristics that will allow it to grow and morph into a series of related, but not identical, configurations. Traditional Old Master paintings feature preliminary drawings that are laboriously corrected and adjusted. These designs are then enlarged, often by a grid measurement system, to produce a pre-conceived final work. By contrast, Goldberg relies on spontaneous, instinctive connections between brain and hand, developed intuitively over decades of painting.

Goldberg's use of automatic techniques brings her back to Abstract Expressionism, one of her longtime passions. Beginning in the late 1940s, the Abstract Expressionist painters adopted the methods of painterly automatism pioneered by the Surrealists, many of whom were exiled in New York City by World War II. The New York abstract painters transformed automatic techniques into monumental paintings that exceeded in sheer visual power the more modest Surrealist experiments. Jackson Pollock's groundbreaking drip paintings are intuitive and immediate, rhythmic and controlled, in a manner that Goldberg finds highly relevant to her art. Pollock created dense works full of pictorial events that have a heritage in Goldberg's recent paintings. He also pioneered a type of composition that eliminates traditional figure/ground relationships while activating every part of the painting surface. This painterly structure, named "all over" painting by the critics, is an additional basis for Goldberg's recent paintings.

Pollock's great drip paintings, like *Autumn Rhythm (Number 30)* of 1950 (Metropolitan Museum of Art, New York), rely much more on his responses to nature than is usually acknowledged in the literature on the artist. However, the Abstract Expressionist most closely associated with transformations of nature is Arshile Gorky. As seen in *Water of the Flowery Mill* (1944) (fig. 7), Gorky created an imaginative world teeming with roots that intertwine, seed pods that explode and germinate, plants that sprout, water that gushes, and hybrid insects that mate.

A powerful motivating force for Gorky's pantheism was the memory of his native land, which he and his fellow Armenians believed to be the original site of the Garden of Eden. That sacred domain had been lost to them when the Ottoman Turks launched the Armenian genocide in 1914, but Gorky found ways of recreating his beloved homeland through his fruitful imagination. While certainly not part of the violent history that Gorky endured, Goldberg's Eden-like paintings, which imagine a dominant and procreative nature, are envisioned in the context of a

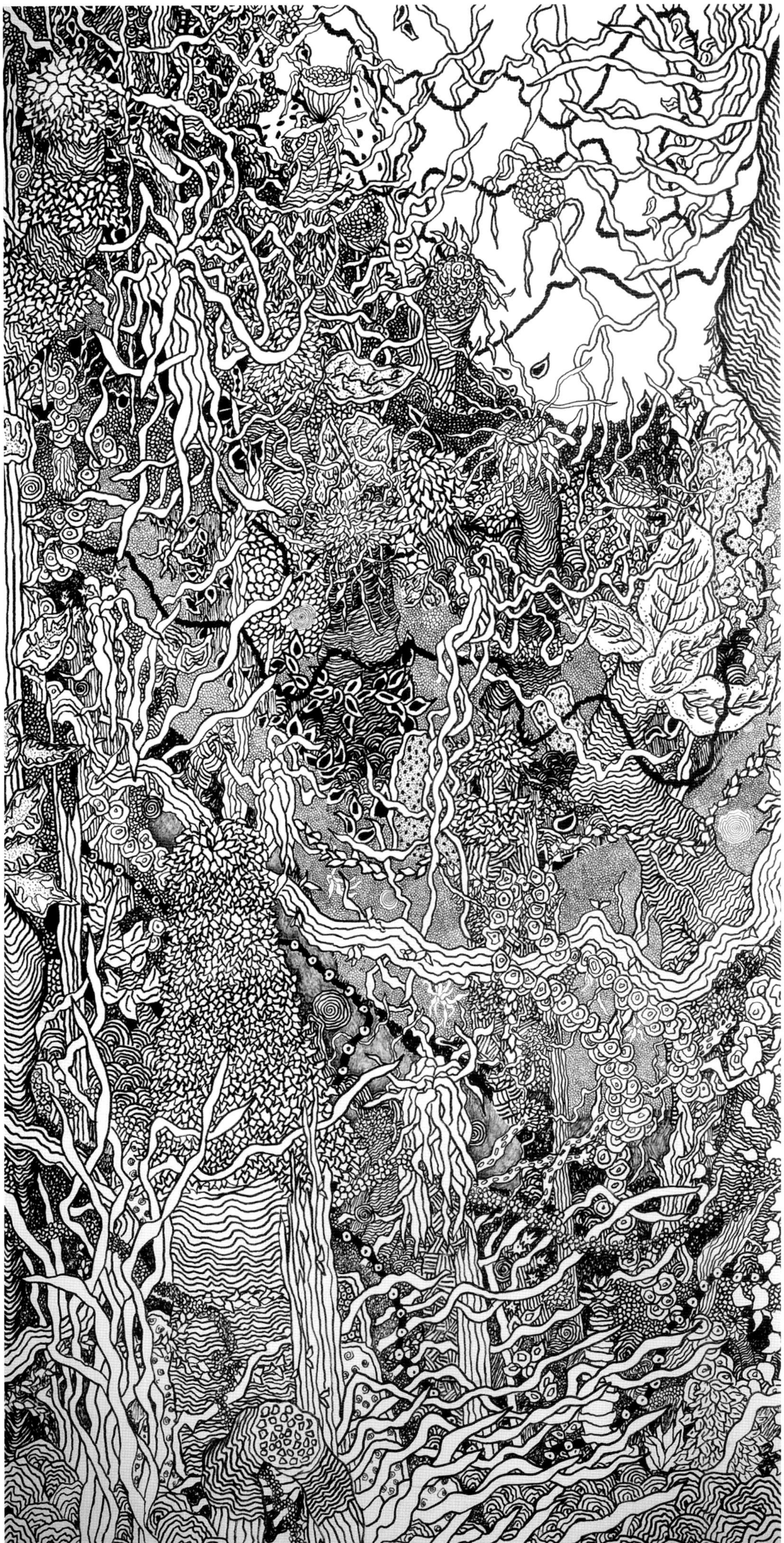

fig. 9
Carol Brown Goldberg
The Fragrance of Entanglements
2016
Acrylic on canvas
72 x 36"
(plate 9, page 43)

worldwide ecological crisis. Stylistically, Gorky's holistic view of nature is developed by way of long, interwoven, fluid lines of pigment that connect all forms in his imaginary universe. Technically, Gorky accomplished this style of painting through his use of long-bristled sign painters' brushes given to him by his closest friend, Willem de Kooning. Similarly, Goldberg's works are defined by entwined lines made possible by her discovery of the acrylic pen—a stylus attached to a cylinder loaded with acrylic paint—which allowed her to paint in long, connected gestures.

Goldberg has had a long and intense interest in science. She is a voracious reader who listens to audio books on science and culture while painting, and she routinely mines the internet for information and images. (One that recently caught her interest was a scientific animation illustrating the elegance with which bacteria flagella assembly occurs.) From 1980 through 1995, Goldberg organized monthly discussion groups at her studio; these included artists, scientists, and intellectuals from a variety of disciplines. In 1989, she produced a sixteen-week lecture series "Voices of Our Time" that brought together such figures as John Carlson, a specialist in archaeological astronomy from the University of Maryland; Margaret Geller of the Harvard-Smithsonian Center for Astrophysics; Margaret Livingstone, Harvard Professor of Neurology and author of the book *Vision and Art: The Biology of Seeing*; and James Yorke, who coined the term "chaos theory." For her recent works, Goldberg has been exploring the intersection of botany and ecosystems, freely exploring images that are metaphors for her ecological concerns.

On the whole, Goldberg's paintings and drawings suggest the botanical concept of a "Climax Community": an intricately progressive relationship among interconnected organisms within an ecosystem, the genesis of which lies in autochthonous energy from the sun. While subsequently elaborated by generations of scientists, this notion was originally advanced by Alexander von Humboldt, who observed during his travels that plants tend to form somewhat discrete associations. They exist in communities of similarly related groups, characterized not only by species but by their occurrence in favorable climatic, edaphic, and biotic conditions.

As a group, Goldberg's paintings and drawings suggest the opulence and richness of tropical vegetation. In her painting *The Fragrance of Entanglements* (fig. 9) (plate 9, page 43), imaginary organisms sprout from a densely packed, nutrient-laden floor. Their rigid lower stems give way at higher levels to more undulating forms, as they strive upwards toward open areas at the top of the canvas. While Goldberg regards these upper expanses as governed by aesthetic decisions (as to the terminus point for her drawing), they also have botanical implications: in tropical forests, vegetation exhibits ordered strata that vary across the expansive height of the canopy. Where upper clearings exist, sunlight can penetrate to support the growth of specimens below, enabling them to thrive.

Goldberg's invented biota range from simple to complex, and depict the gradient of microscopic to monumental scales, all gathered together in her unitary biosphere. In *Thank you Franz* (plate 5, page 35) (a reference to the black-and-white paintings of Franz Kline), the left

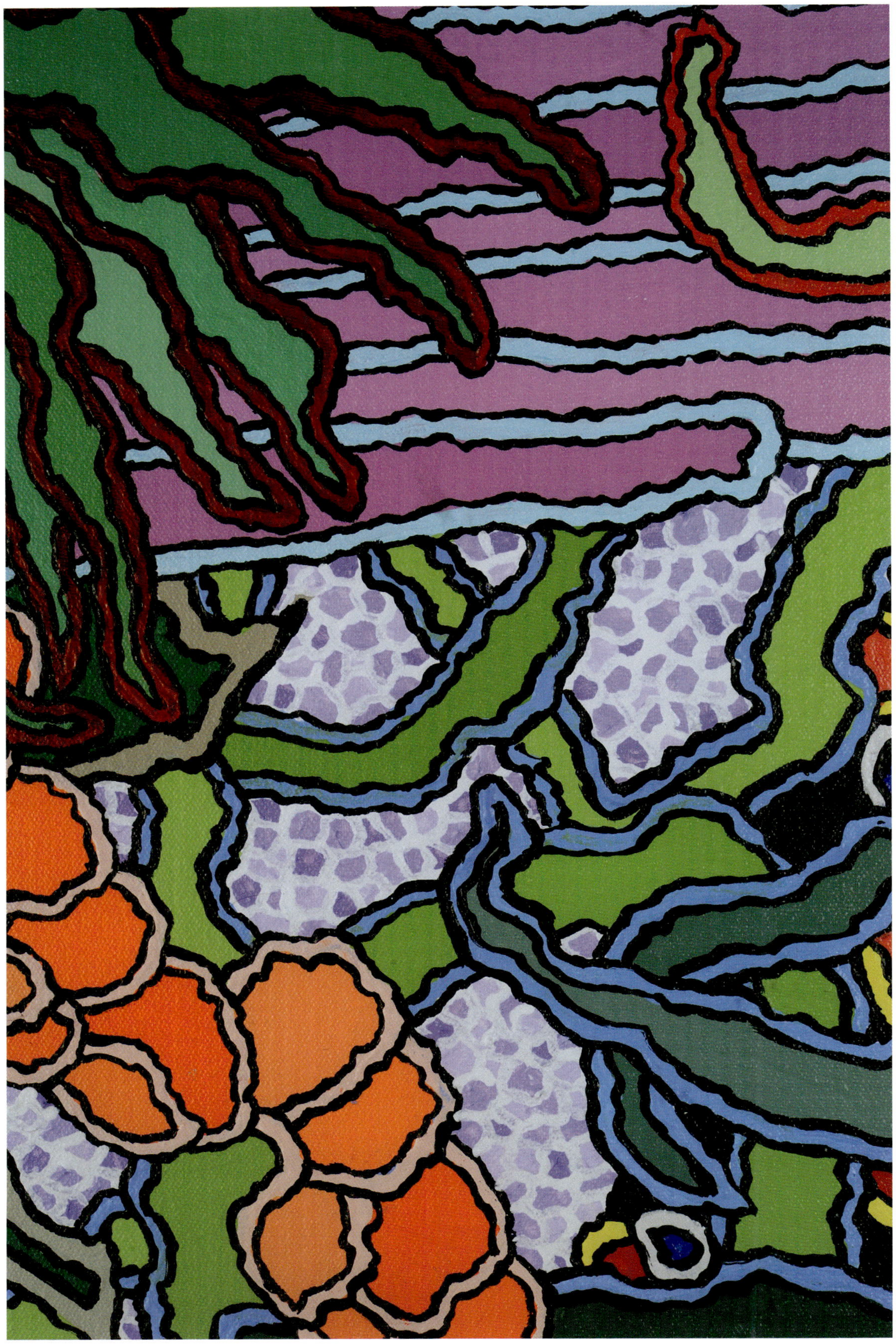

fig. 10
detail of
Carol Brown Goldberg
The Garden of the Moon-god
2015
Acrylic on canvas
36 x 24"
(plate 18, page 61)

side of the canvas exhibits the redolent stem and leaf configurations of vascular plants. At the center of the composition, vertical tubular forms resemble flower spikes with inflorescences crowded along fleshy axes, the very symbol of procreative energy. Other cone-shaped forms resemble fungi interspersed as in nature—where they enable decomposition processes that transform energy and enable nutrient cycling. While upper tendrils appear similar to vines, they also seem reflective of microscopic flagella, those fine hair-like plant cellular projections that are in reality only about 0.2 microns in diameter.

Additionally, Goldberg's forms seem layered, attaching themselves one to another in patterns that suggest epiphytes, those organisms that grow on plant surfaces without being parasitic. Epiphytes can include mosses, lichens, algae, ferns, and orchids, and derive their nutrients from air, rain, and organic debris that accumulates in their vicinities. Thus, they exist in a symbiotic relationship with the plant; such interdependence is a central theme in Goldberg's art. The perspective in this particular work places the viewer at the base of an impressive array of living organisms that towers over our sensibilities and elevates nature to a greater significance.

Goldberg's black-and-white paintings are accompanied by others of opulent color. While some appear to be terrestrial (land-based) organisms, others suggest the freely floating character of aquatic plants like bladderwort: plants whose innate buoyancy permits them to drift in response to water currents. This reference becomes particularly relevant in the washed blue tones of works like *Passive Resistance* (plate 3, page 31). *The Day After* (plate 8, page 41) is the pendant in red for that work. Seen together, these two paintings allude to minuscule blue-green and red algae.

At the same time, Goldberg's paintings have social/political implications. *The Day After* (plate 8, page 41) was painted immediately following the surprise Republican victory in the 2016 American presidential election, and *Passive Resistance* (plate 3, page 31) was painted shortly afterwards. The current administration's denial of the present-day global, ecological crisis is among its many policy positions that profoundly concern Goldberg.

Many of the most vibrantly colored works by Goldberg, such as *The Garden of the Moon-god* (fig. 10) (plate 18, page 61), occupy the beginning of her *Entanglement* series. They are filled with the diverse hues found in formal contemporary horticultural planting, but their forms are more primal, suggesting the ancient microscopic shapes typical of cellular

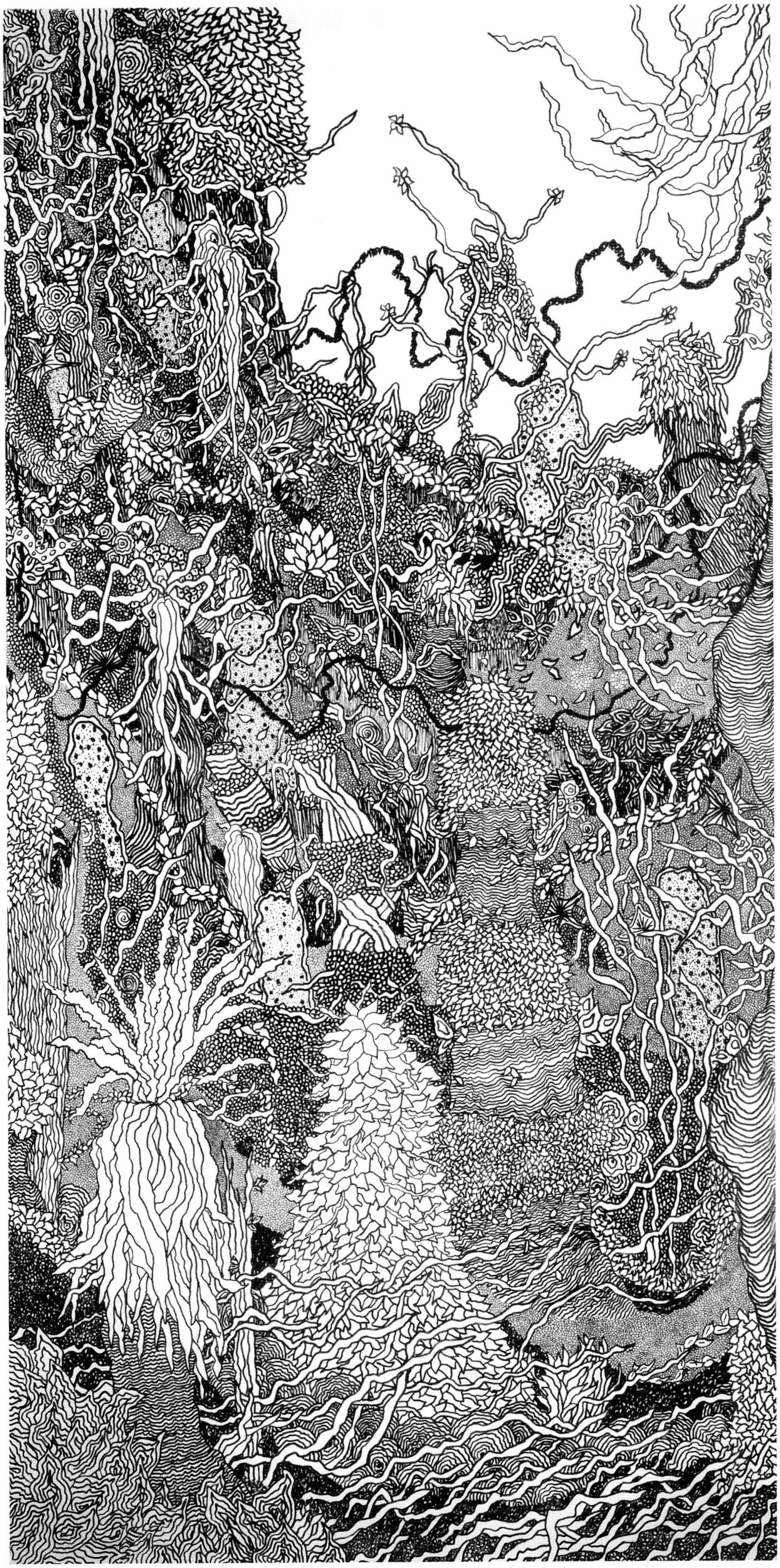

fig. 11
Carol Brown Goldberg
What We Cannot Touch
2016
Acrylic on canvas
72 x 36"
(plate 11, page 47)

membranes and plane epidermal tissues. And Goldberg's work is not immune to the influences of popular culture; these bountiful color-rich paintings bring to mind the riot of propagating abstractions popularized in the famous "Rite of Spring" sequence of Walt Disney's *Fantasia* (1940).

The life cycle itself is symbolized throughout *Entanglement*, as realized in works like *What We Cannot Touch* (fig. 11) (plate 11, page 47). Goldberg's imaginary botanical organisms drop seeds and discharge spores. They germinate, pollinate, swell, and grow. Fantasy plants, vines, and grasses reach toward nourishing sunlight in order to mature and disperse seeds for the next generation. The succession of growth seems not only fruitful but inexhaustible. The fecundity of the natural world permeates each piece individually as well as collectively.

Goldberg's *Entanglement* series is named after a key term developed by the physicist John Stewart Bell (1928–1990). In 1964, Bell set forth his "Bell's Theorem," which proposed that quantum physics be defined as an "entangled system" in which quantum states cannot be described as a product of their local constituents; that is, they are not explained by individual particles but are an inseparable whole. In essence, Bell argued for an intelligent universe in which all elements are related and interdependent. A common expression goes, "As is above, so it is below." In the *Entanglement* series, Goldberg envisions the natural world as a symbiotic and mutually dependent system of the highest order. Finally, Goldberg does not depict nature so much as cultivate a style of unhampered and pantheistic profusion that is a metaphor for both the interrelated abundance of nature and the profusion of human creativity. In our age, which grapples with increasingly urgent environmental threats and social/political/ethnic fracture, these works give us reason for hope.

Dr. Robert S. Mattison is the Marshall R. Metzgar Professor of Art History at Lafayette College. His books include *Robert Motherwell: The Formative Years; Grace Hartigan: A Painter's World; Masterworks: Jasper Johns, Ellsworth Kelly, Roy Lichtenstein, Robert Rauschenberg and Frank Stella in the Robert and Jane Meyerhoff Collection; Robert Rauschenberg: Breaking Boundaries; Arshile Gorky: Works/Writings;* and *Franz Kline: Coal and Steel.* His forthcoming book (2018) is *Ronald Bladen: Sculpture.*

“I see in nature the mirror of how we can flourish and live.”

Paintings

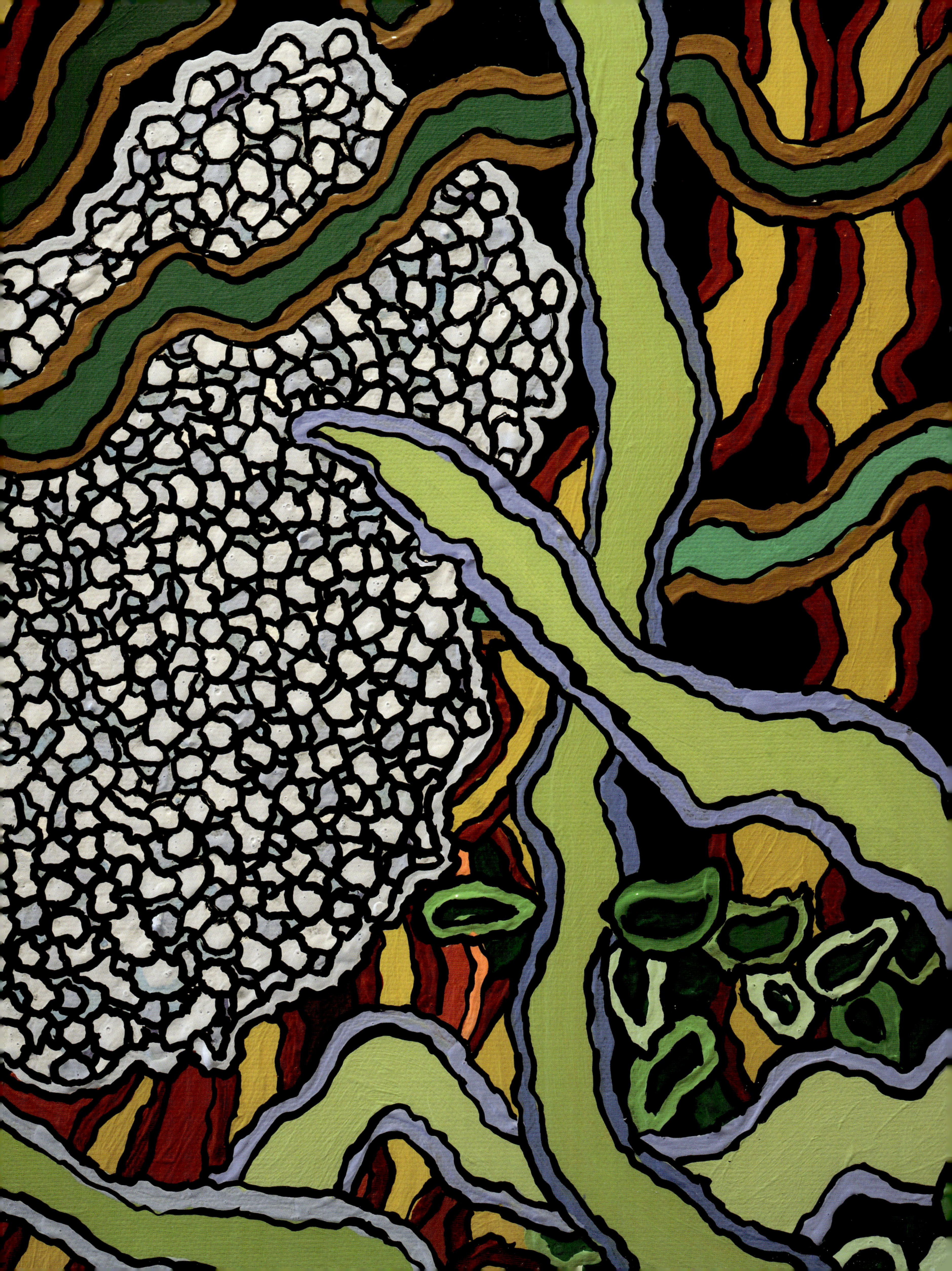

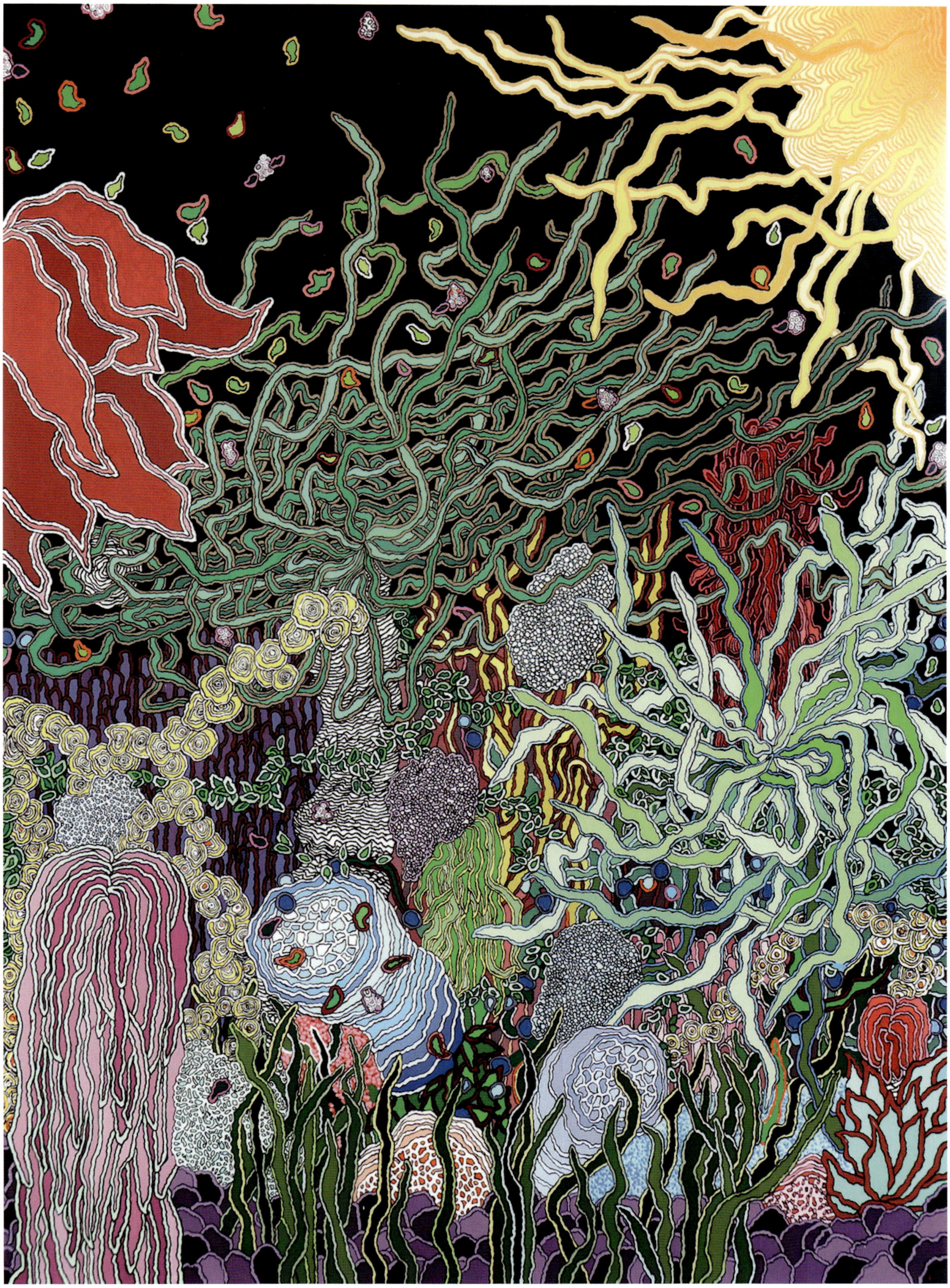

1 *Maggie on my Mind,* 2015, Acrylic on canvas, 79 x 58"

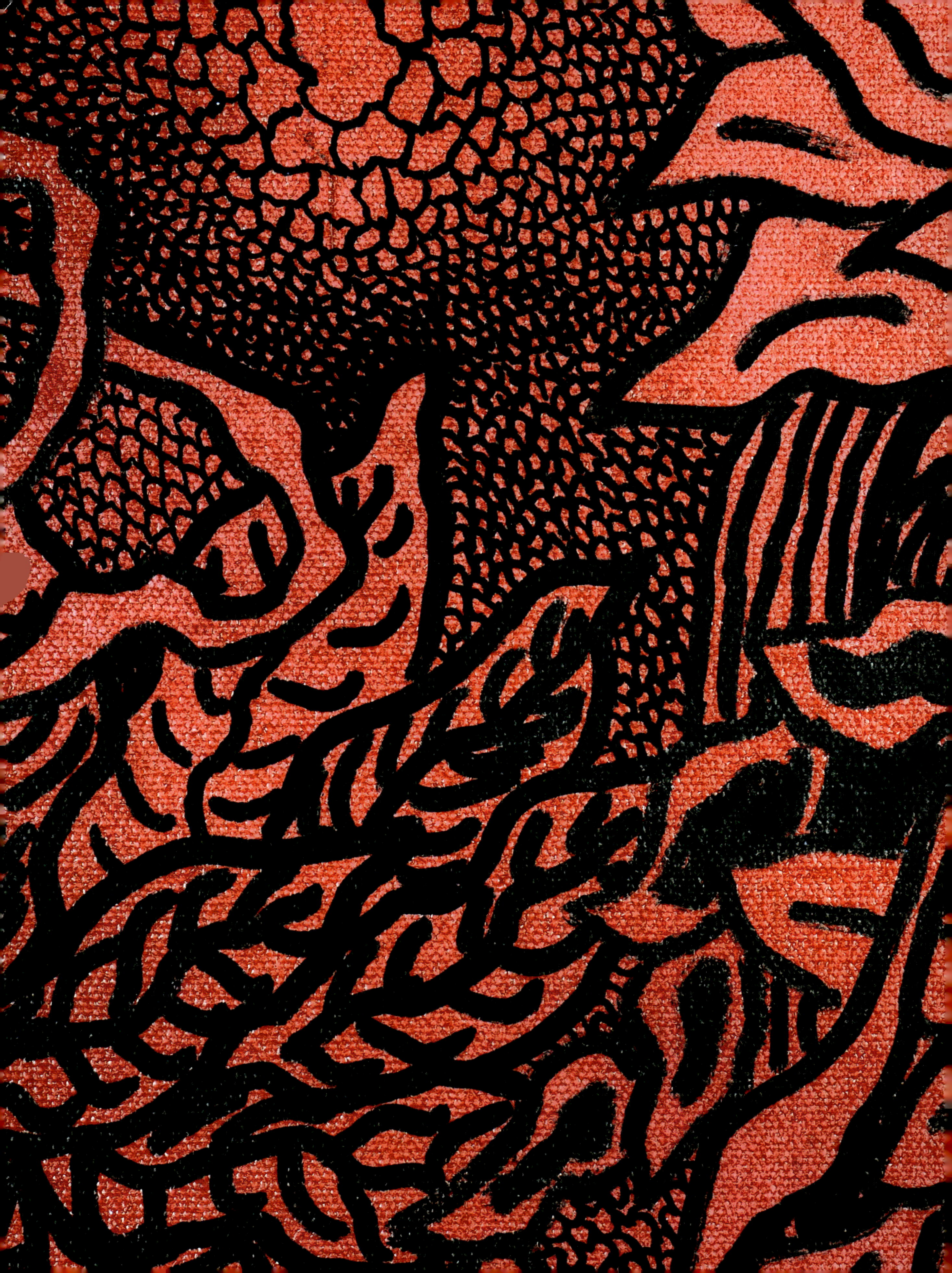

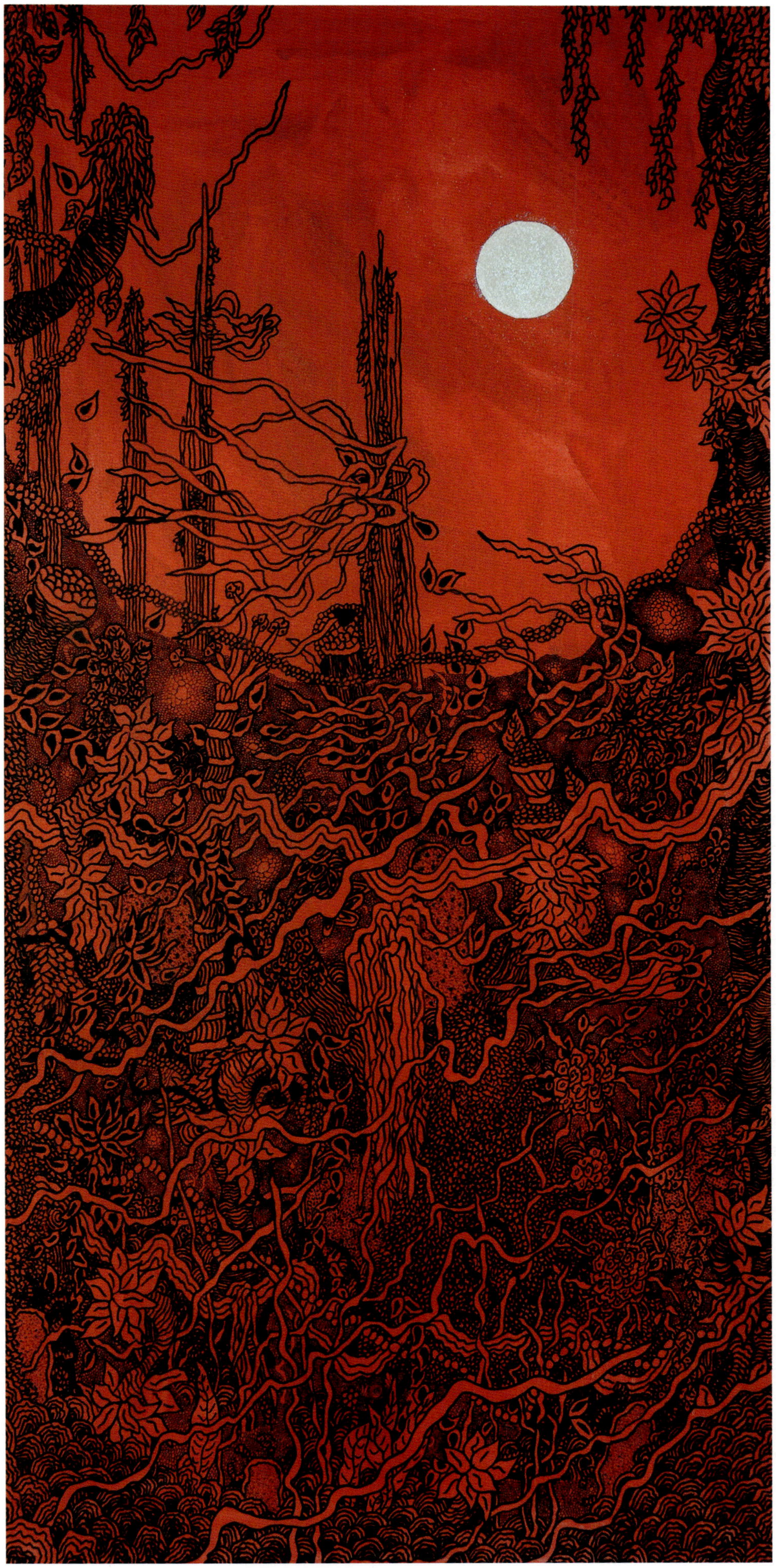

2 *Miami Blush,* 2017, Acrylic on canvas with polymer particles, 72 x 36"

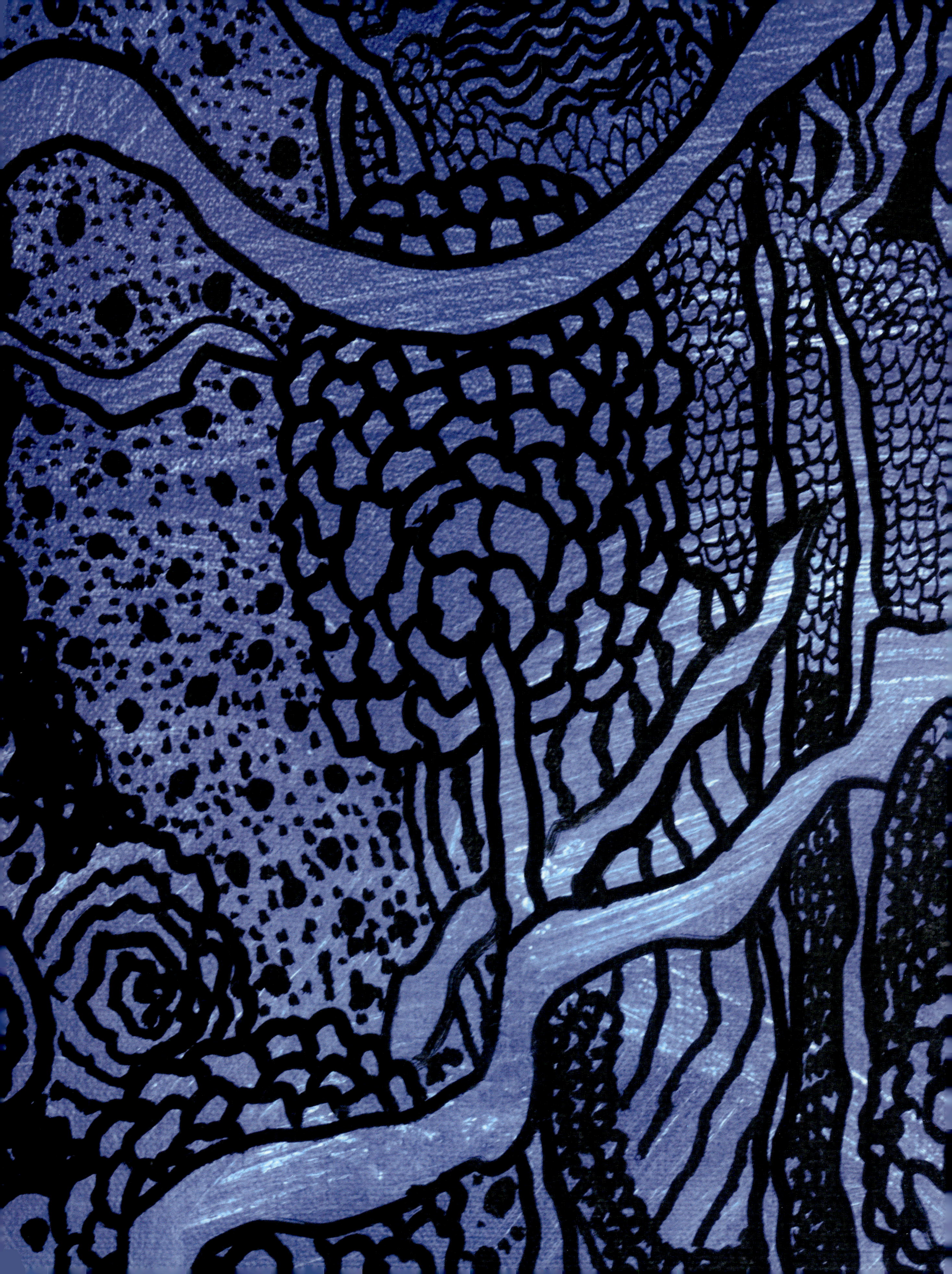

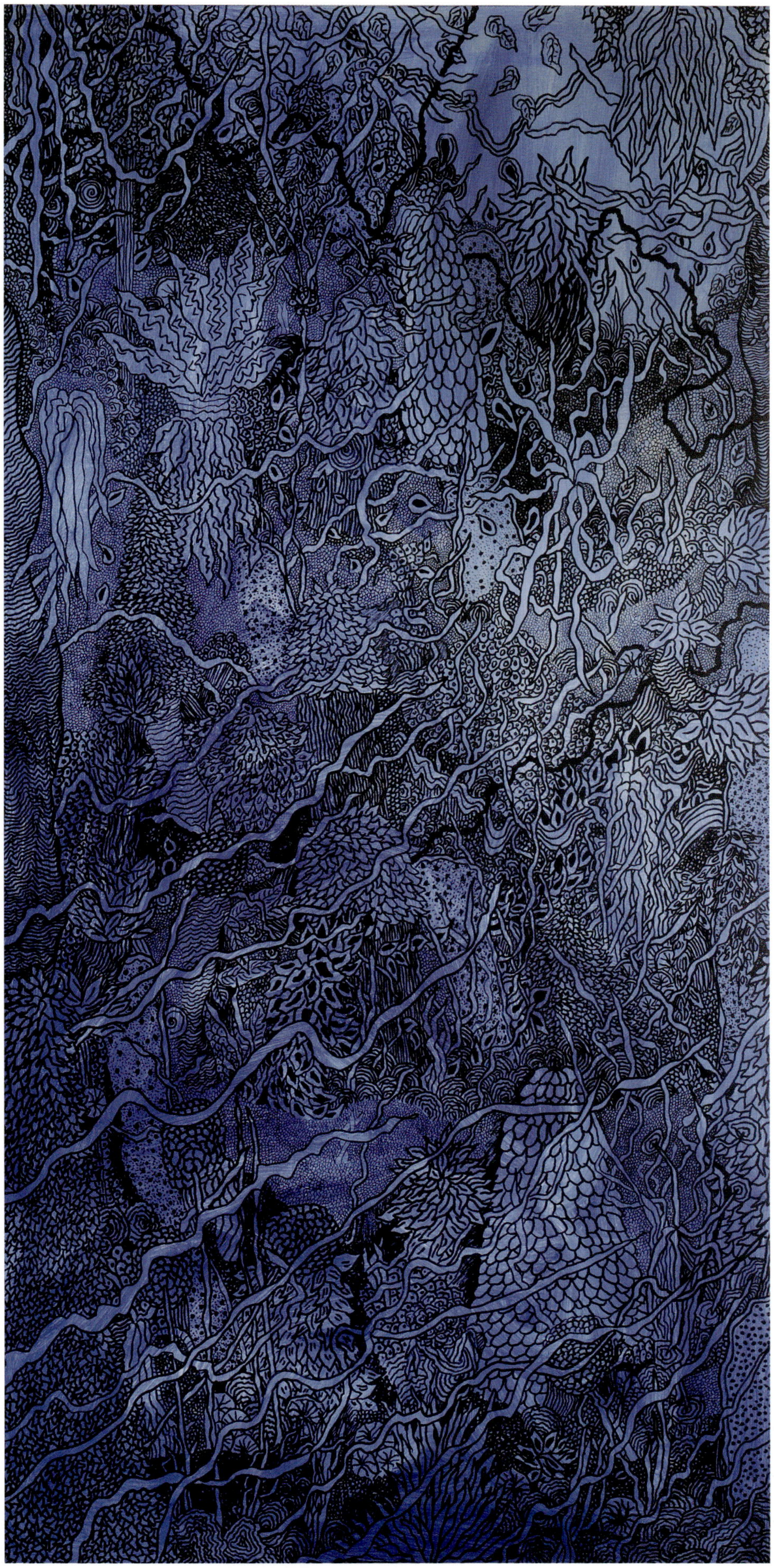

3 *Passive Resistance*, 2016, Acrylic on canvas, 72 x 36"

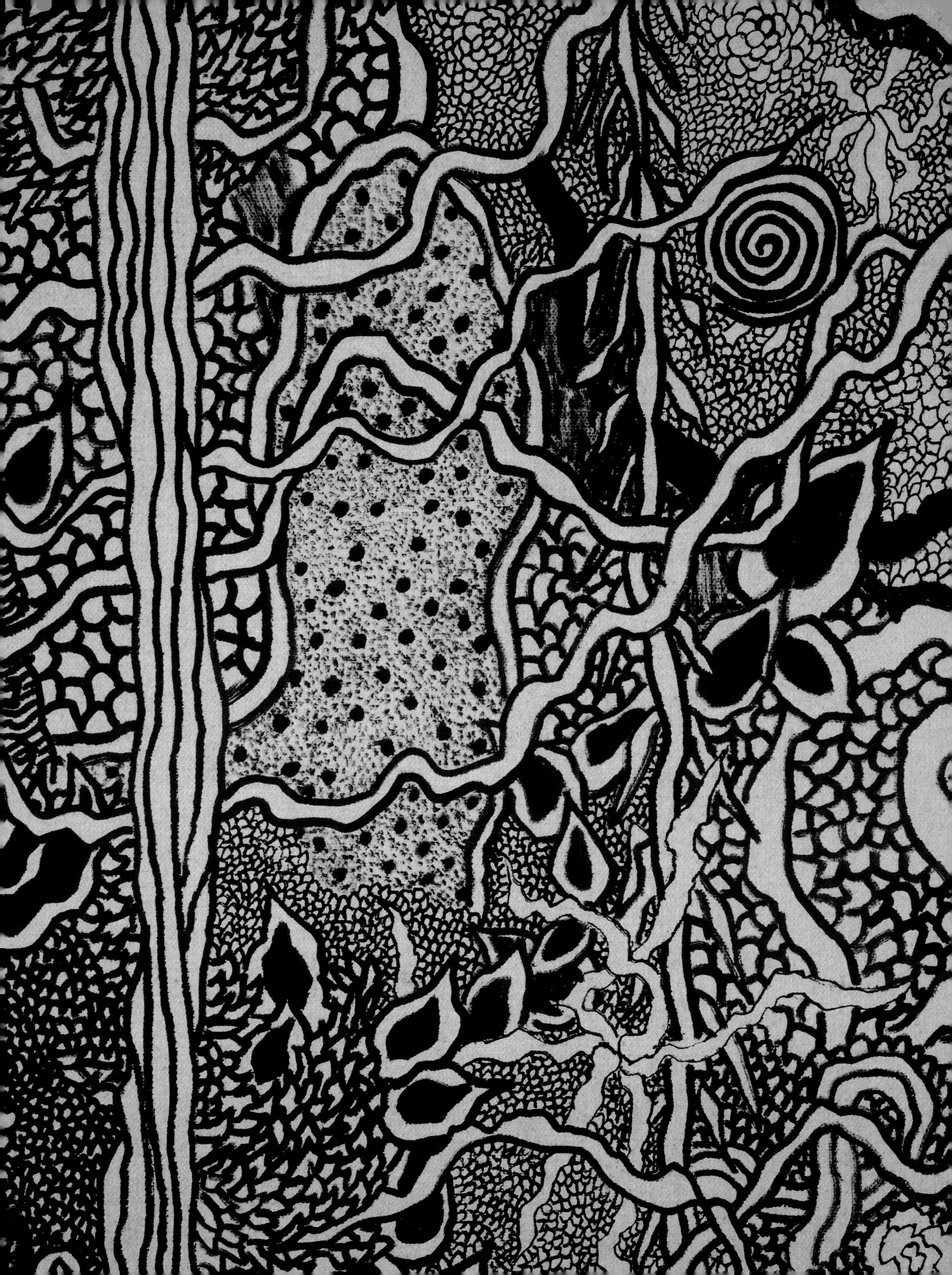

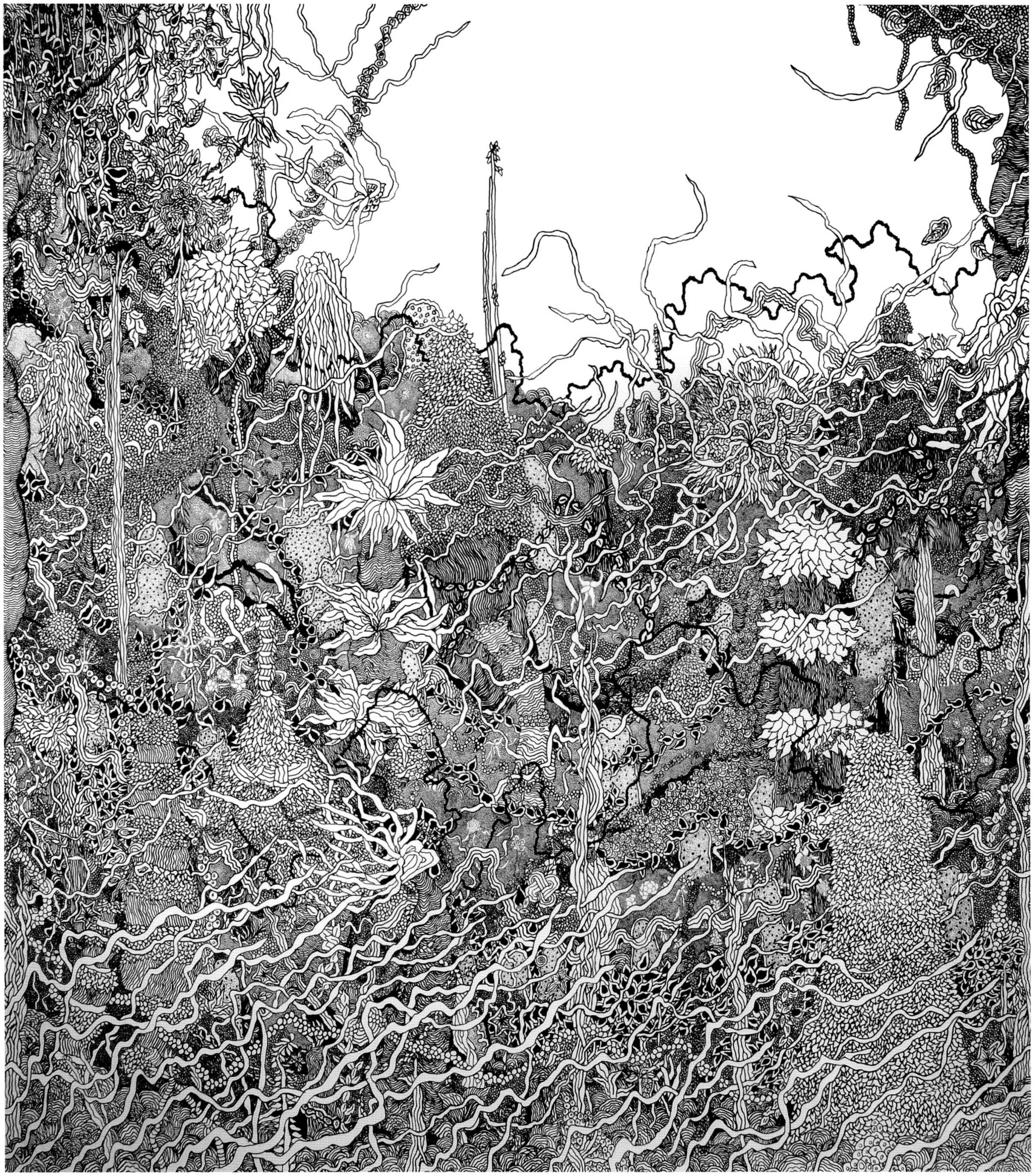

4 *Thank you Ad,* 2016, Acrylic on canvas, 96 x 84"

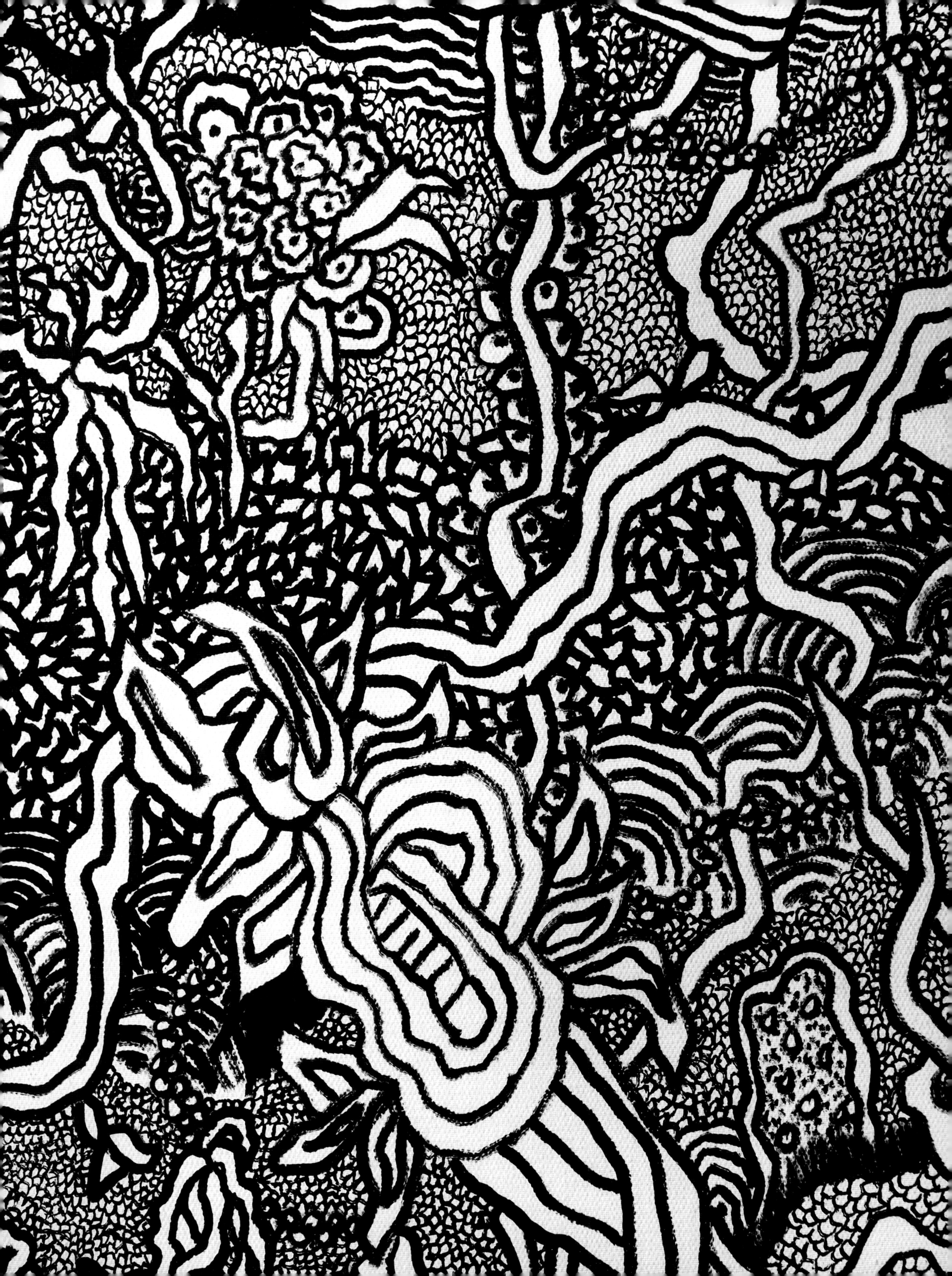

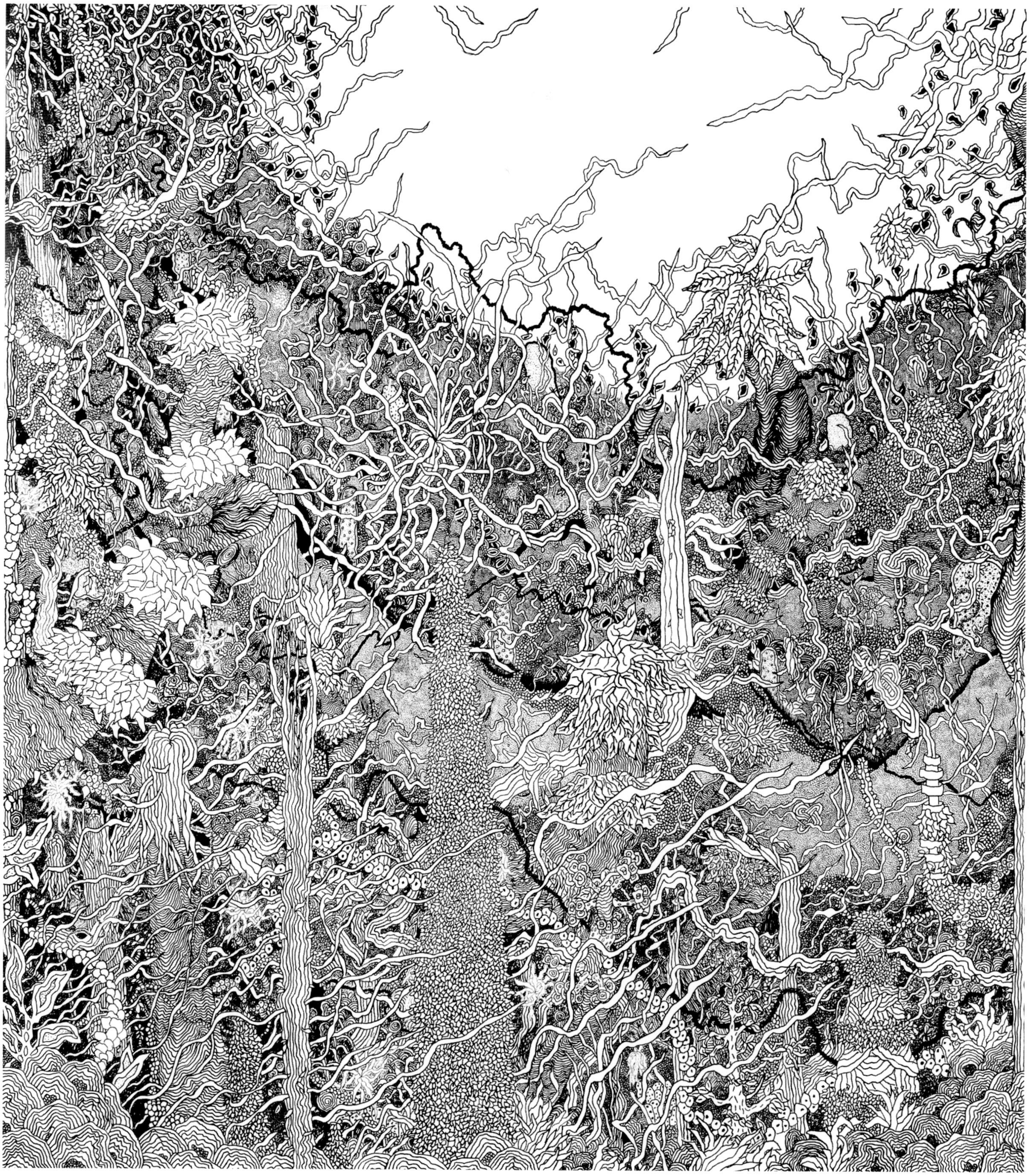

5 *Thank you Franz,* 2016, Acrylic on canvas, 96 x 84"

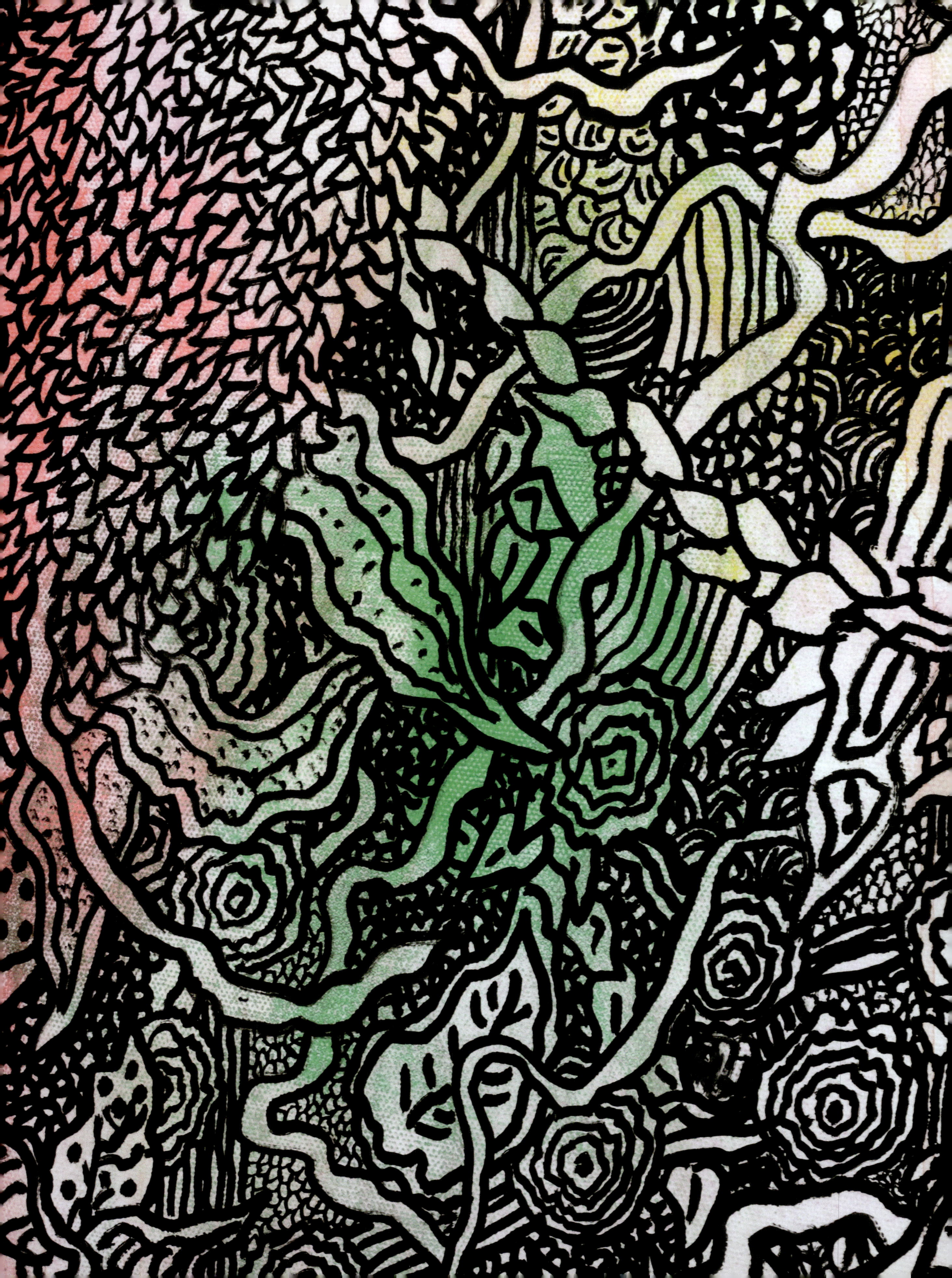

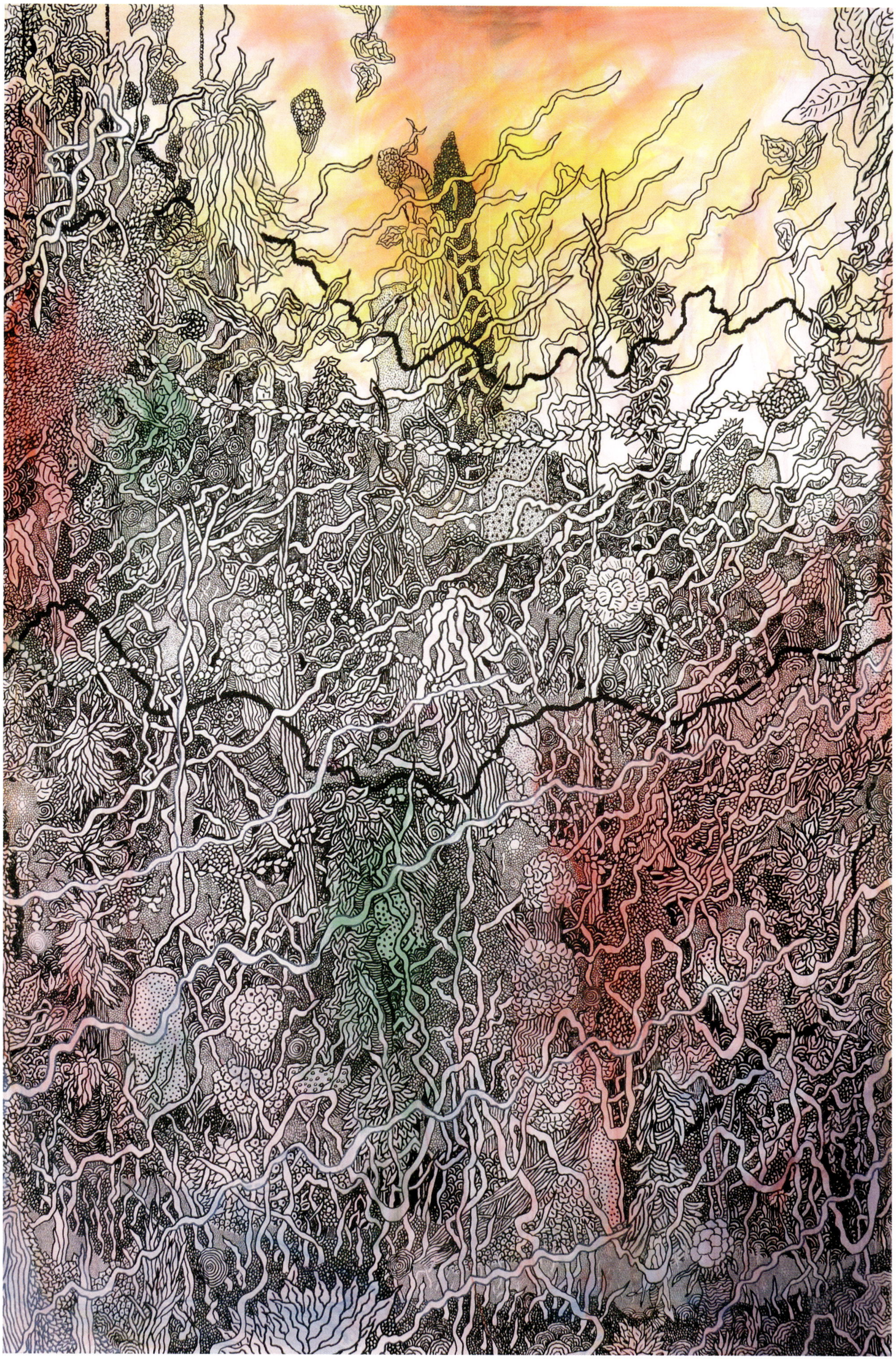

6 *The Biology of Wonder,* 2017, Acrylic on canvas, 72 x 48"

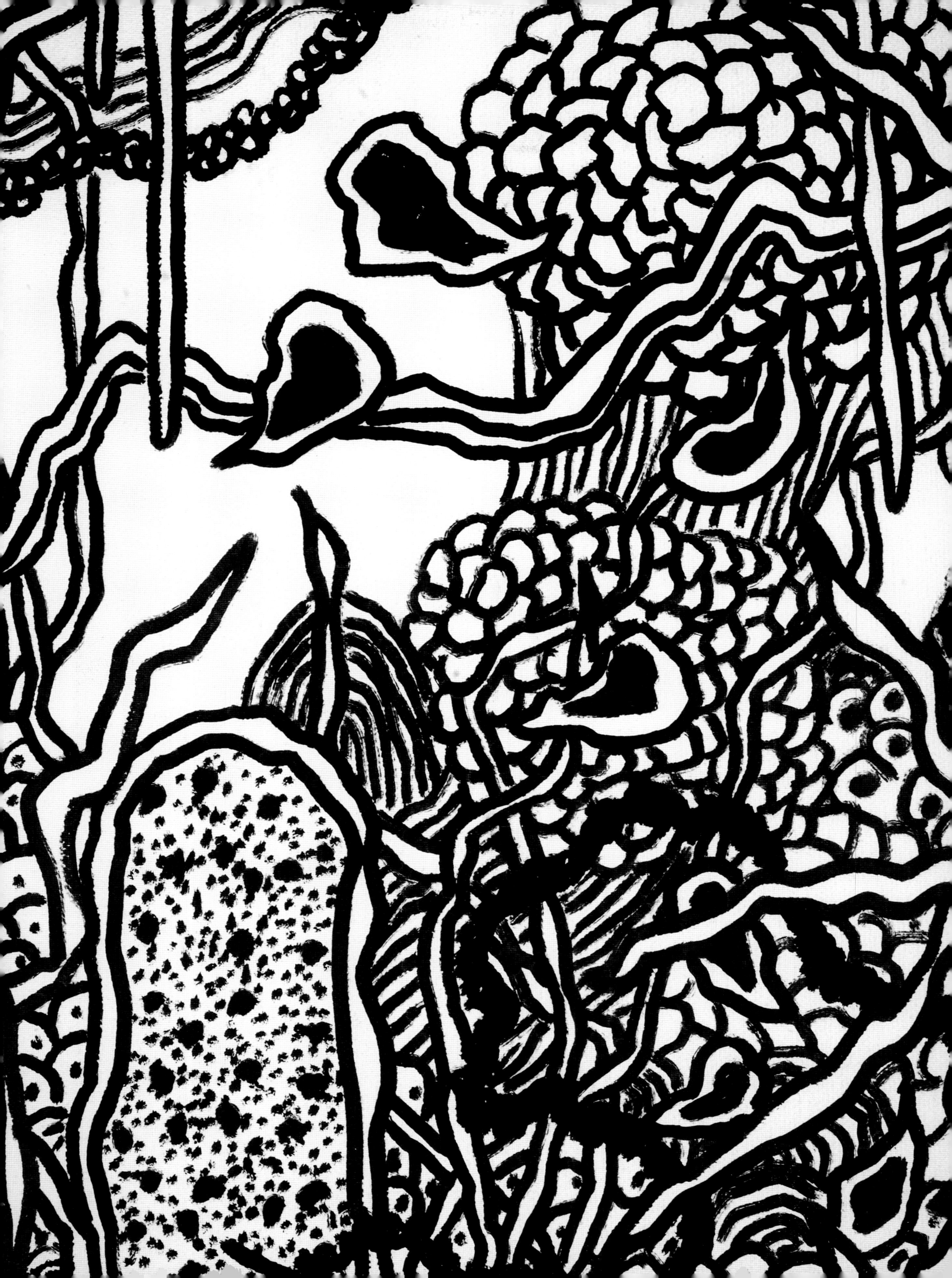

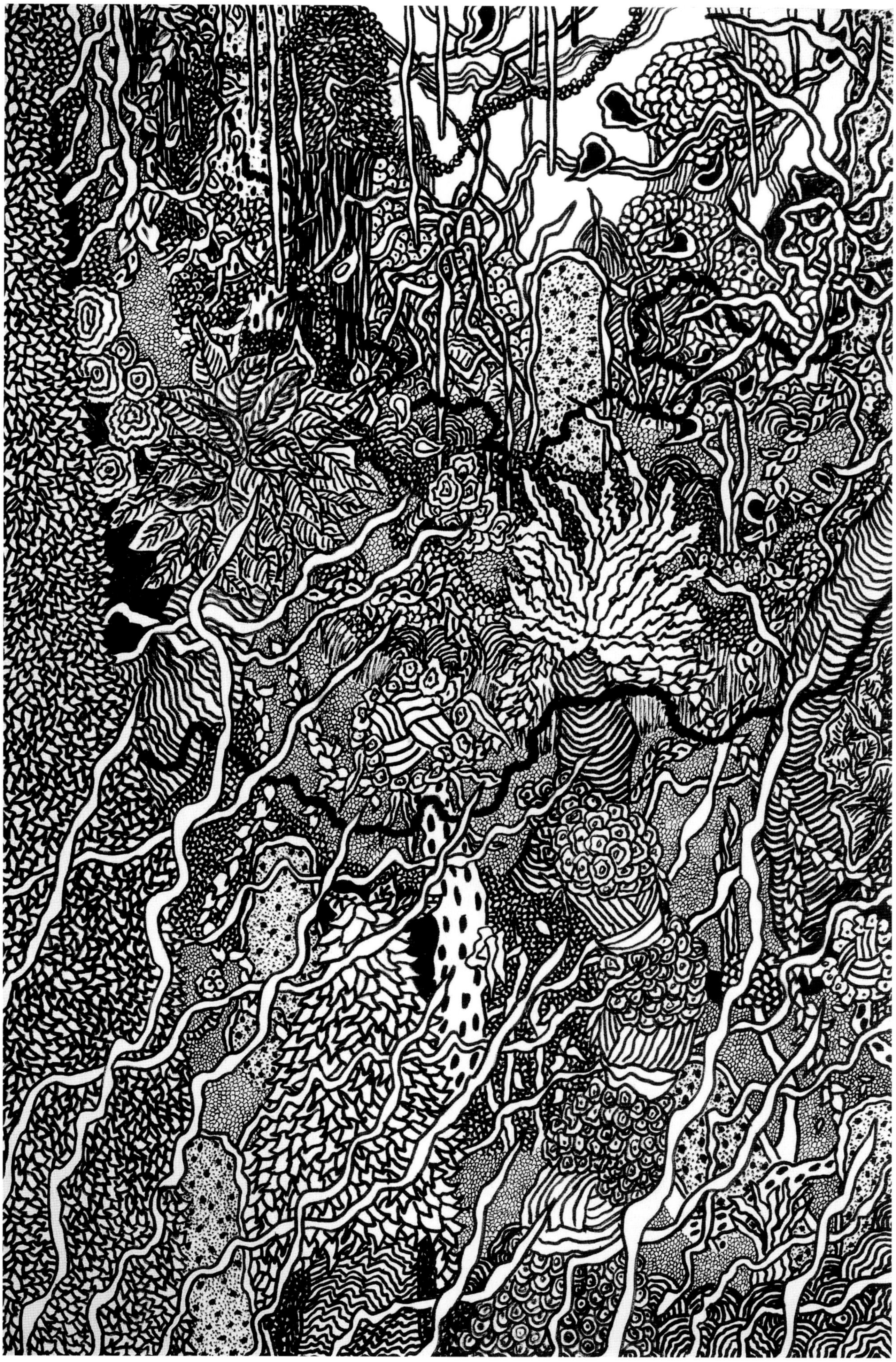

7 *The Botany of Romance,* 2016, Acrylic on canvas, 36 x 24"

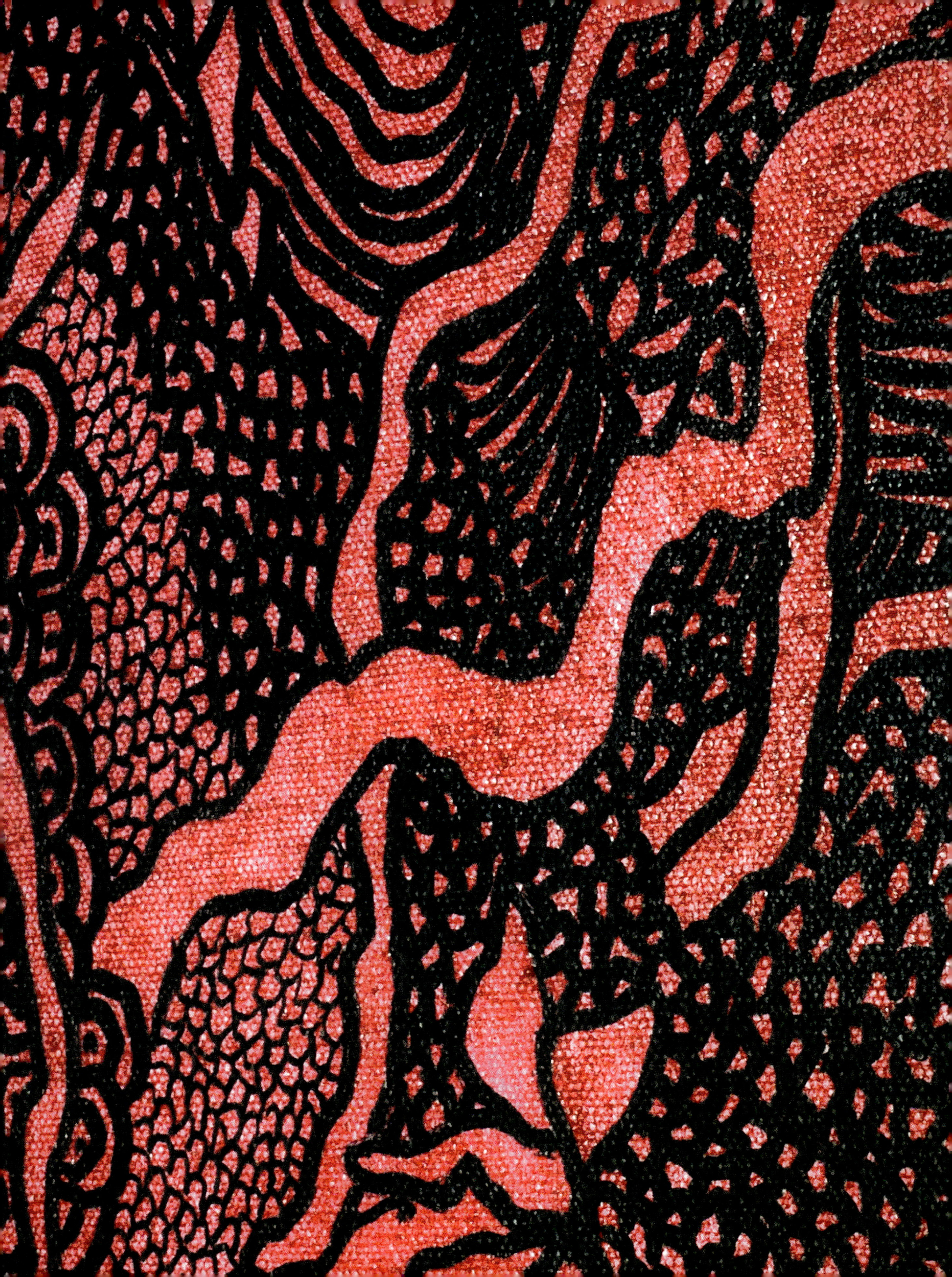

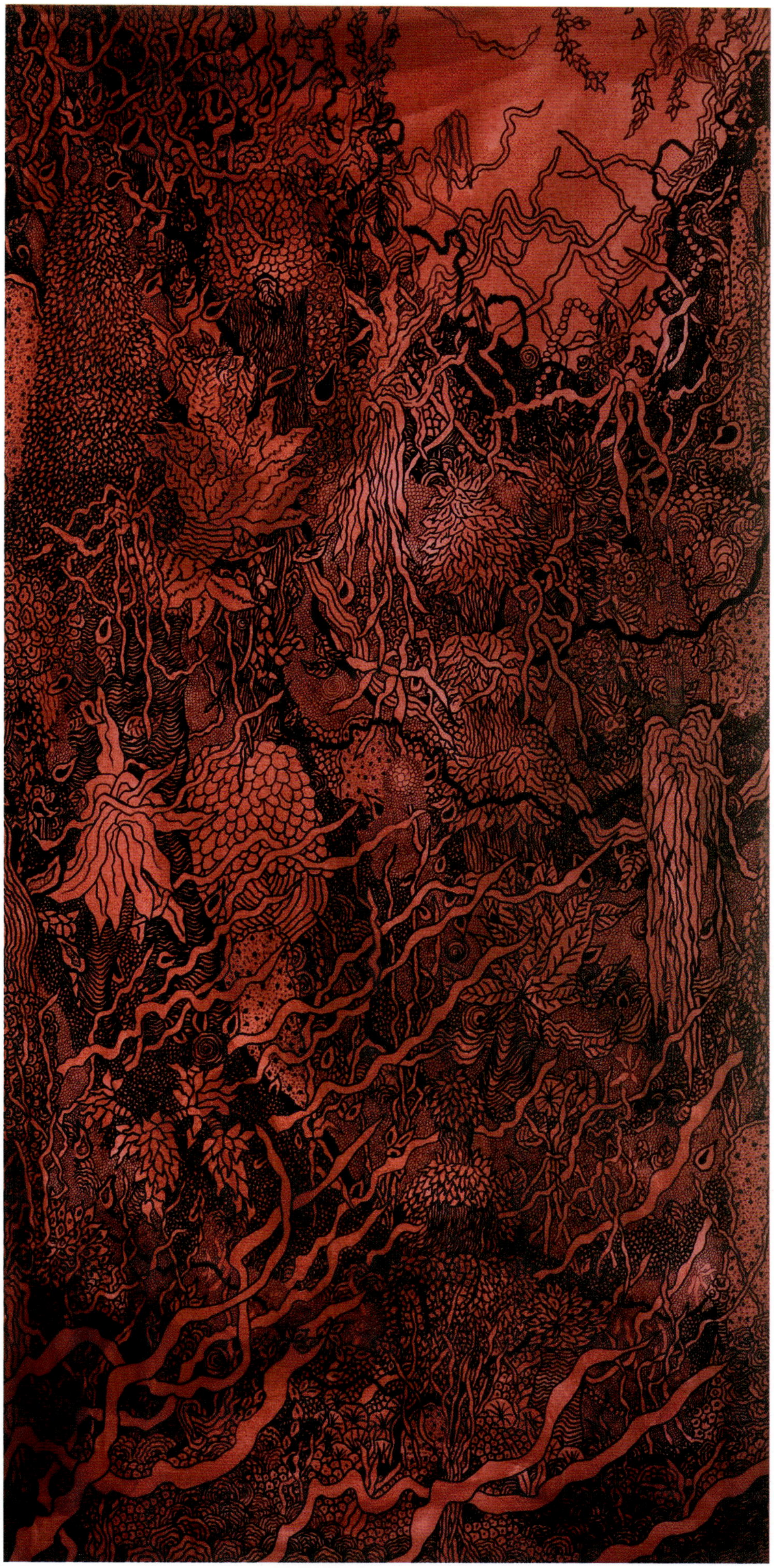

8 *The Day After,* 2016, Acrylic on canvas, 72 x 36"

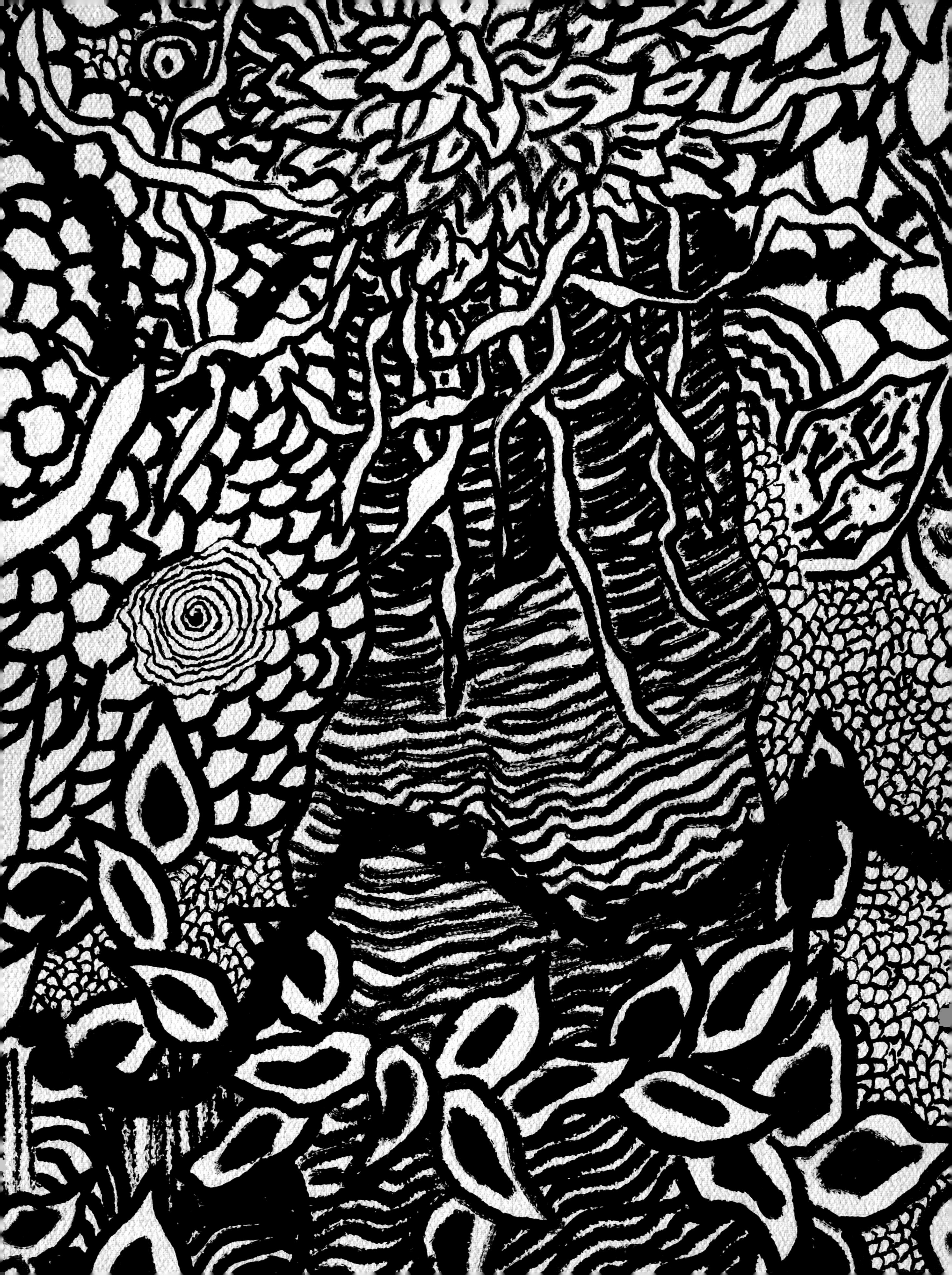

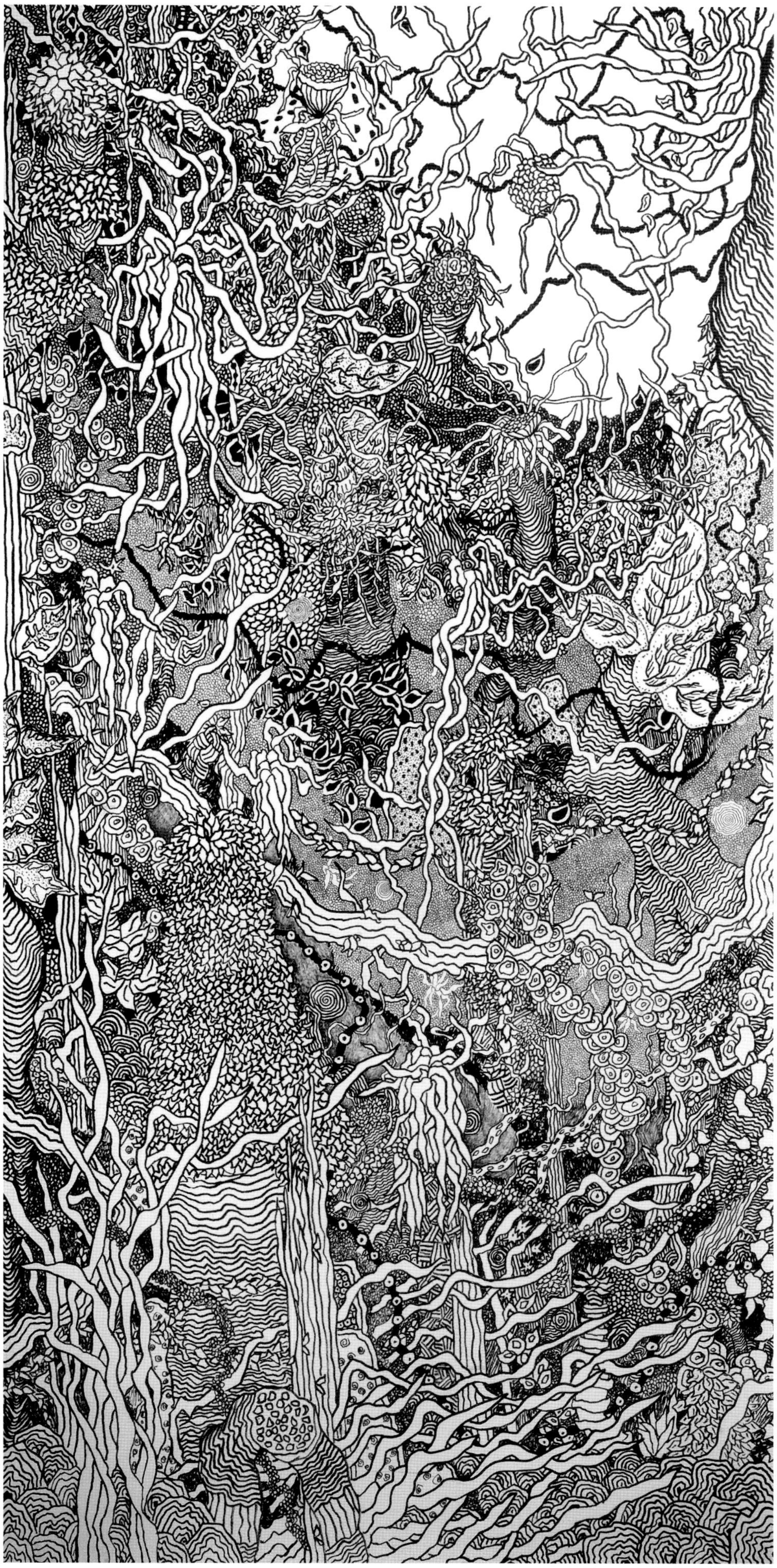

9 *The Fragrance of Entanglements,* 2016, Acrylic on canvas, 72 x 36"

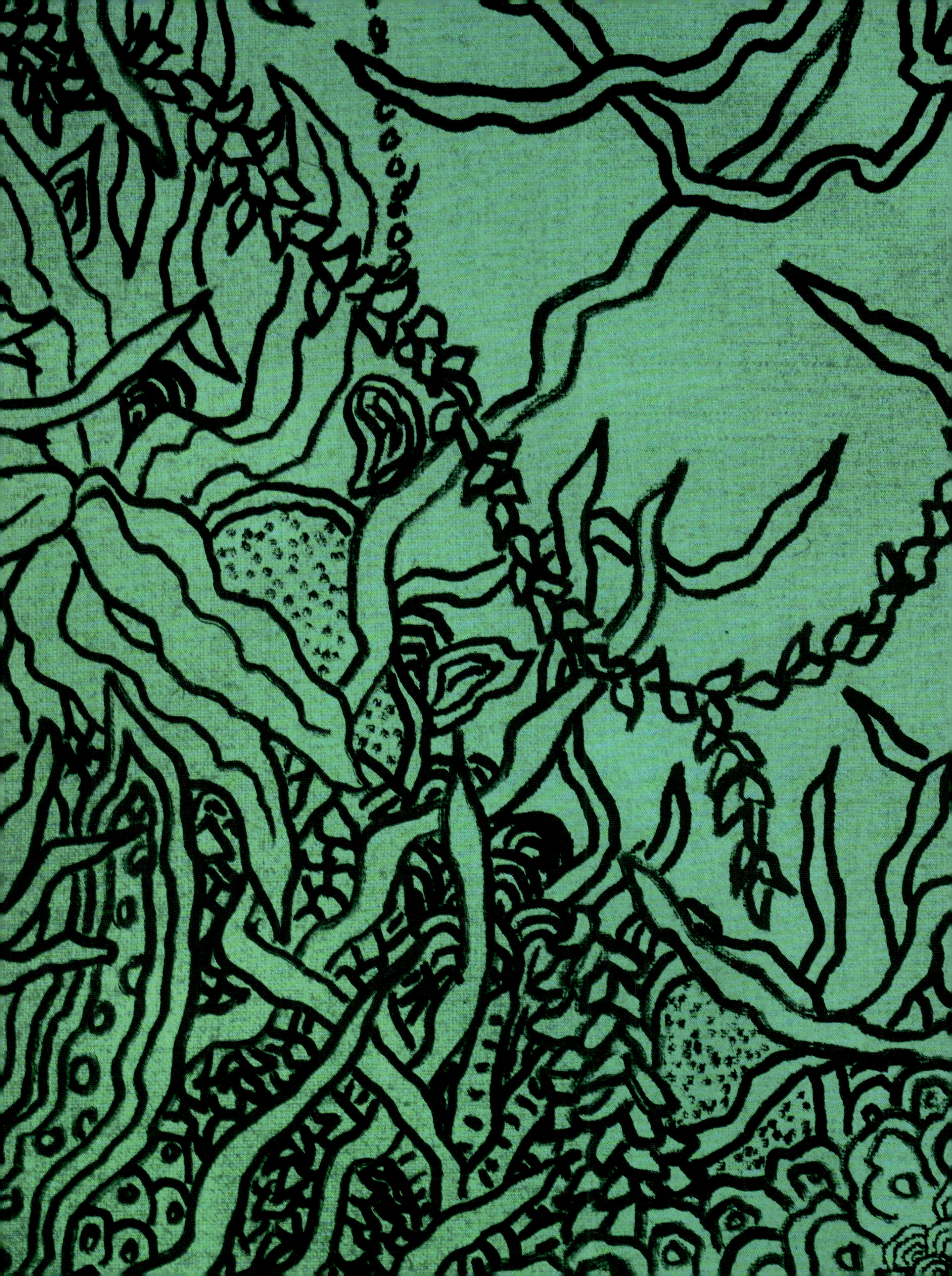

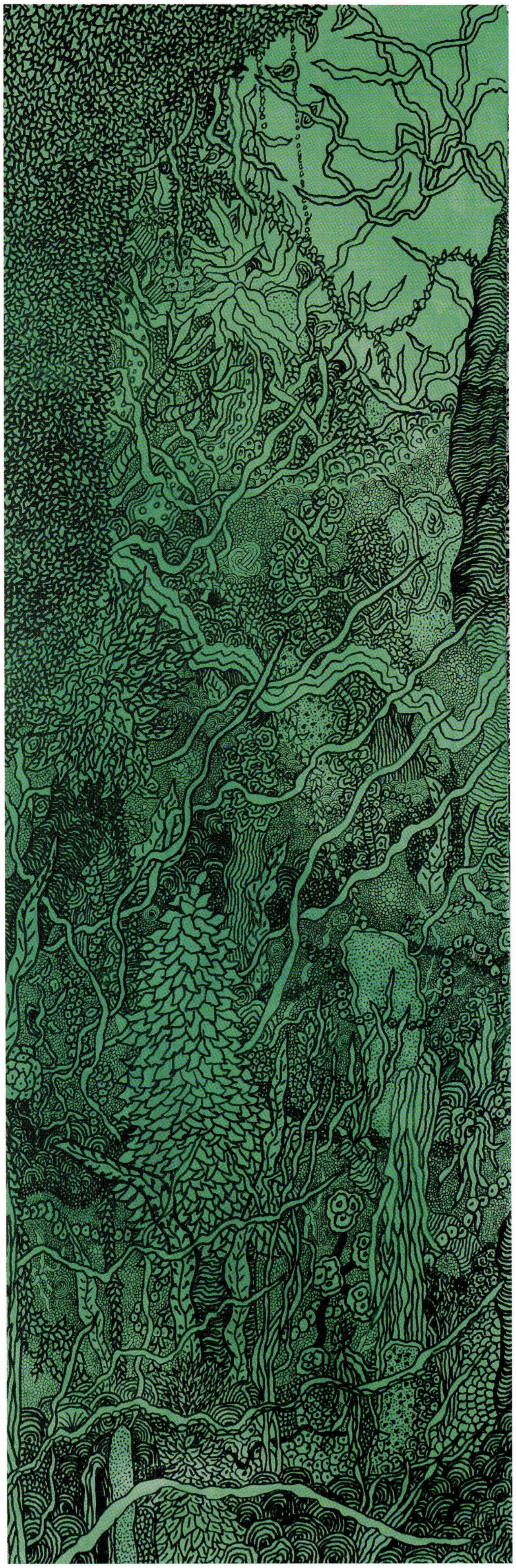

10 *The Mystery of Evolution,* 2017, Acrylic on canvas, 60 x 20"

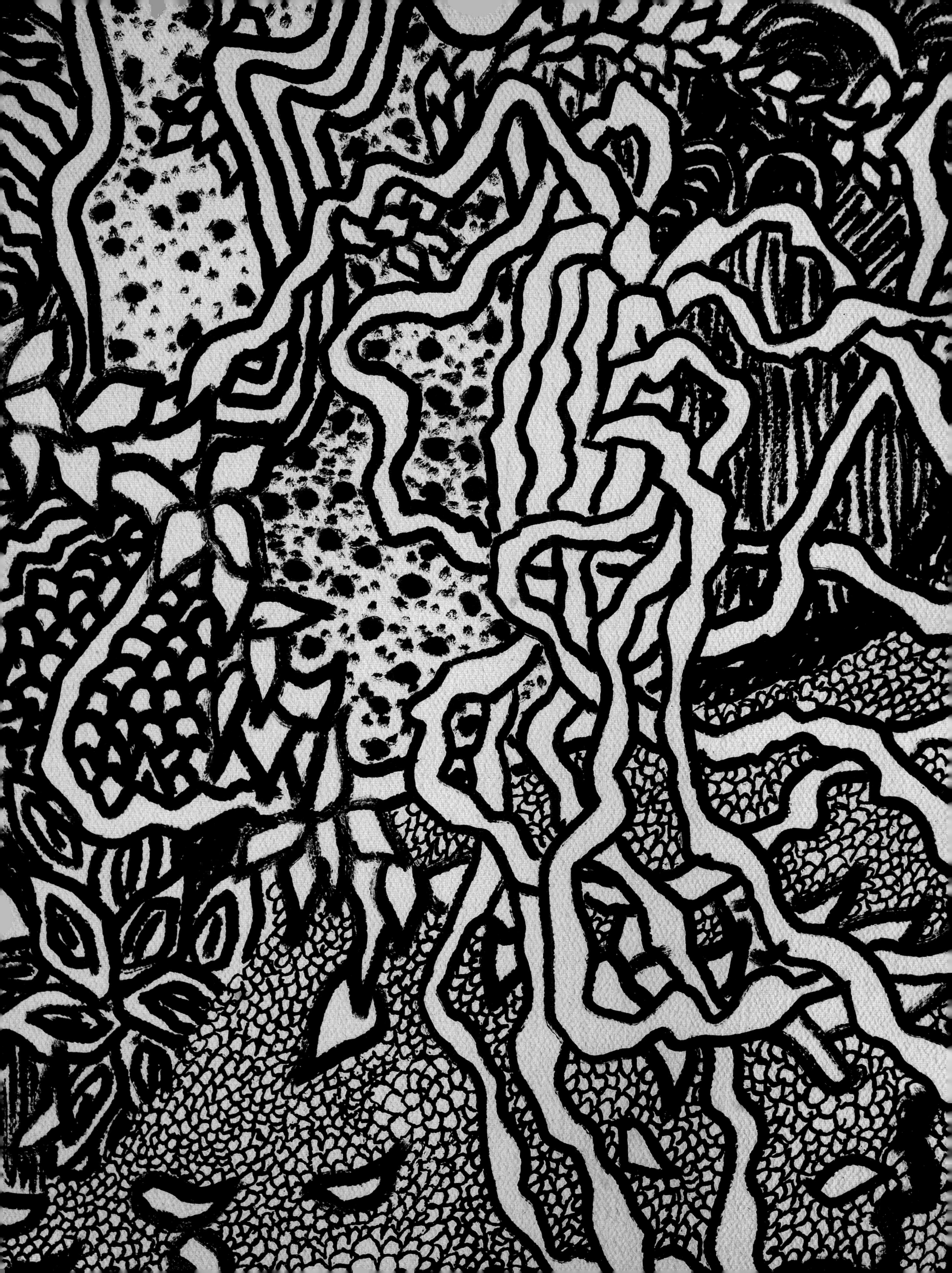

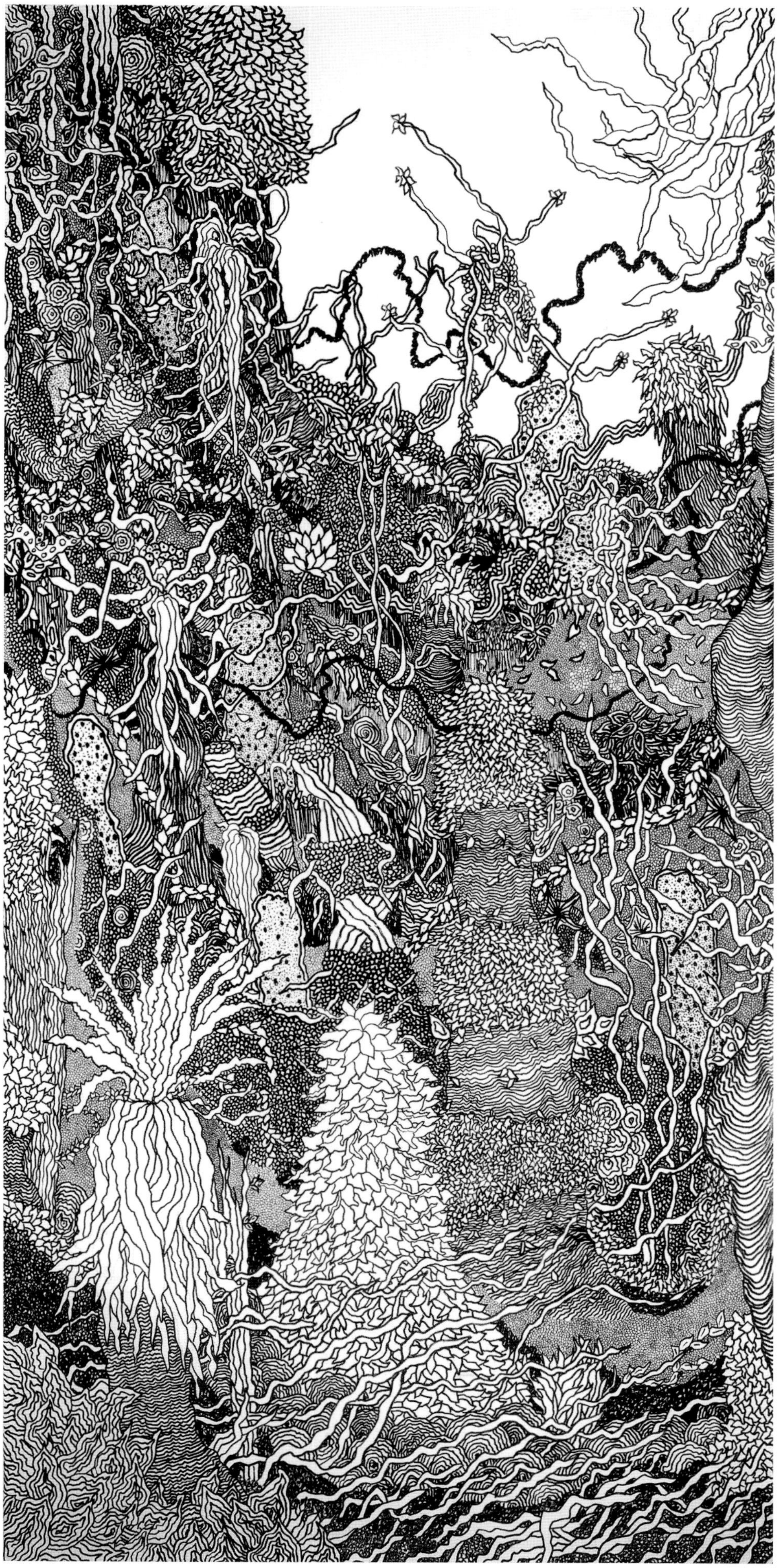

11 *What We Cannot Touch,* 2016, Acrylic on canvas, 72 x 36"

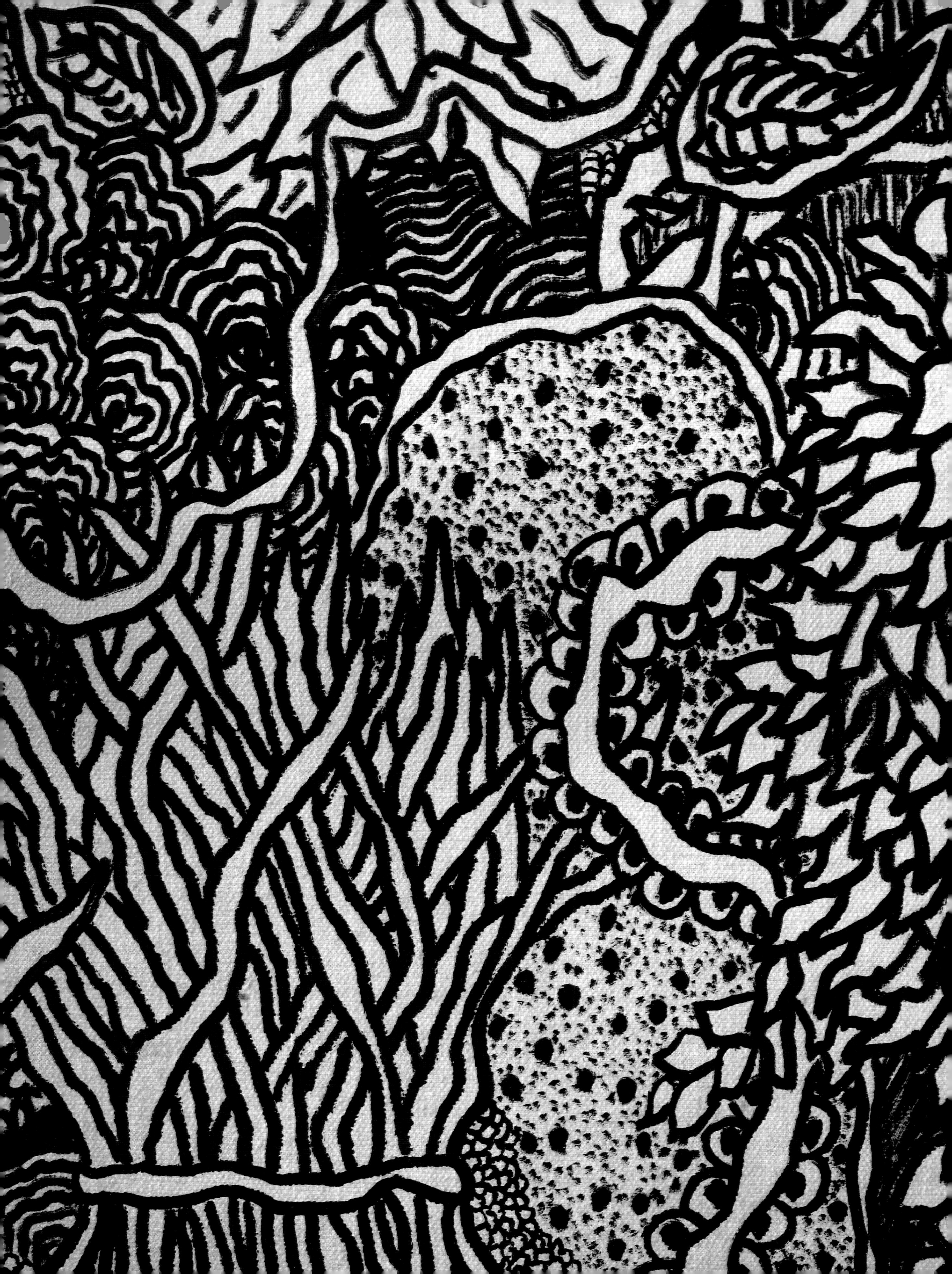

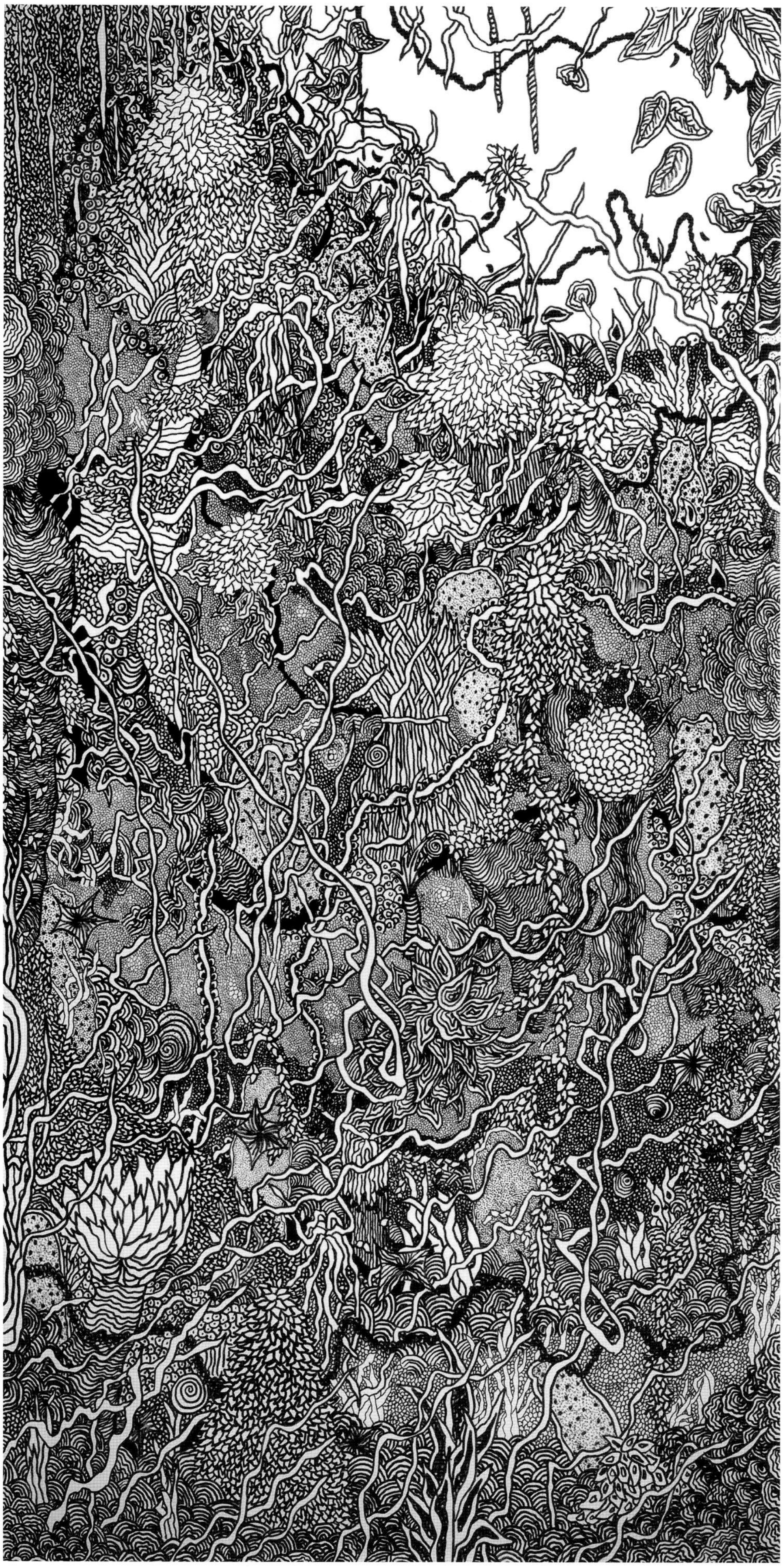

12 *What We Do Not See,* 2016, Acrylic on canvas, 72 x 36"

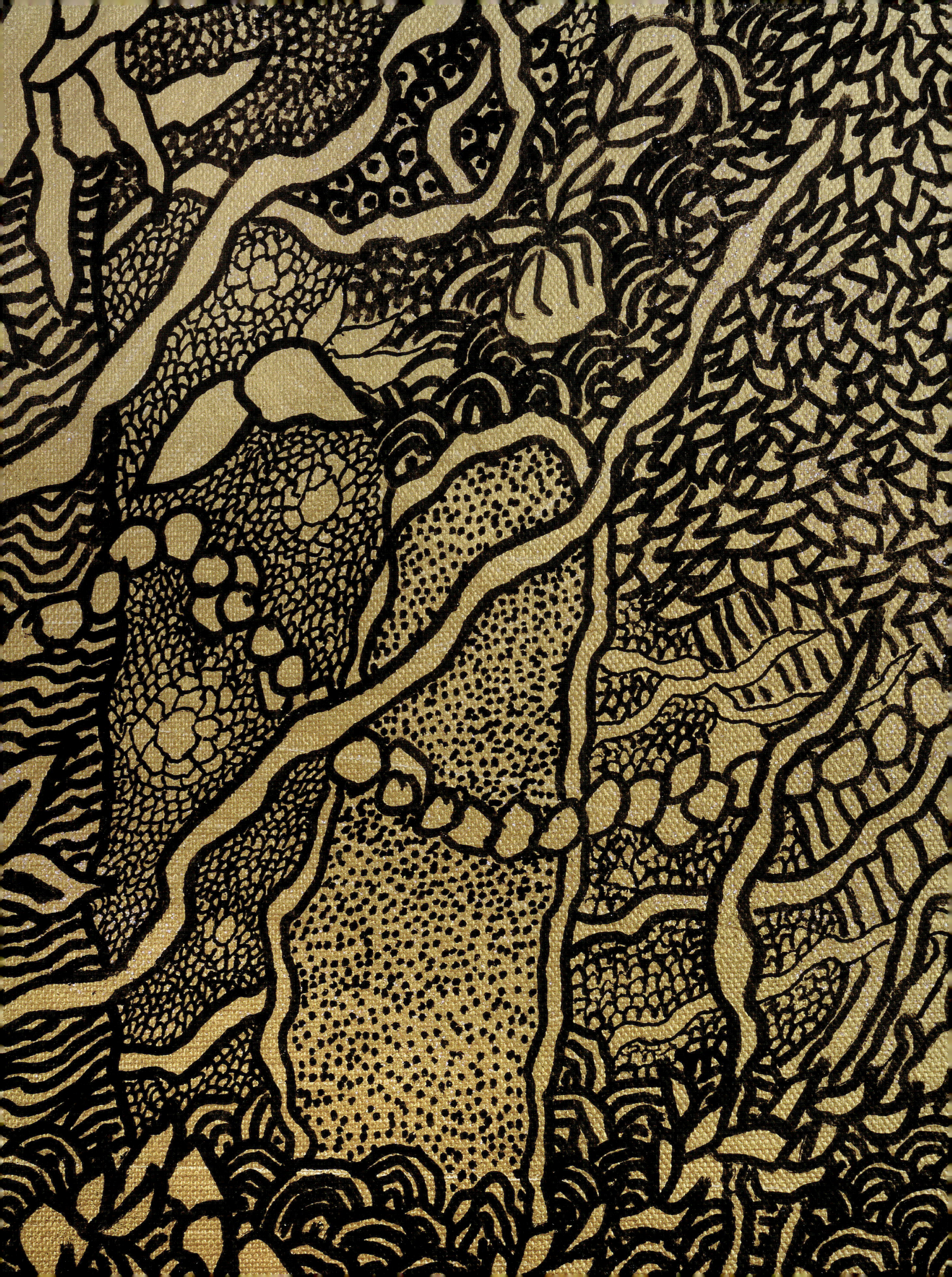

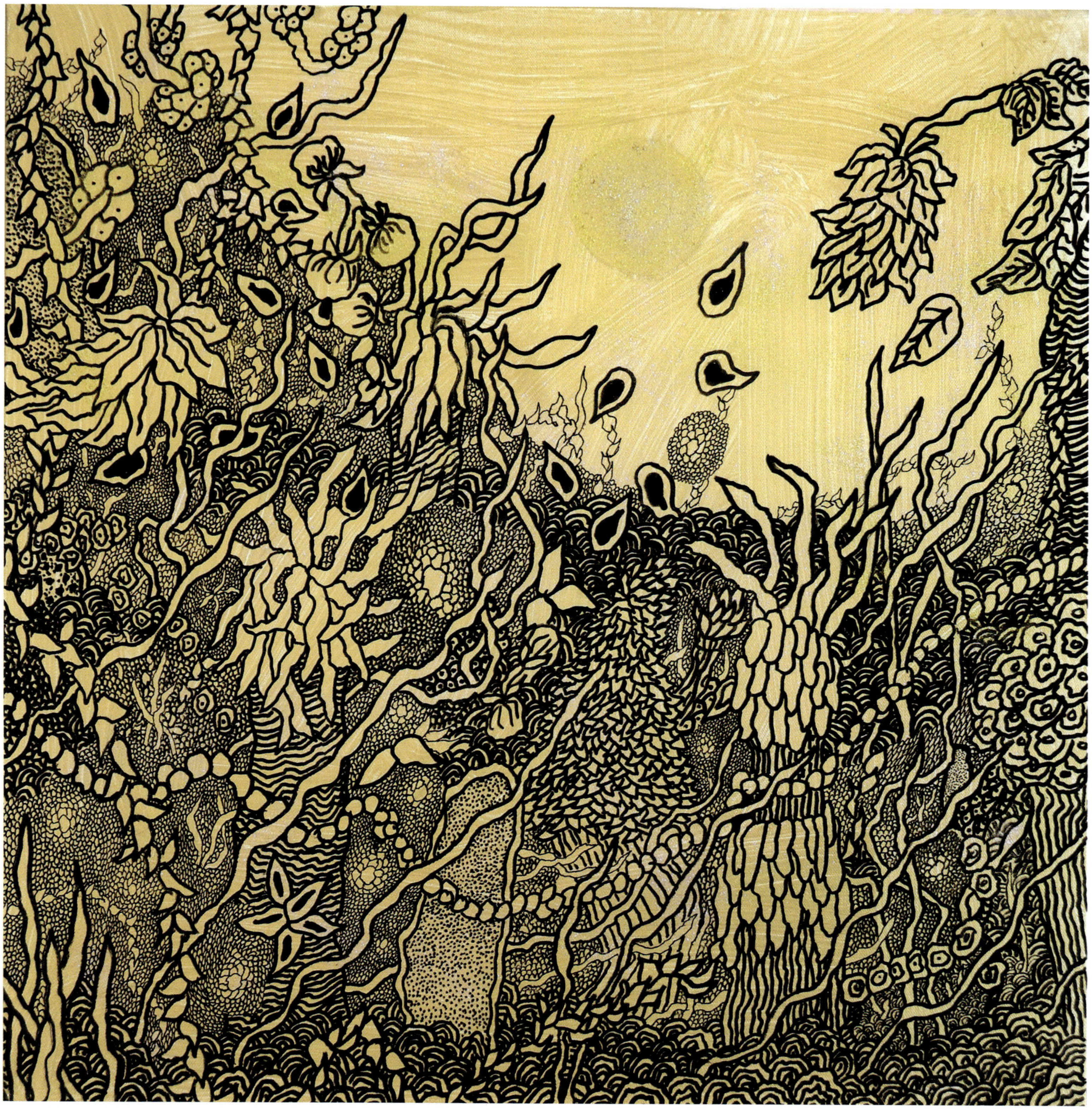

Painting in honor of dear friend, Trish Vradenburg, whom we lost in Spring 2017.

13 *She is the Gold in the Glittering Moon,* 2017, Acrylic on canvas with polymer particles, 24 x 24"

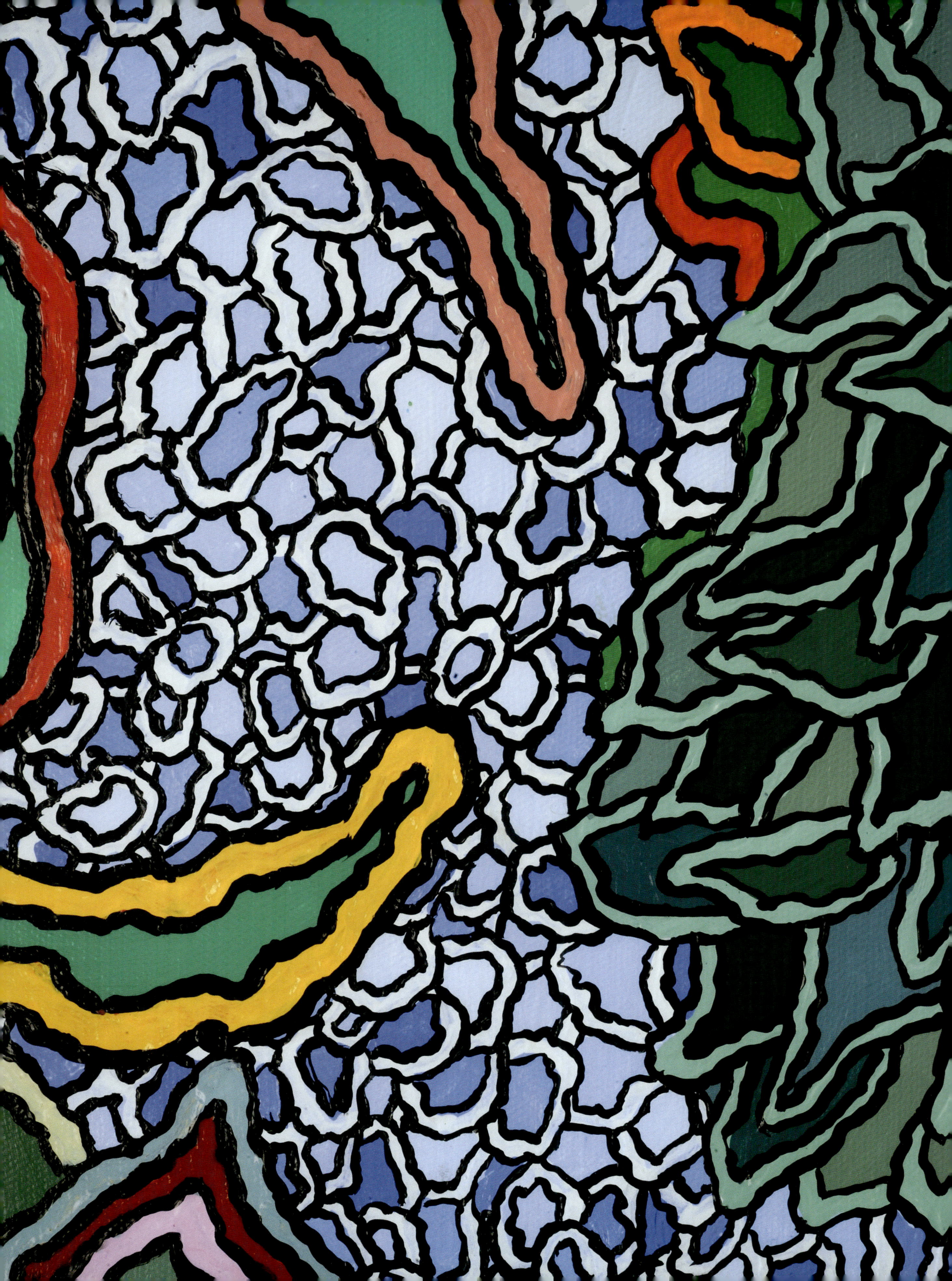

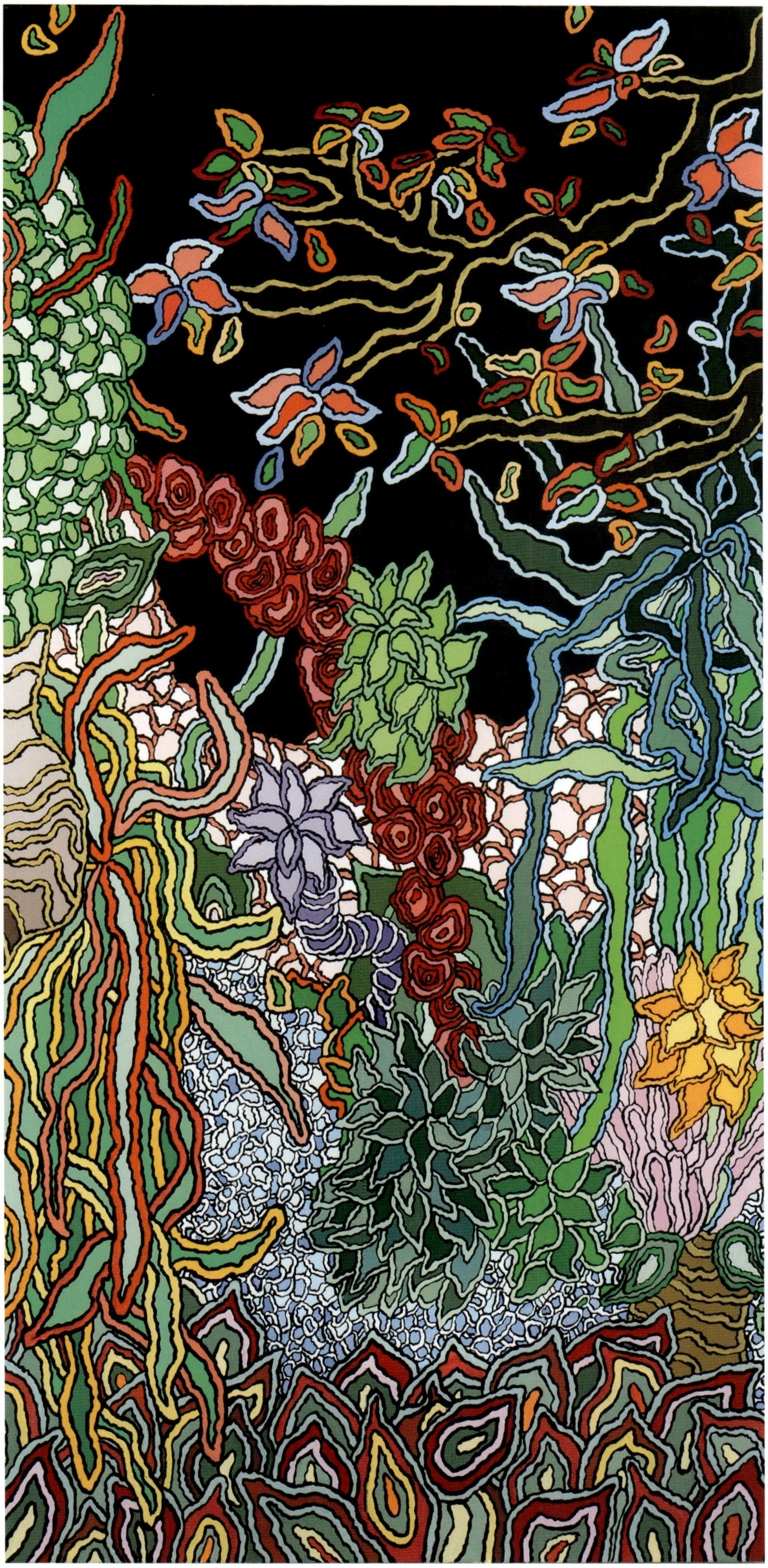

14 *Beverly's Garden,* 2015, Acrylic on canvas, 48 x 24"

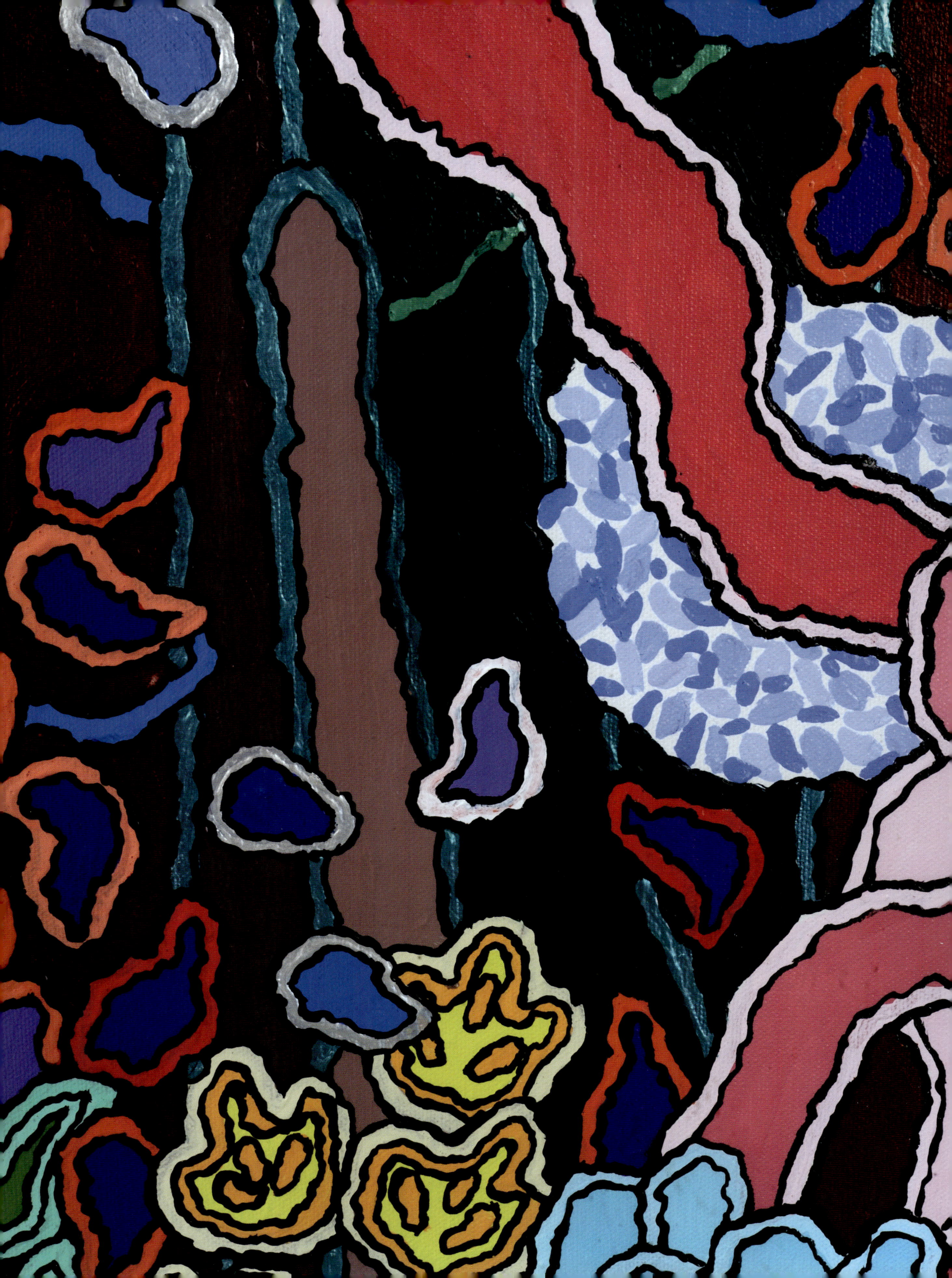

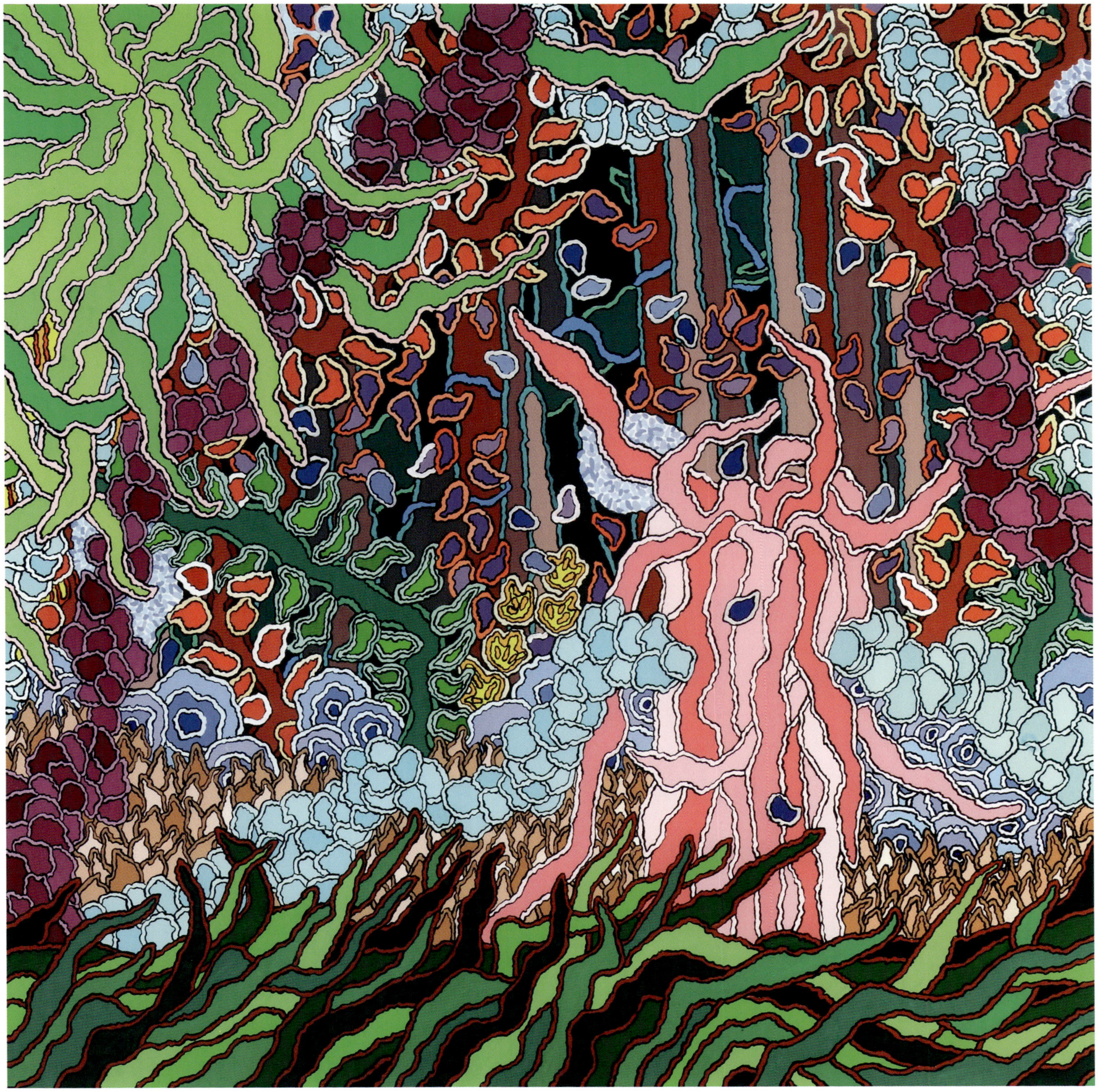

15 *Garden Behind the White Picket Fence,* 2015, Acrylic on canvas, 48 x 48"

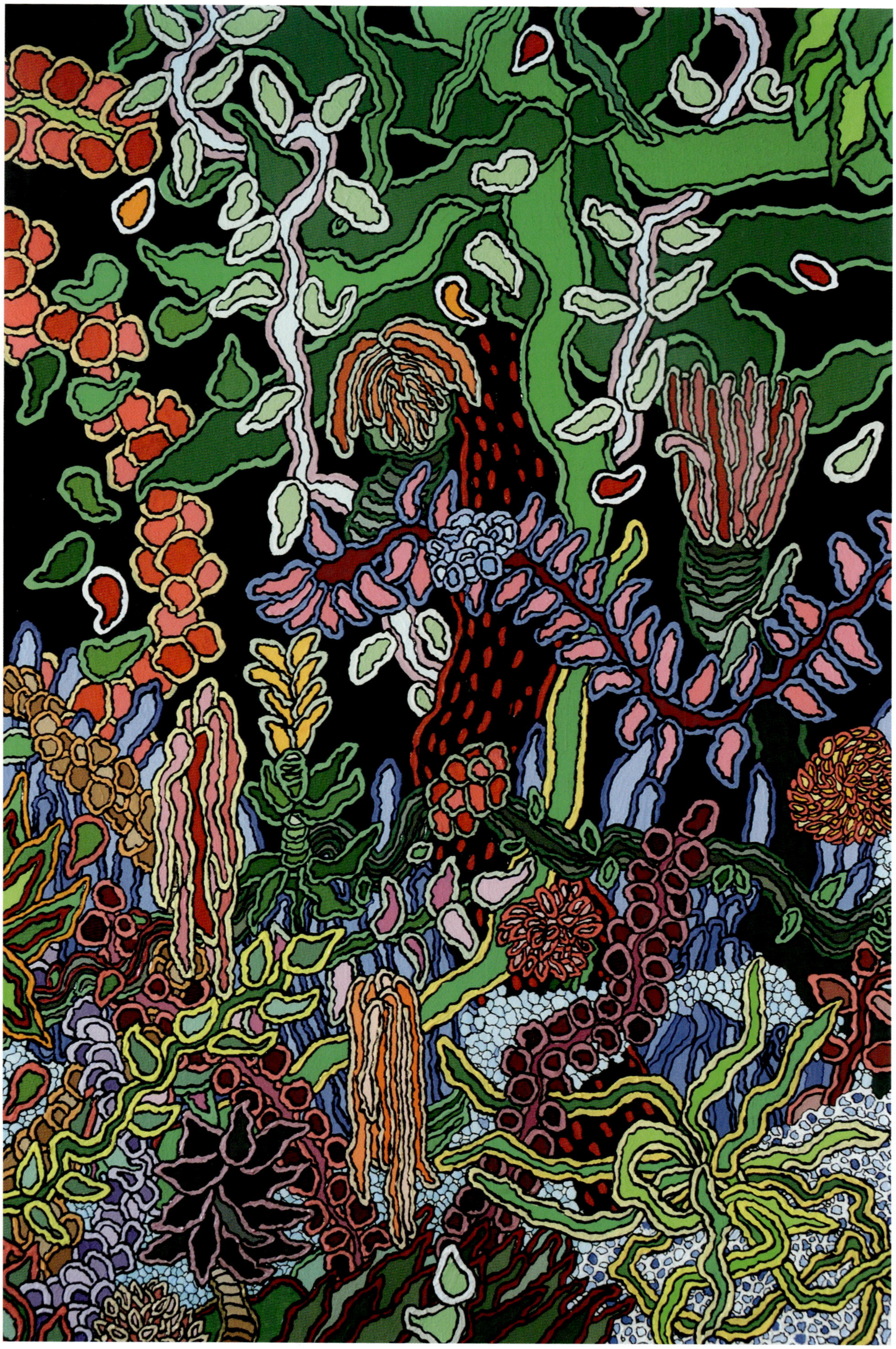

16 *The Garden of Enkidu,* 2015, Acrylic on canvas, 36 x 24"

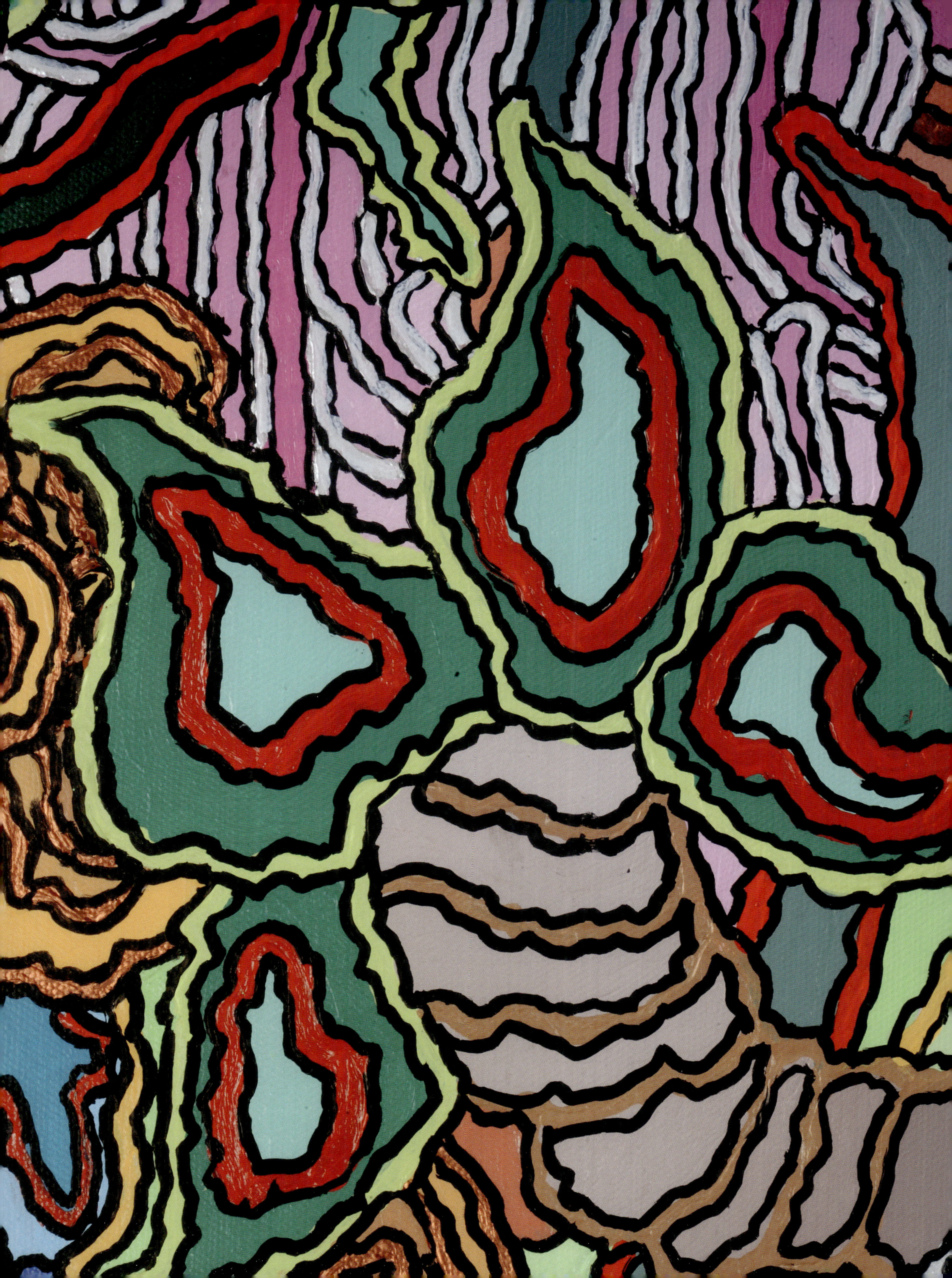

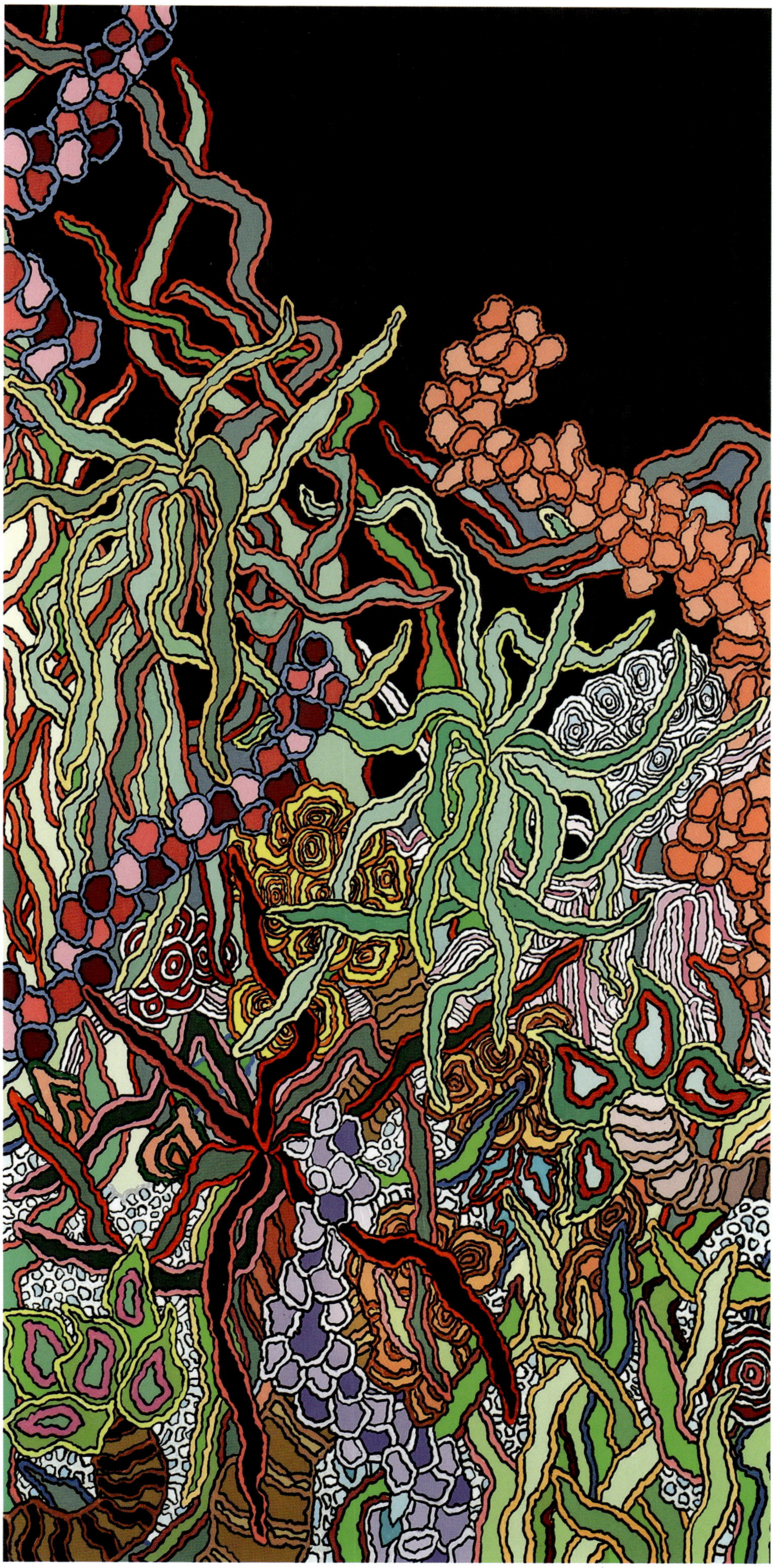

17 *The Garden of Sumer,* 2015, Acrylic on canvas, 48 x 24"

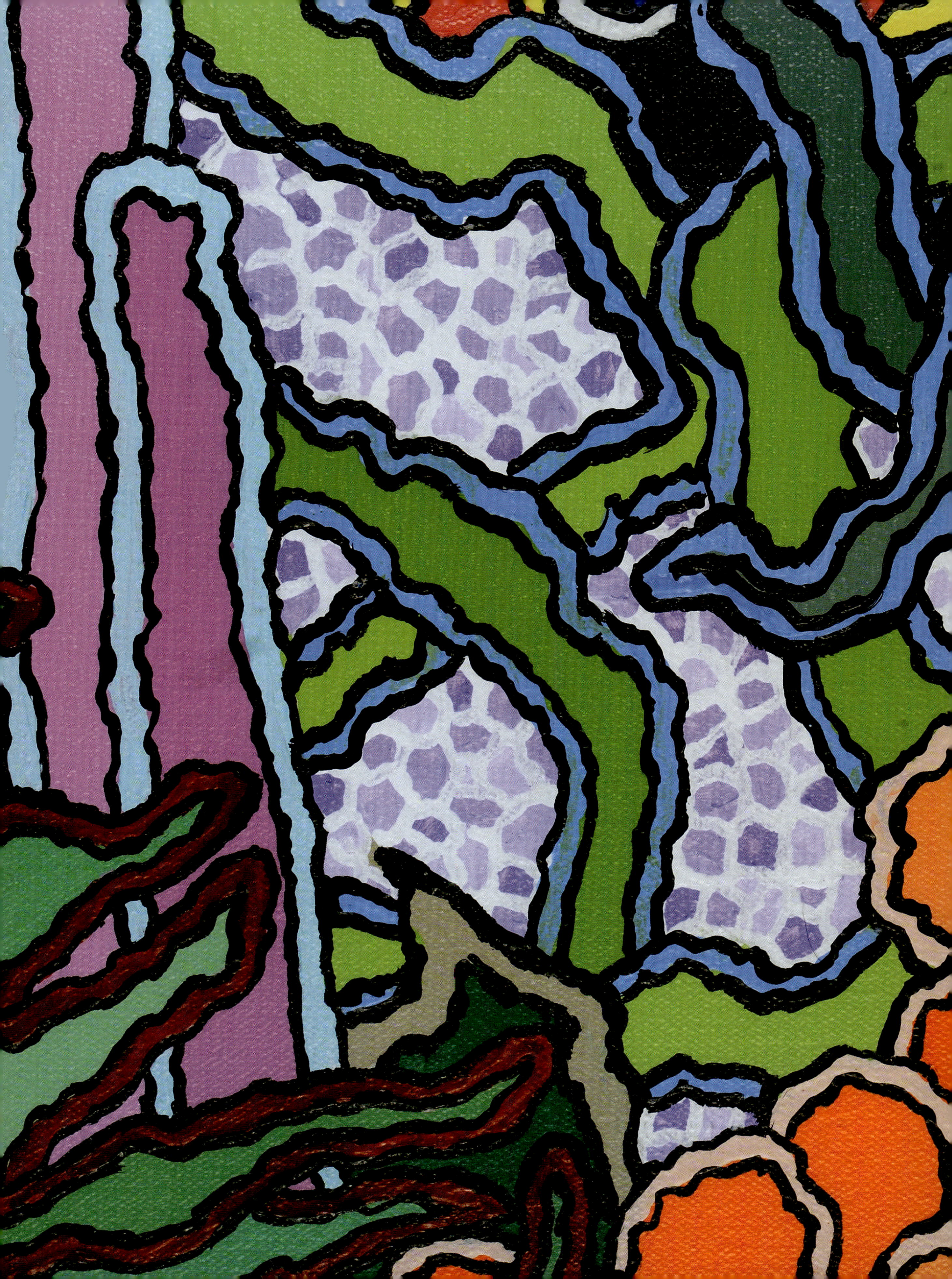

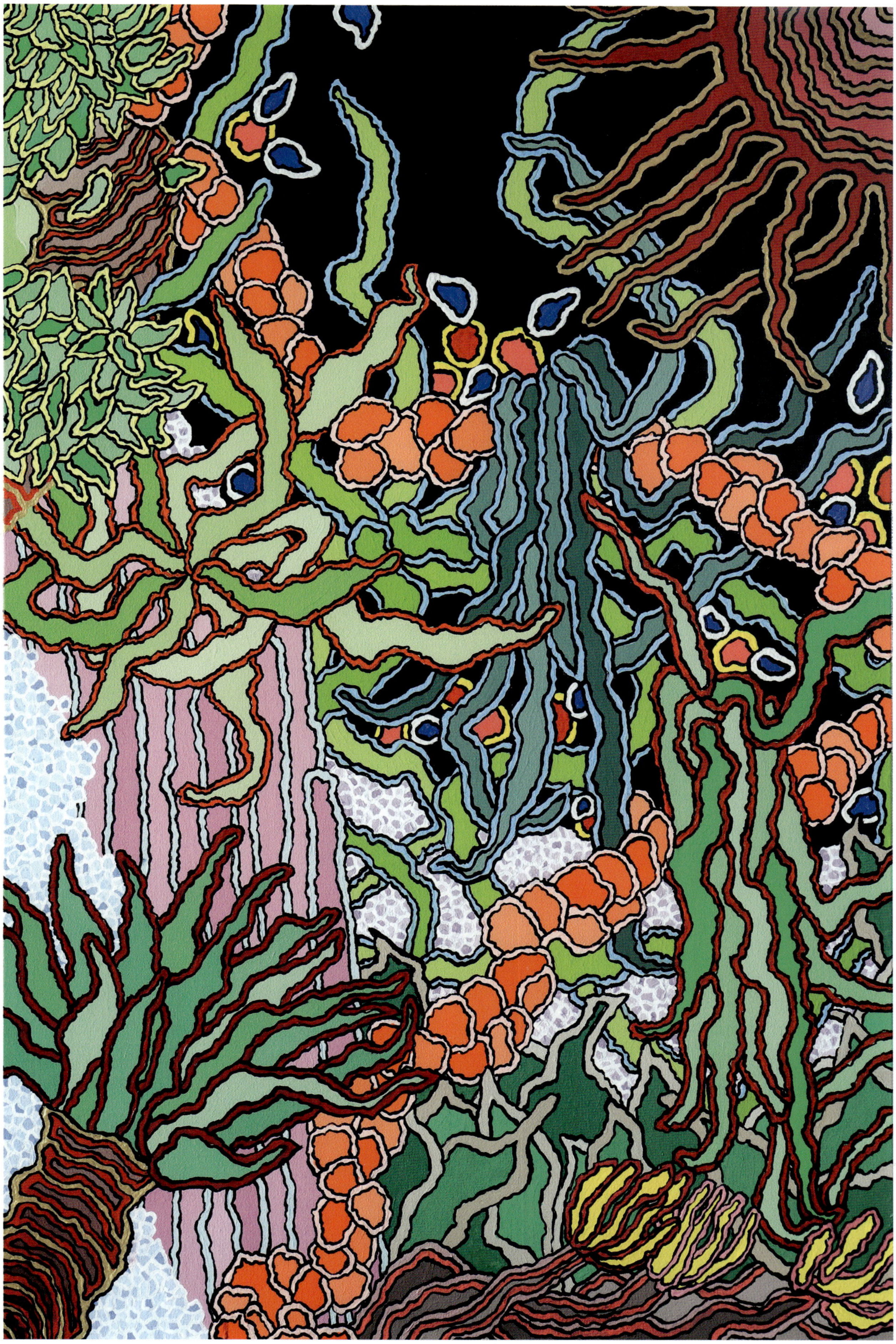

18 *The Garden of the Moon-god,* 2015, Acrylic on canvas, 36 x 24"

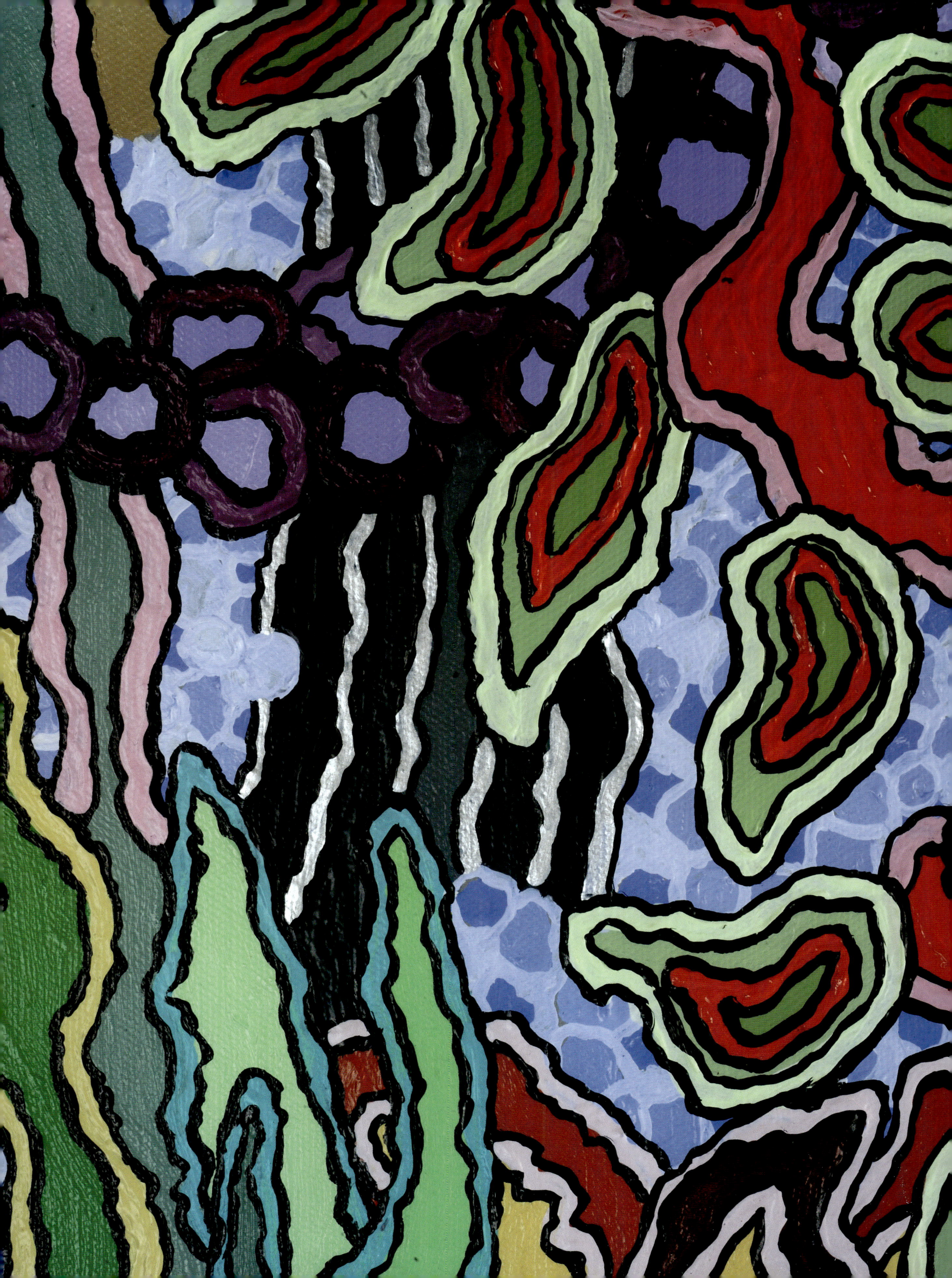

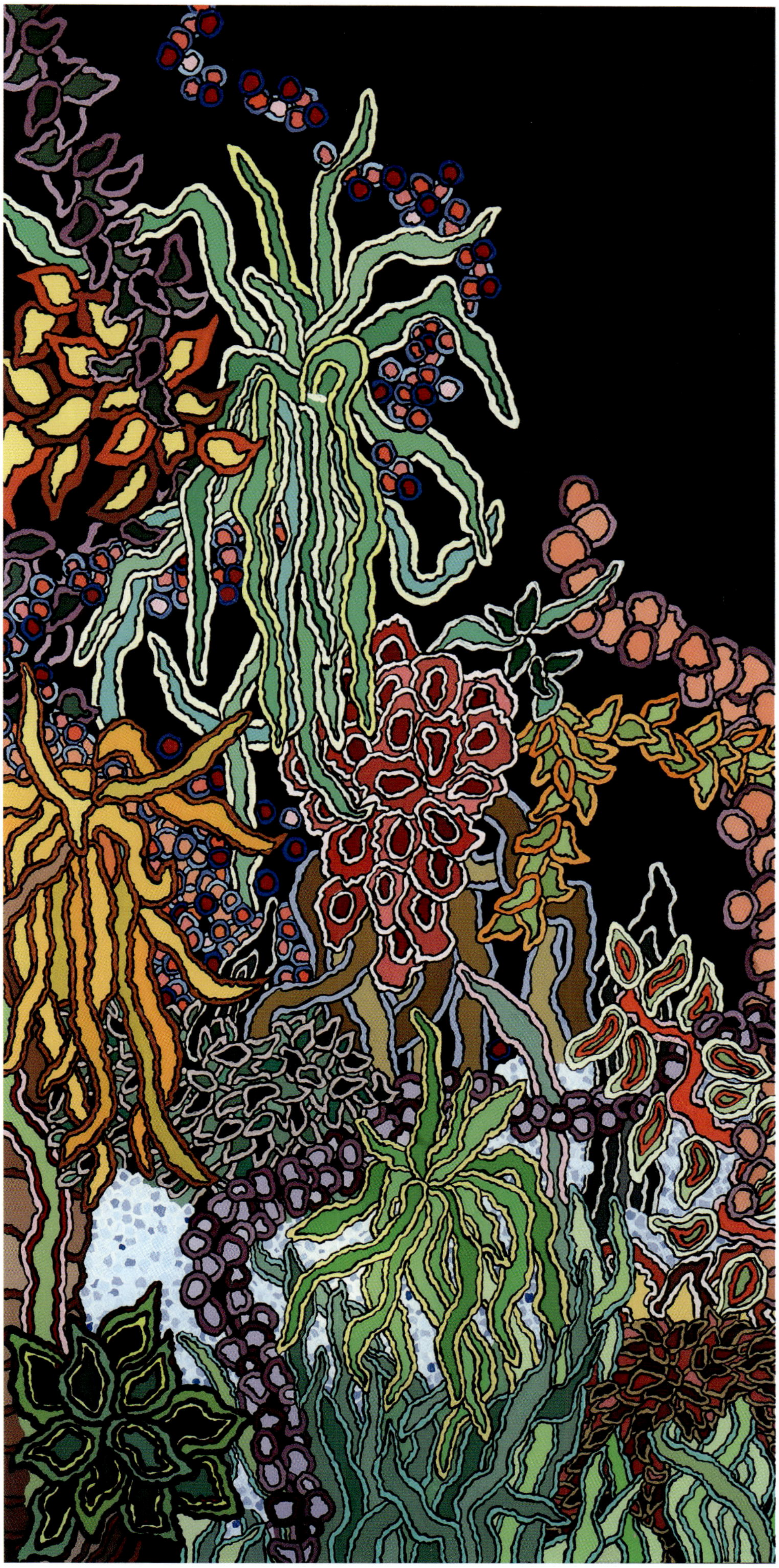

19 *The Garden of Uruk,* 2015, Acrylic on canvas, 48 x 24"

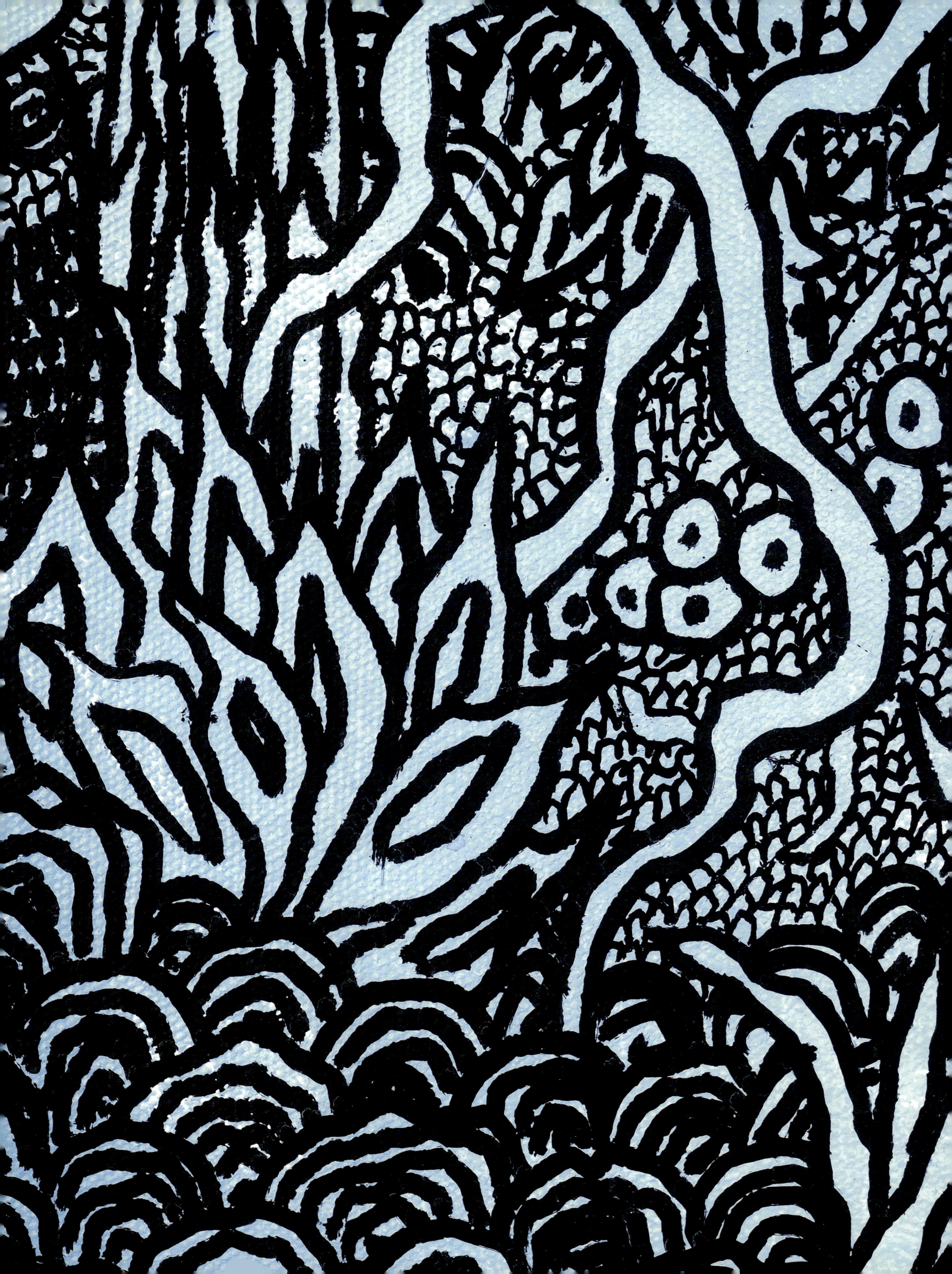

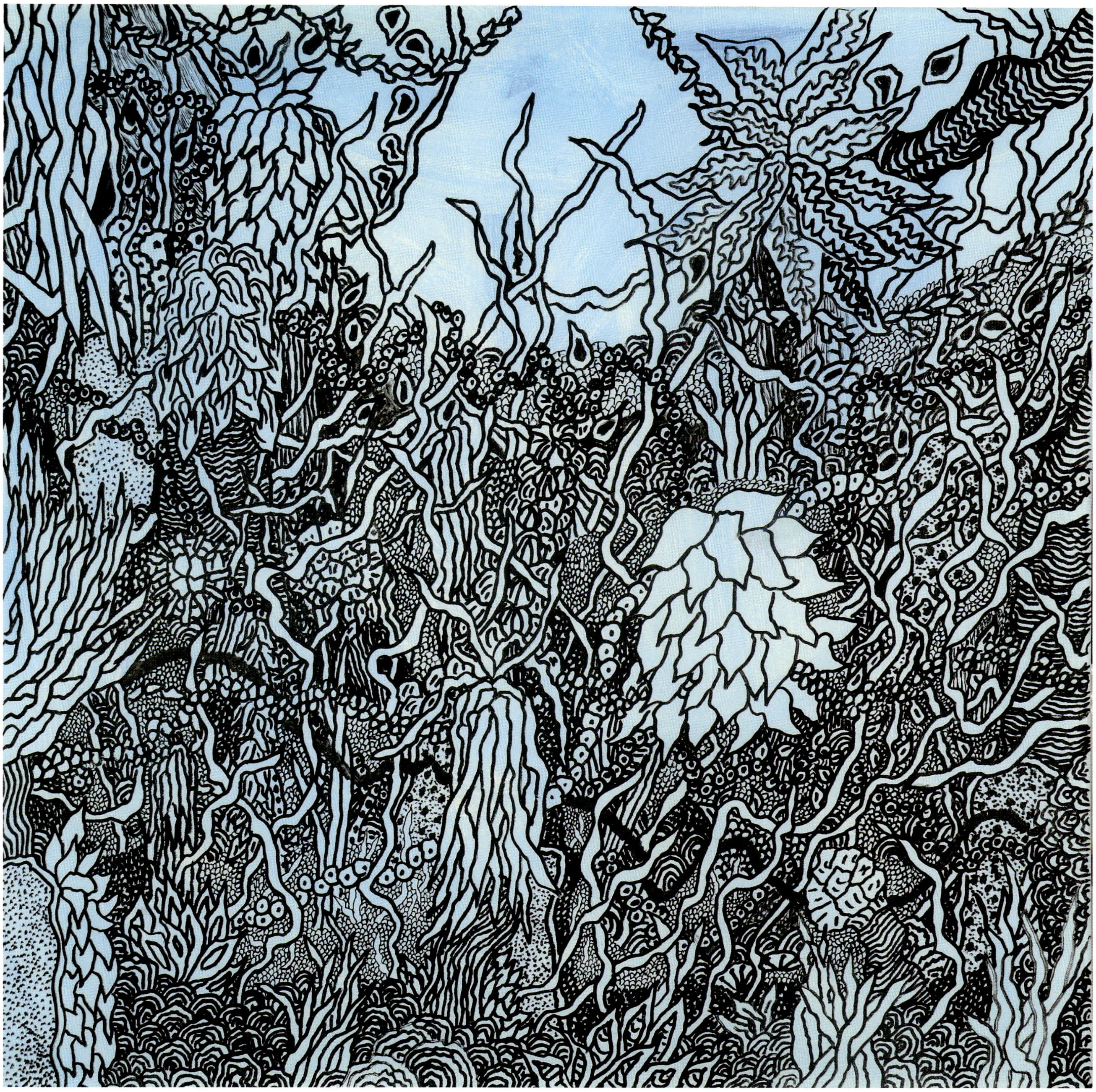

20 *I See Through the Moon,* 2017, Acrylic on canvas, 24 x 24"

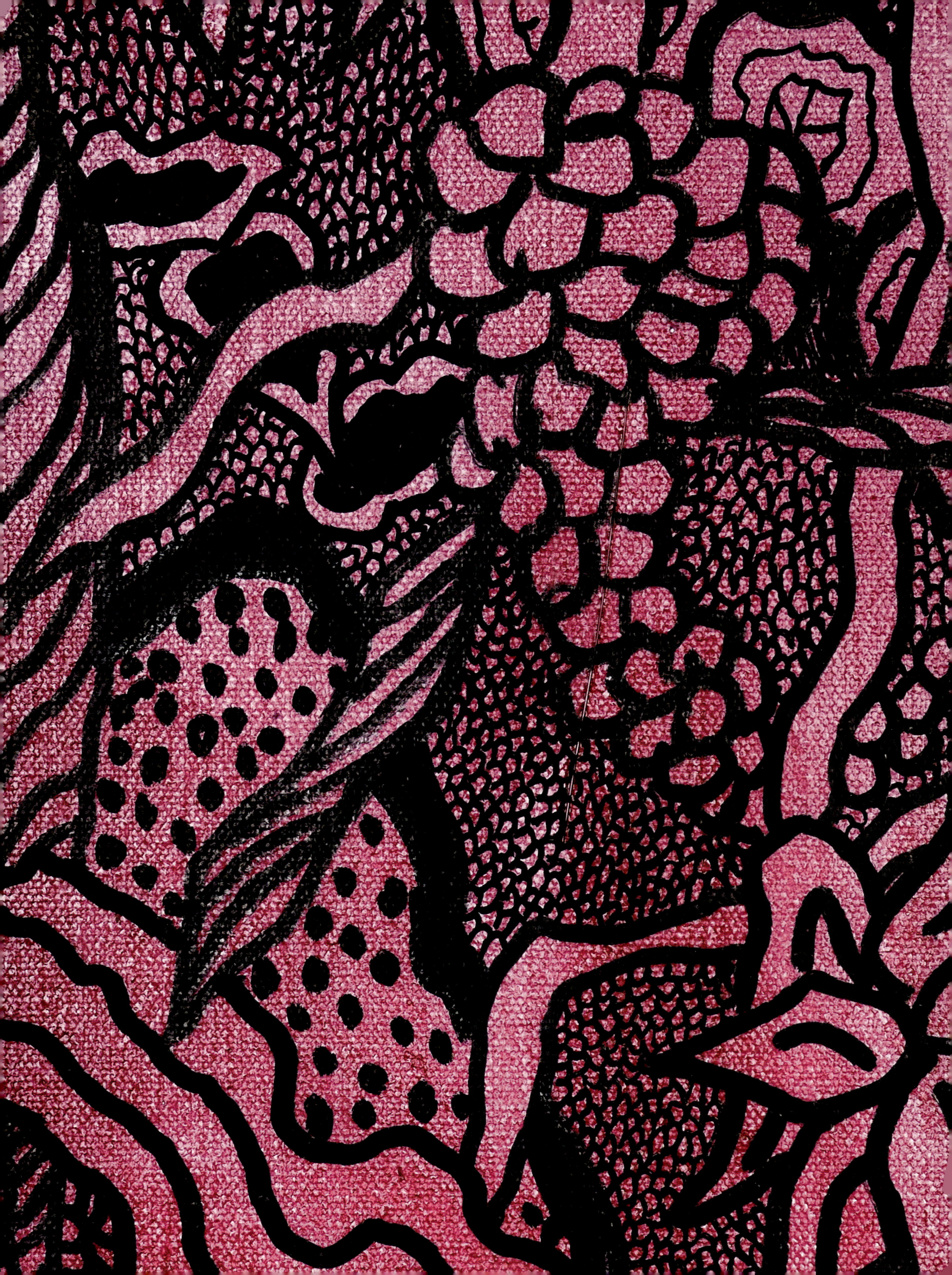

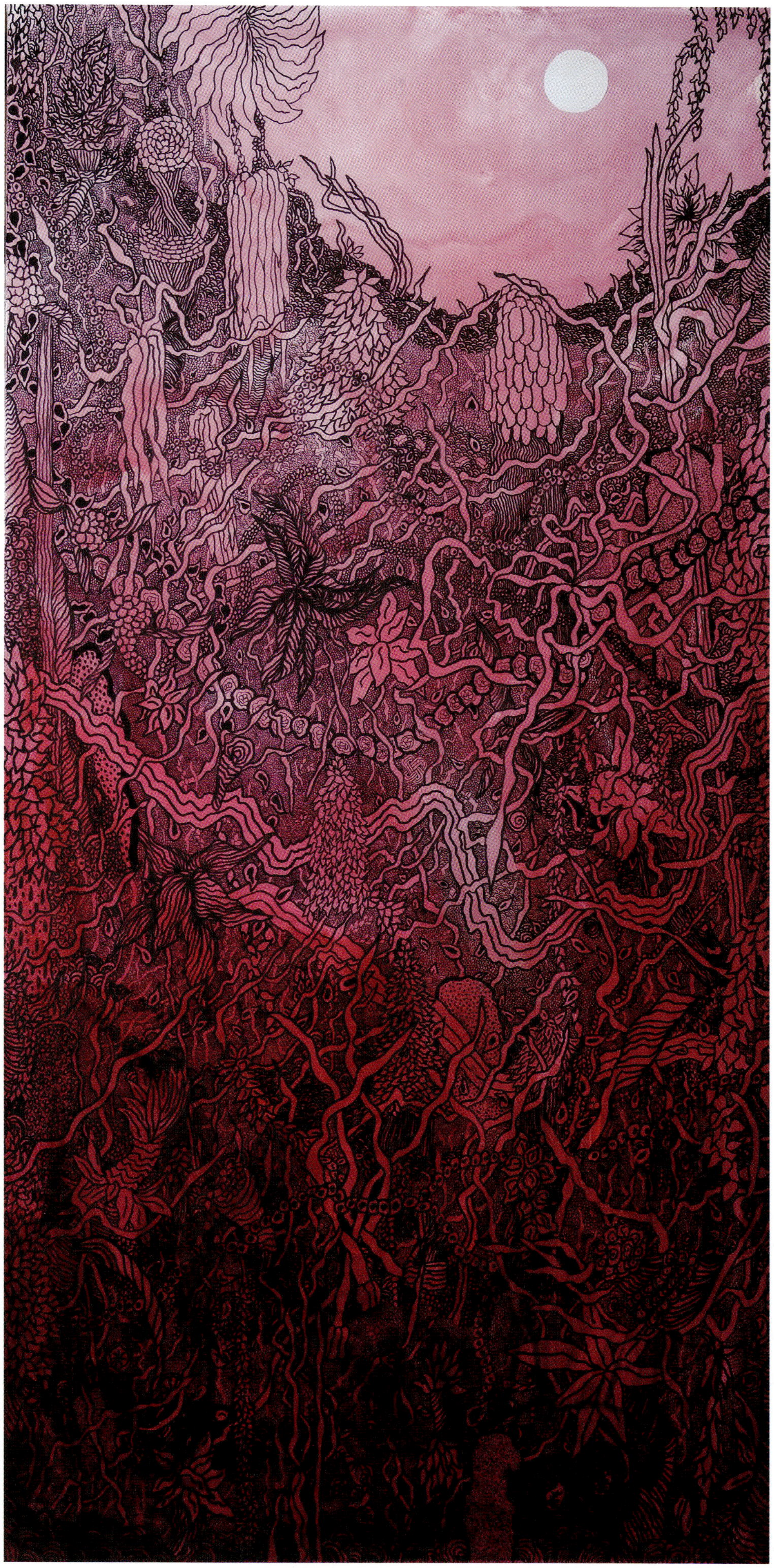

21 *Magental Moonlight,* 2017, Acrylic on canvas, 72 x 36"

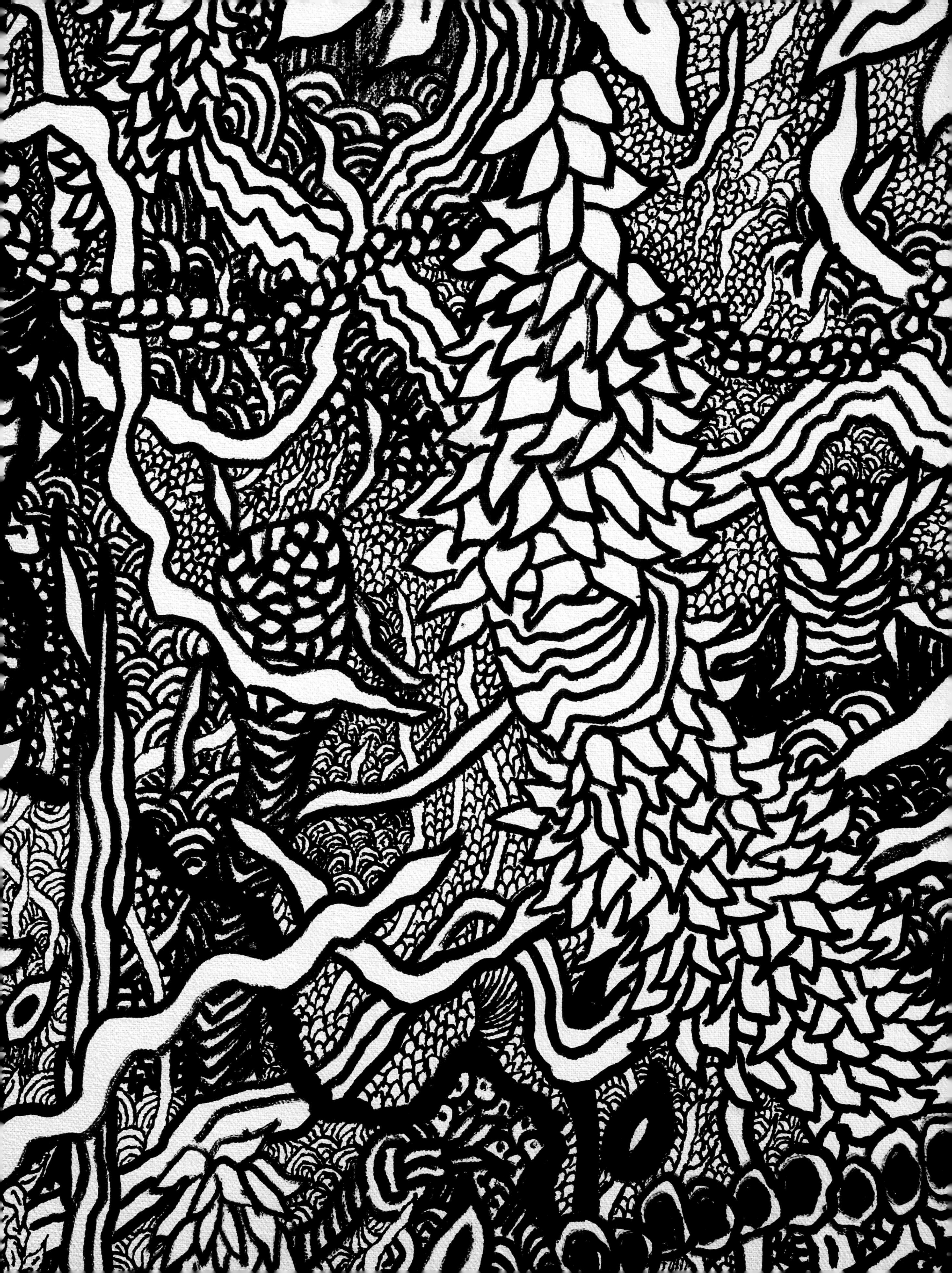

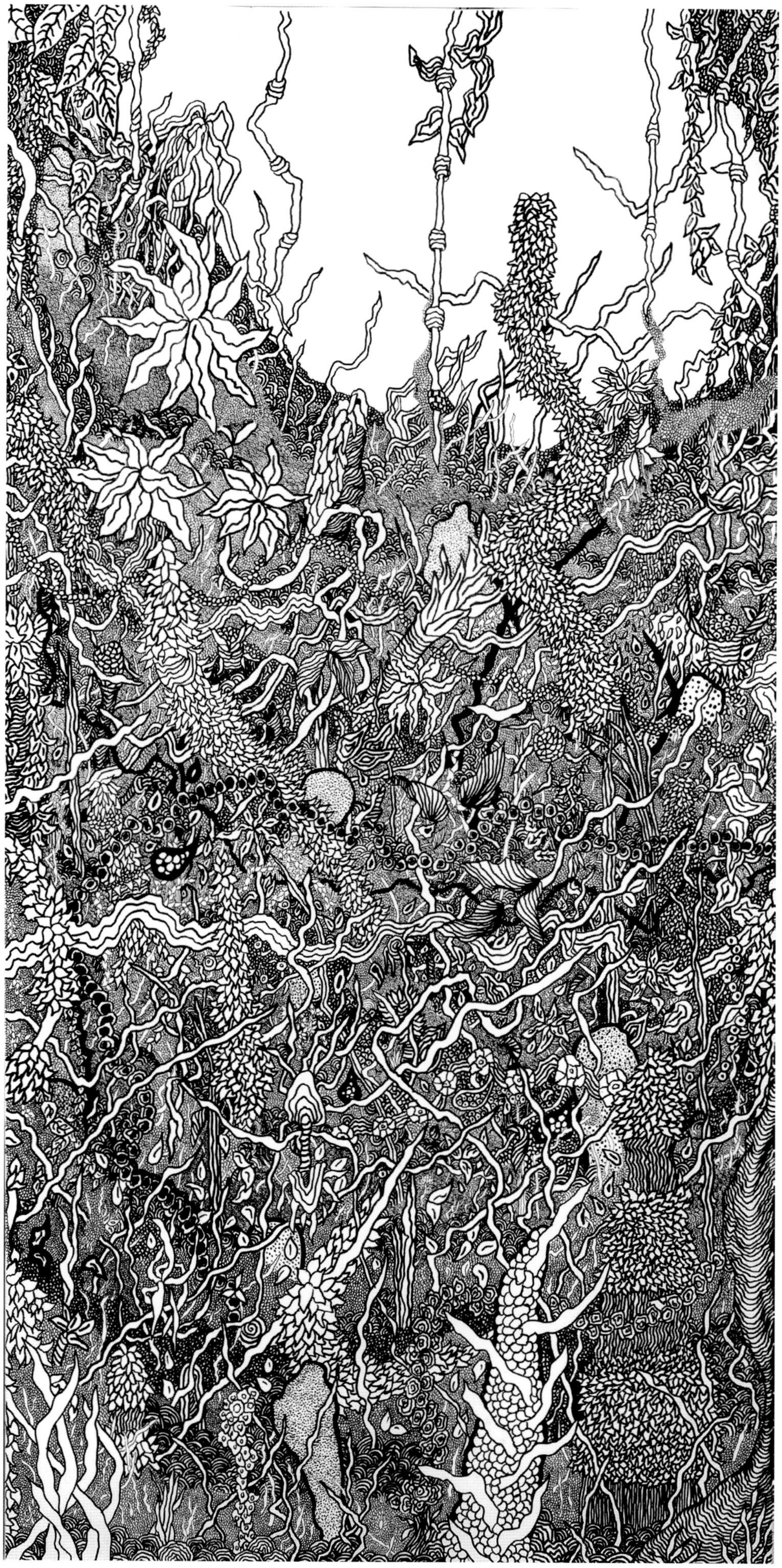

22 *Motionless Presence,* 2017, Acrylic on canvas, 72 x 36"

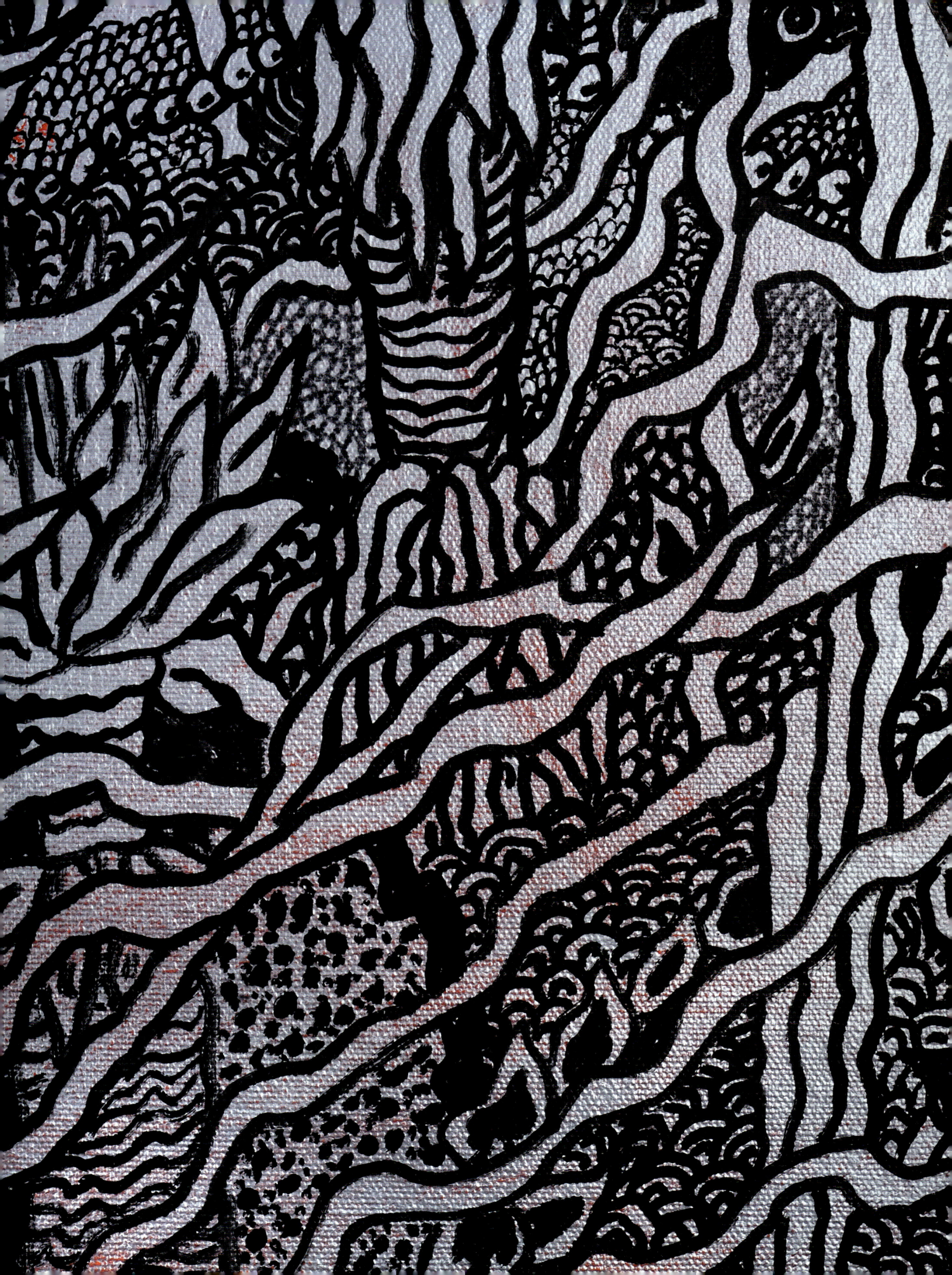

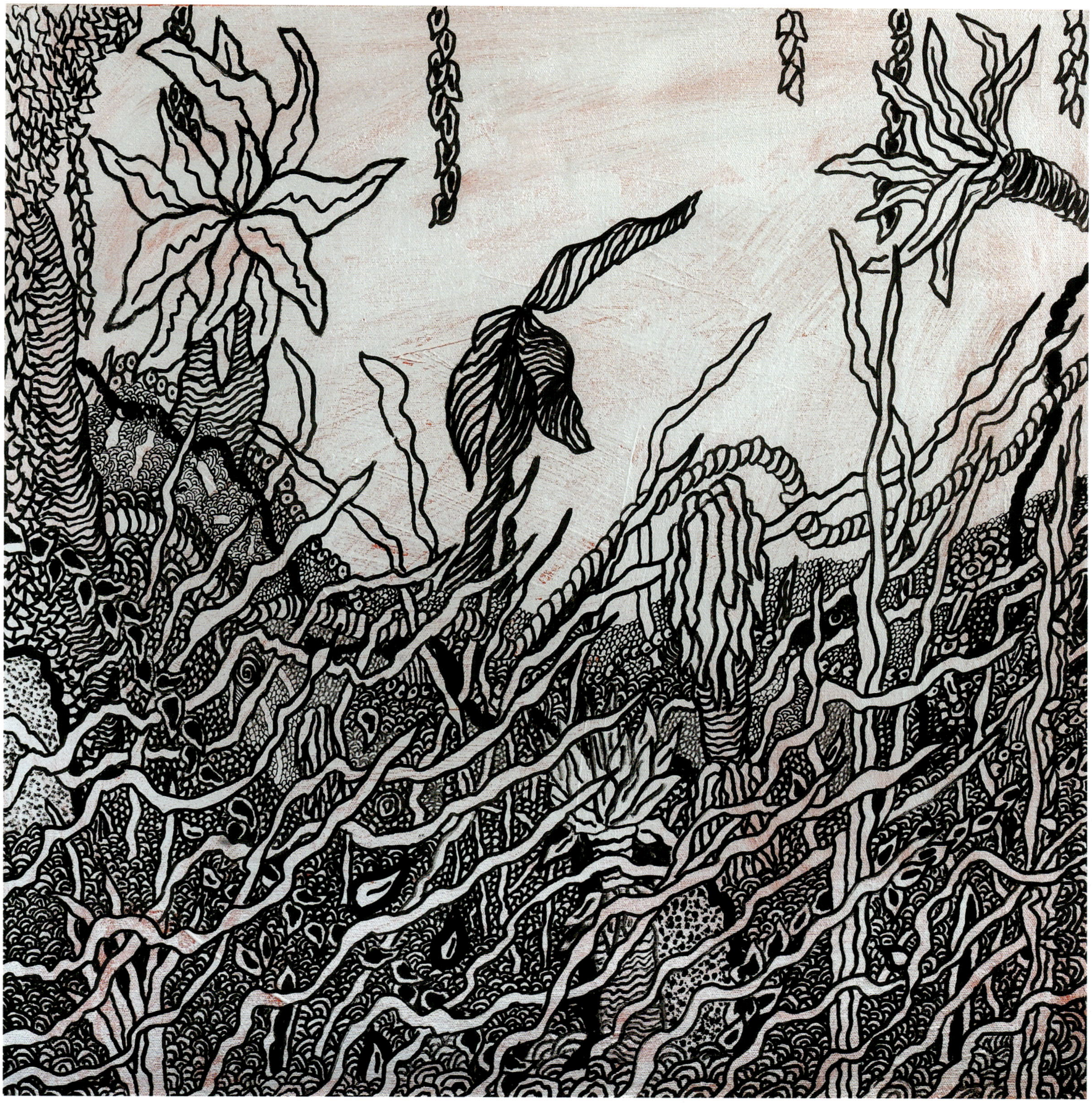

23 *Silken Garden,* 2017, Acrylic on canvas, 24 x 24"

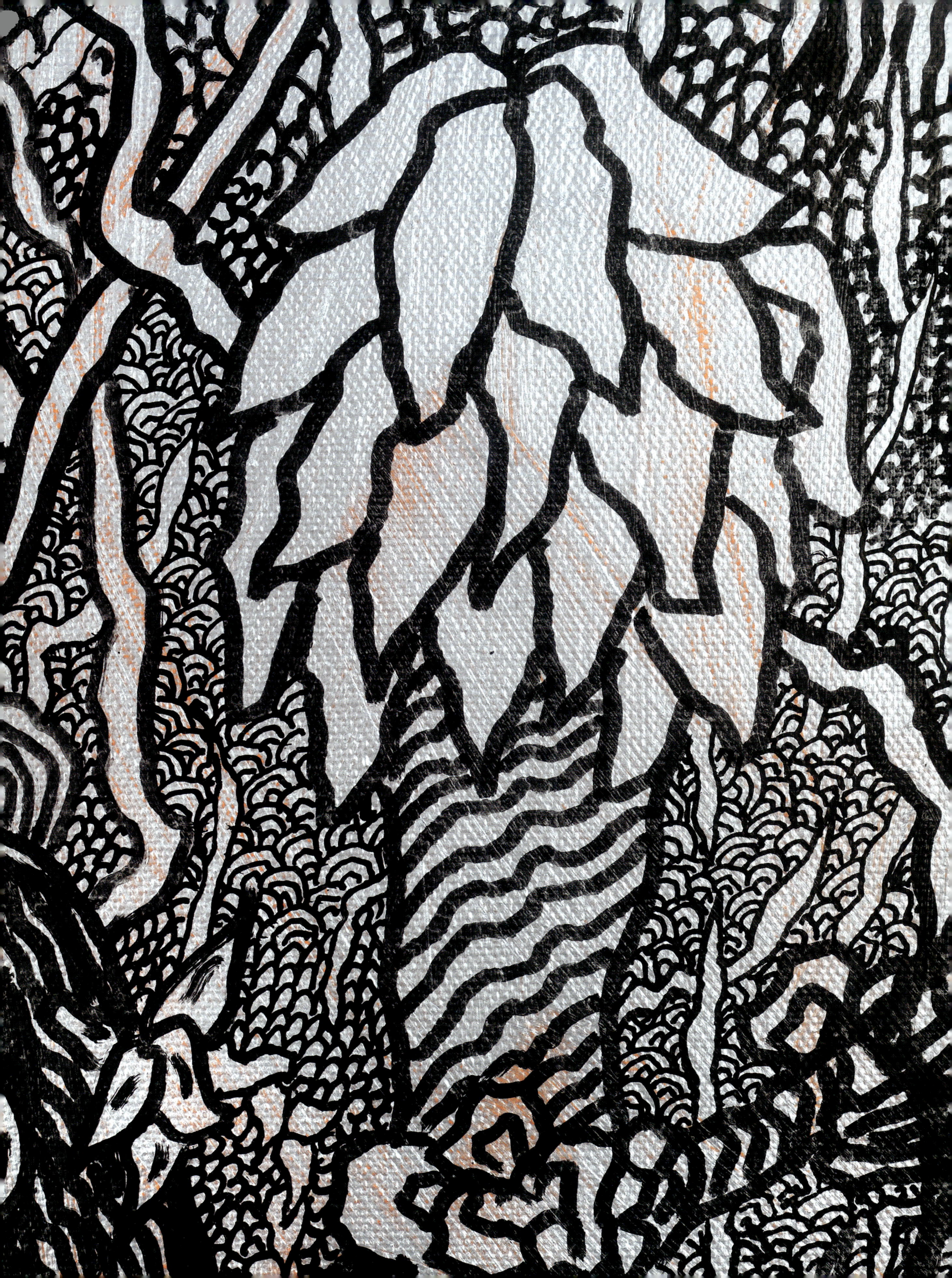

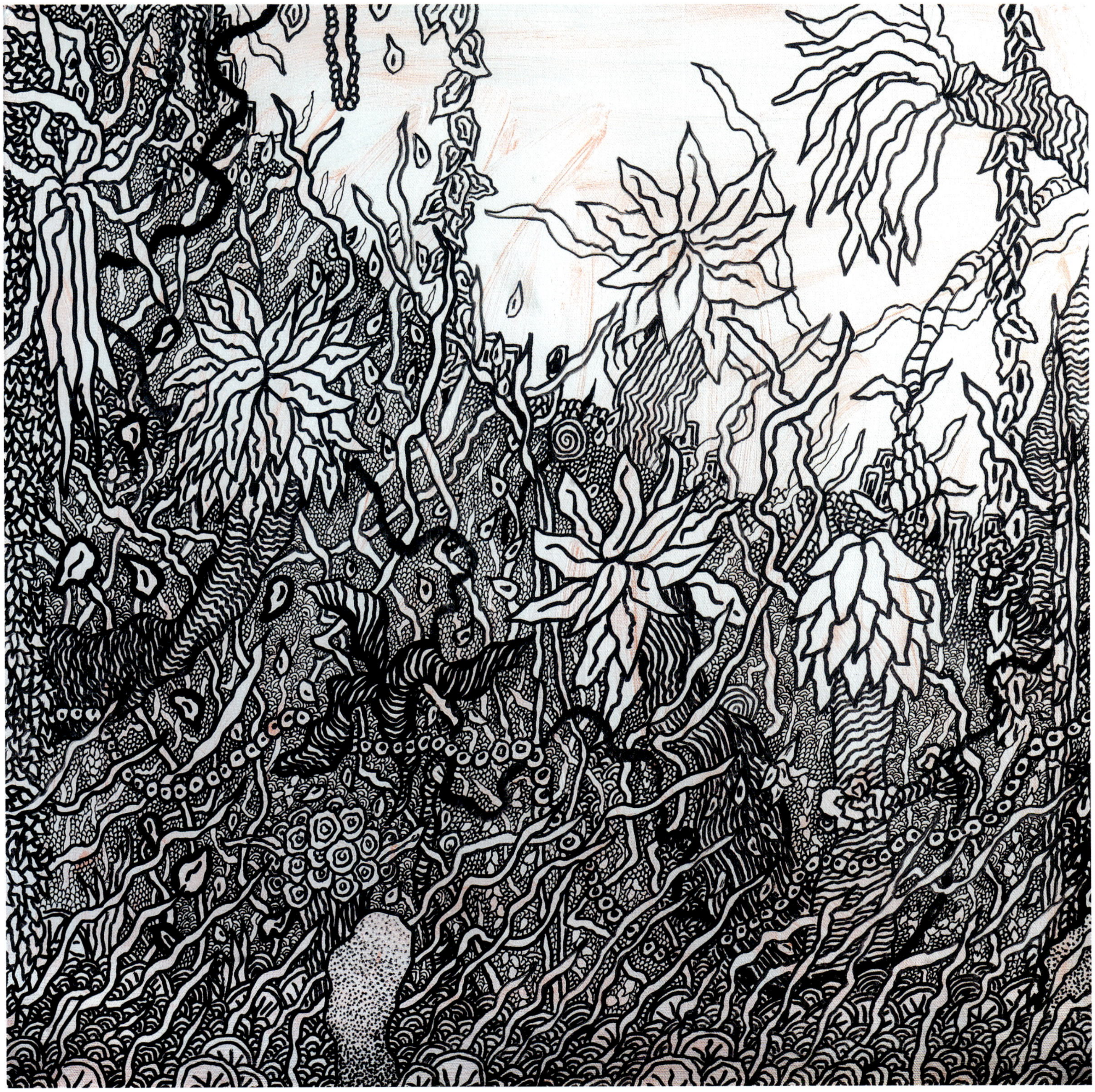

24 *Twilight of the Grasses,* 2017, Acrylic on canvas, 24 x 24"

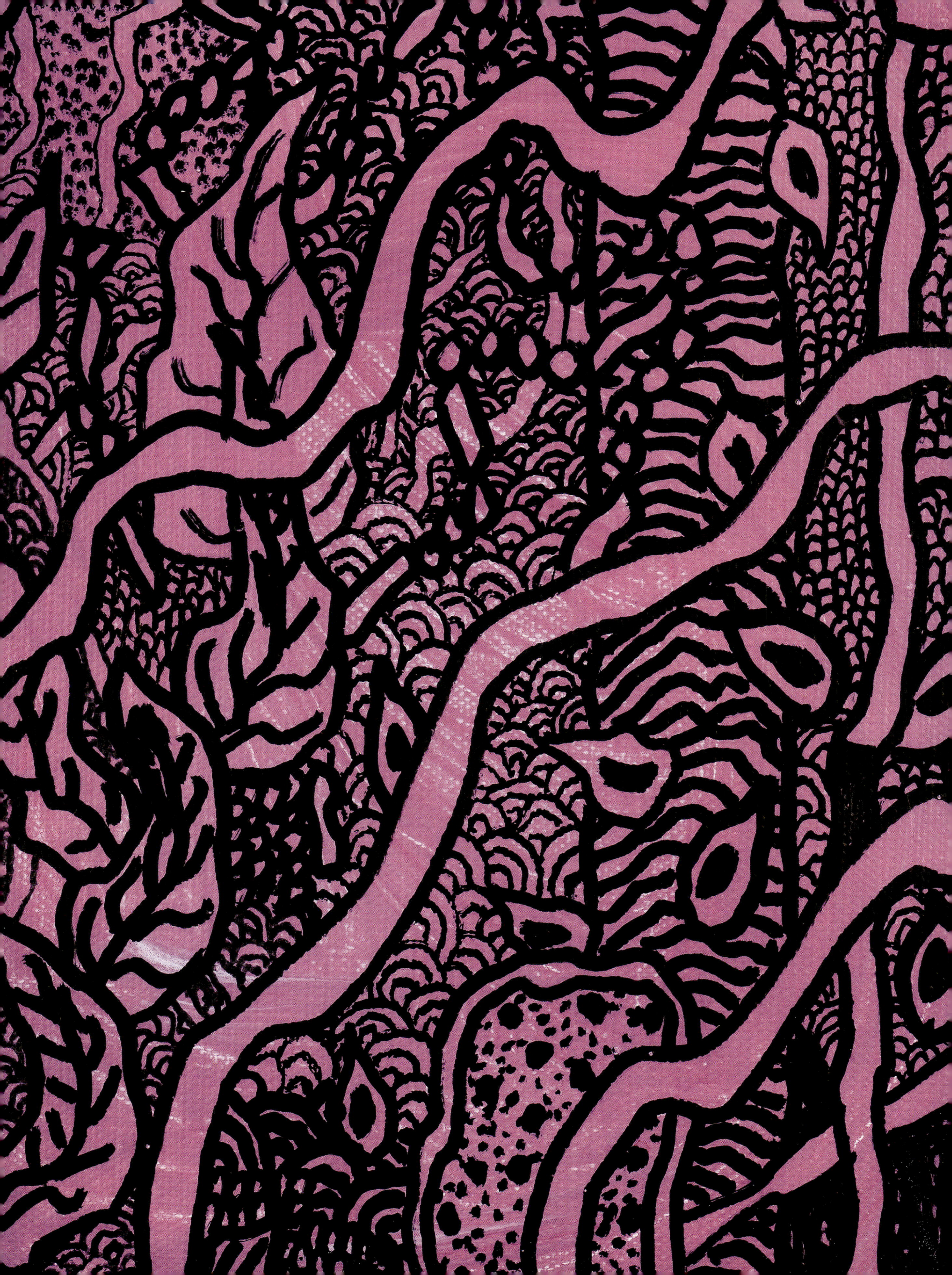

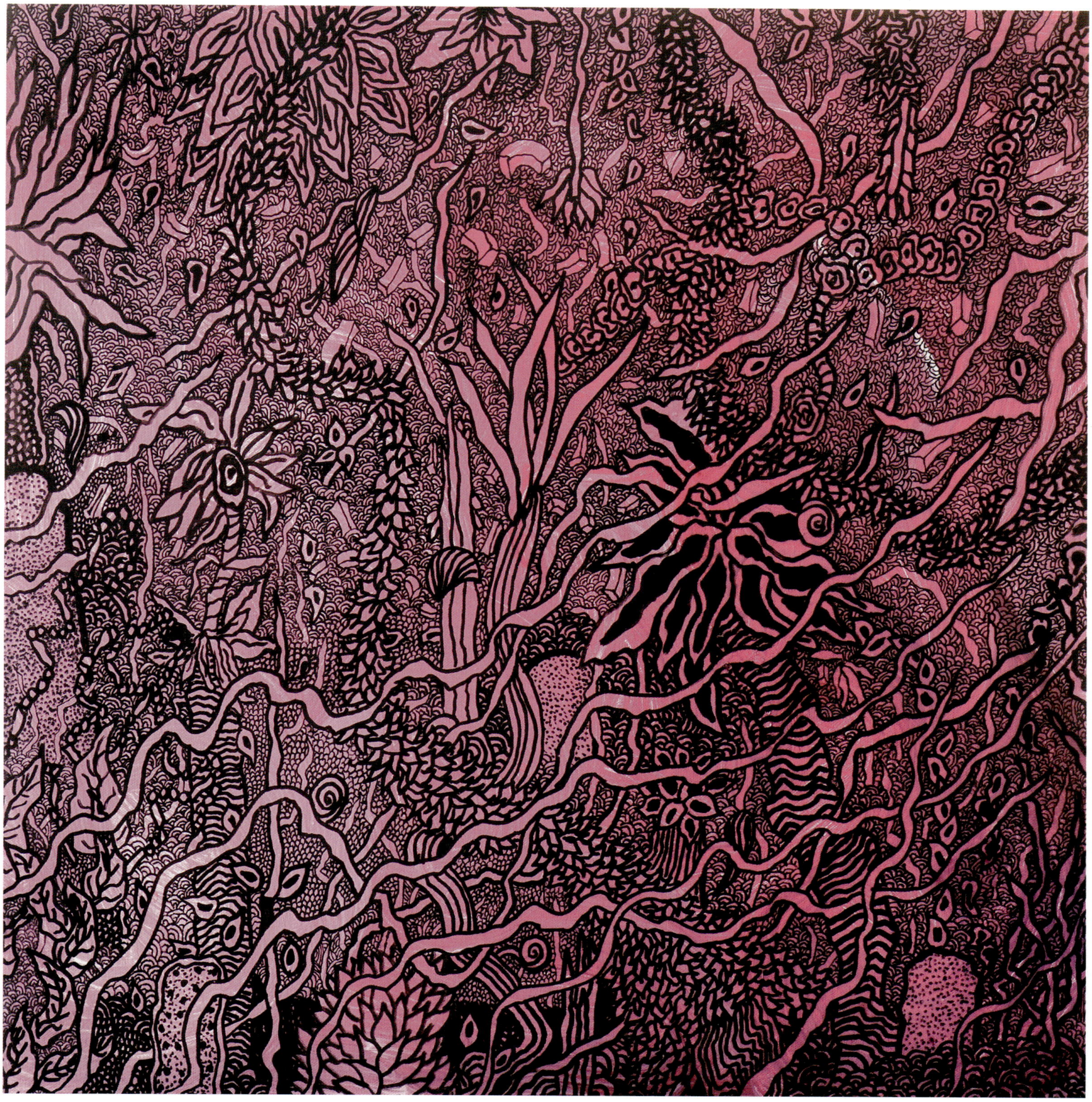

25 *Sunsets Past,* 2017, Acrylic on canvas, 24 x 24"

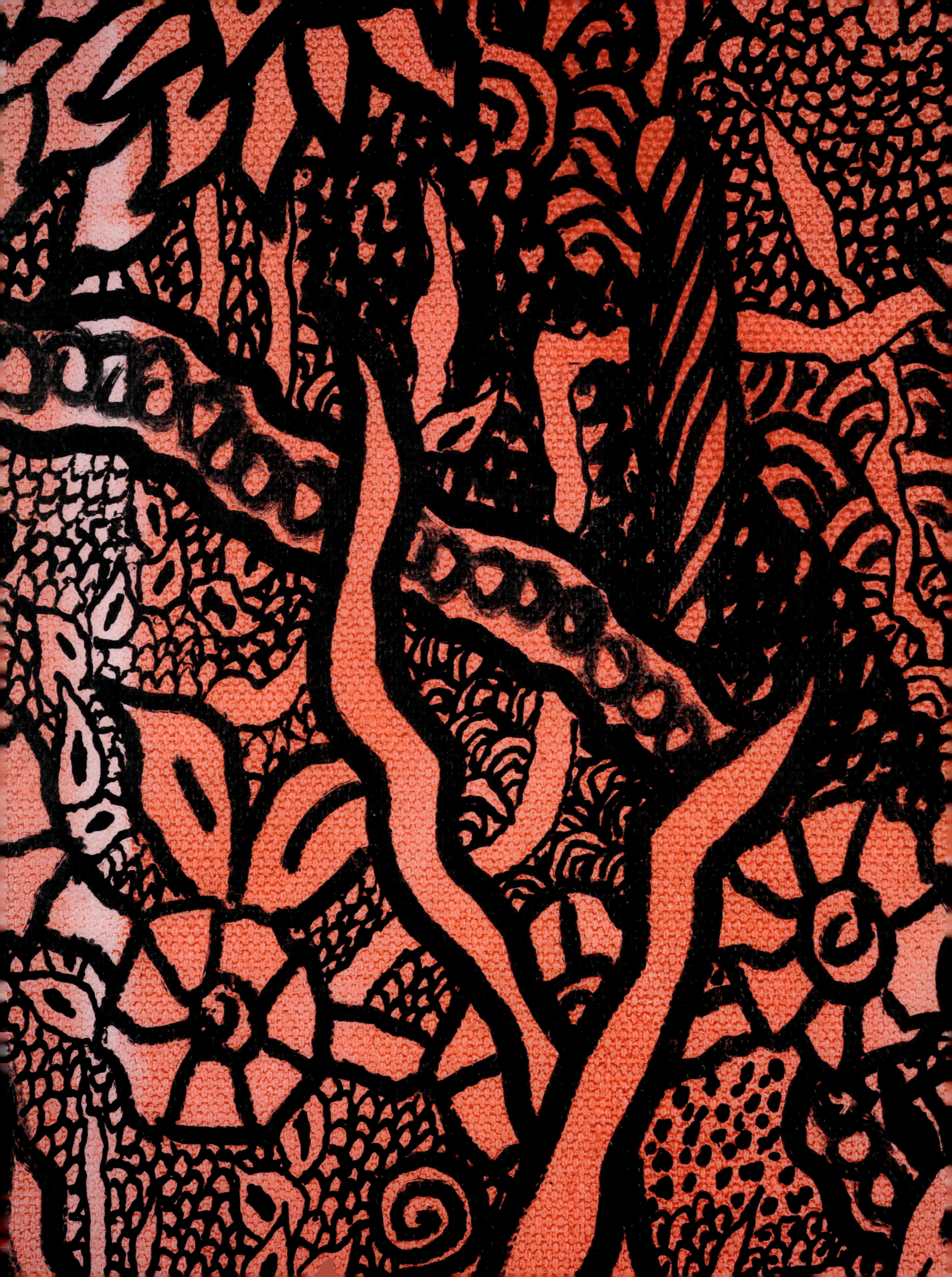

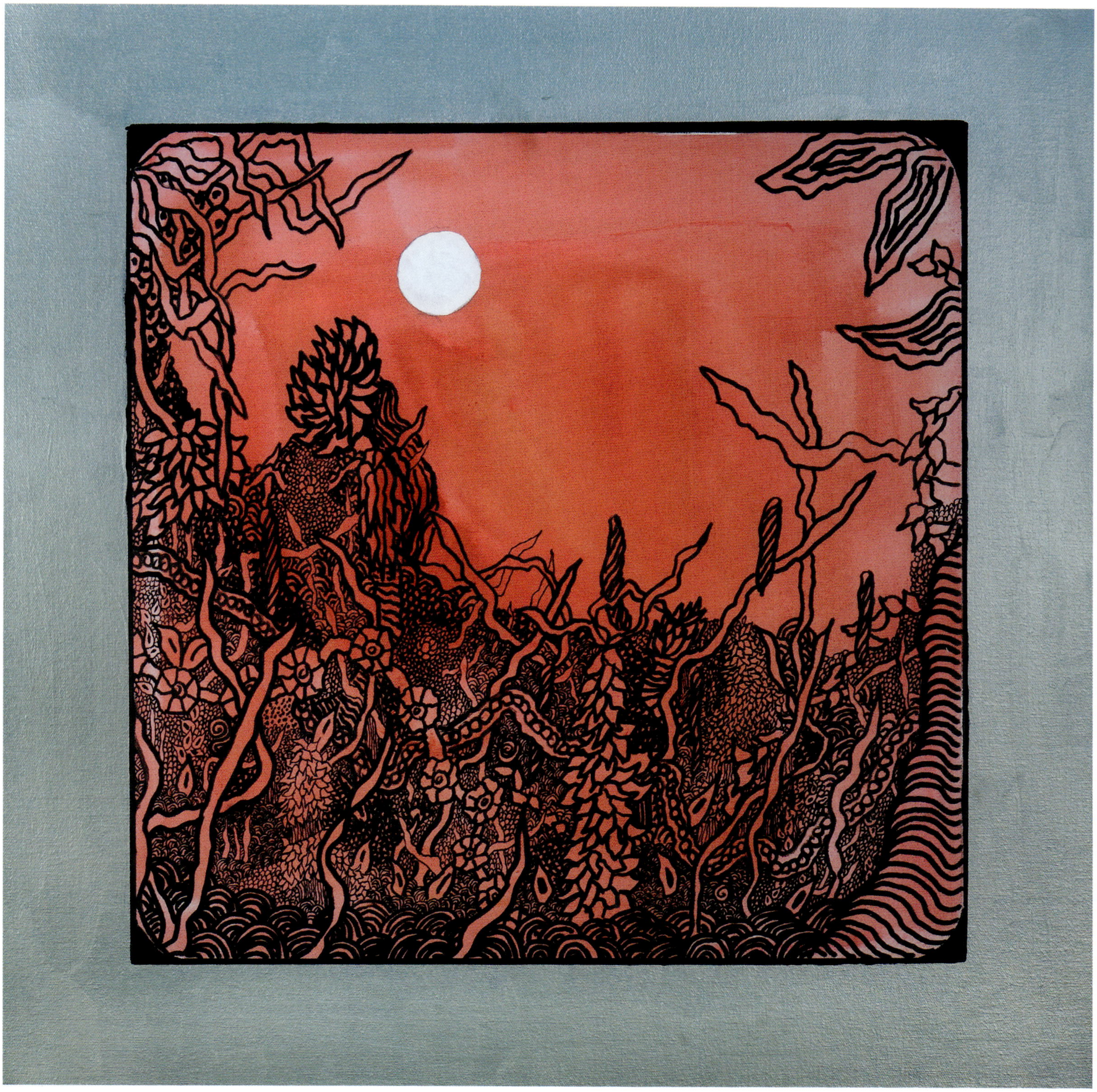

26 *Sky Fire,* 2017, Acrylic on canvas, 24 x 24"

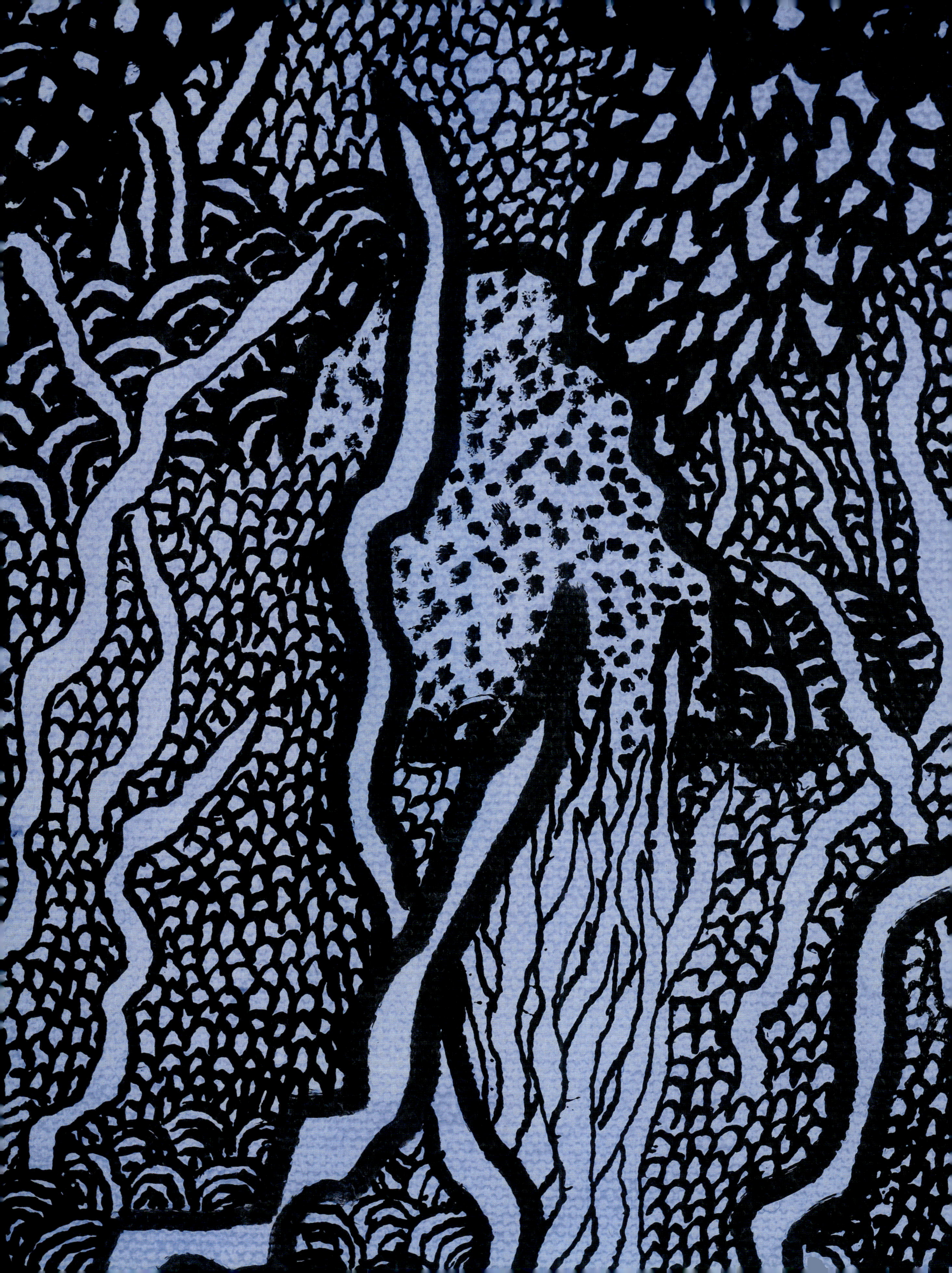

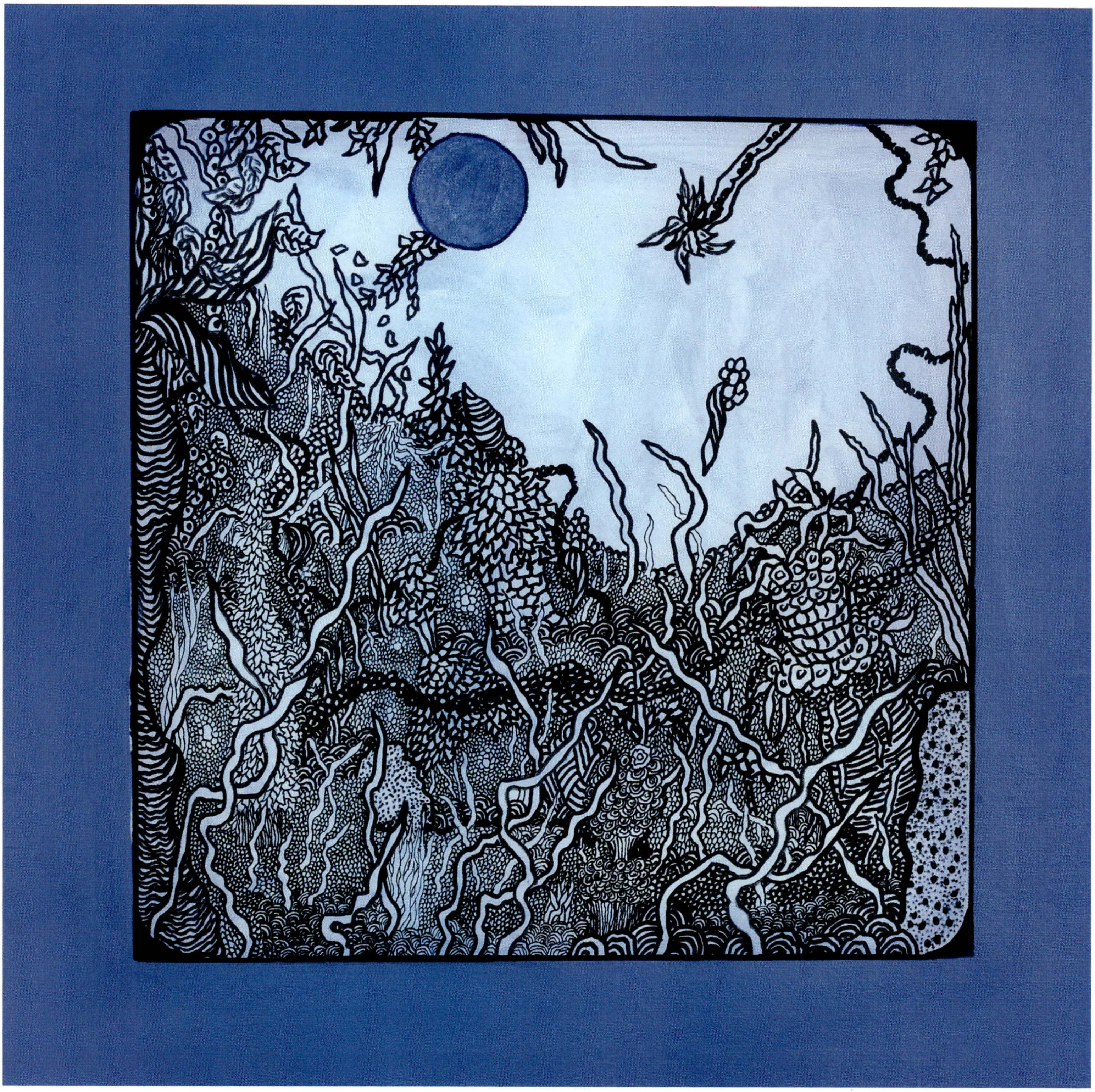

27 *The Sky Has Fallen Asleep,* 2017, Acrylic on canvas with polymer particles, 24 x 24"

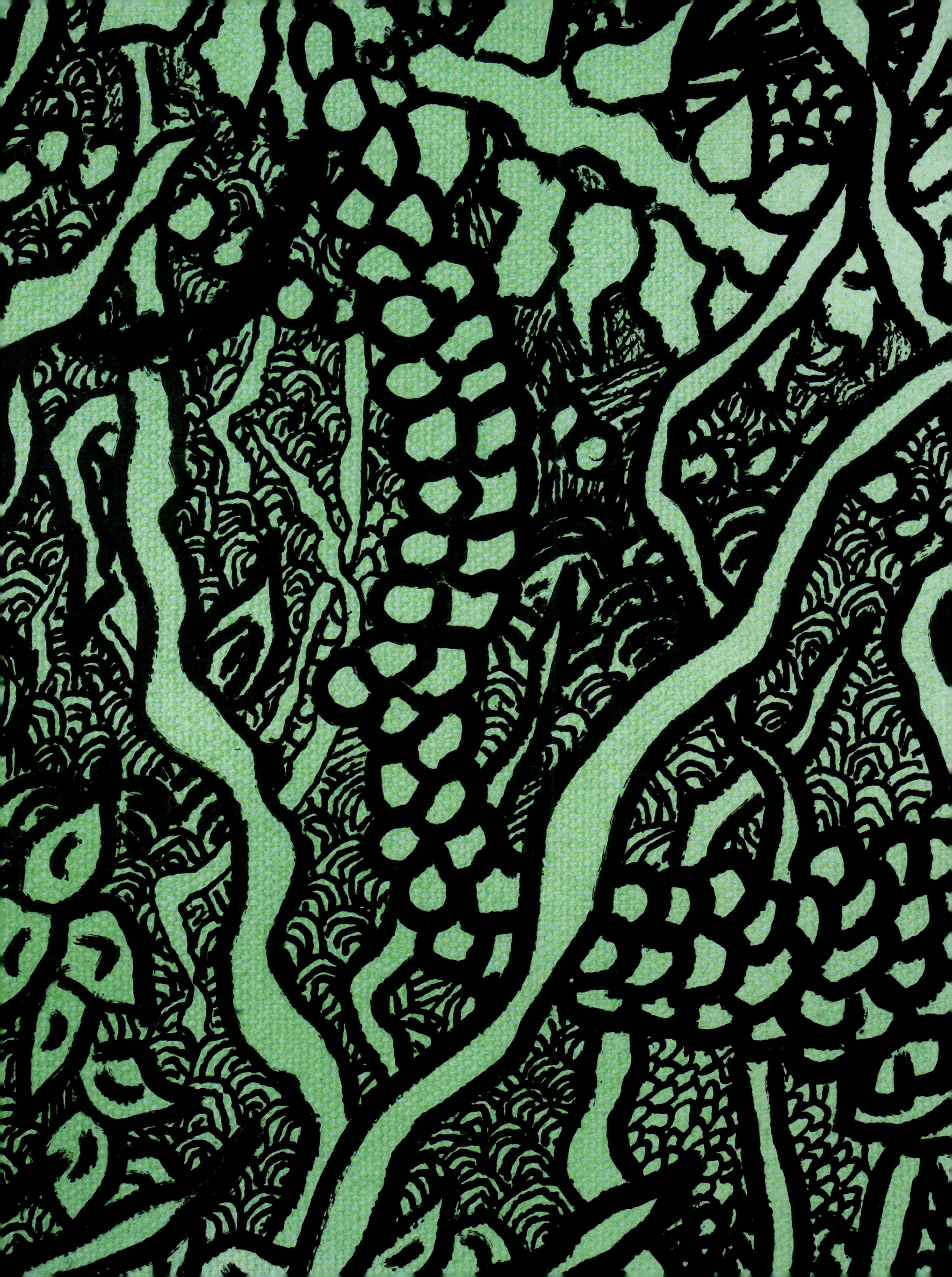

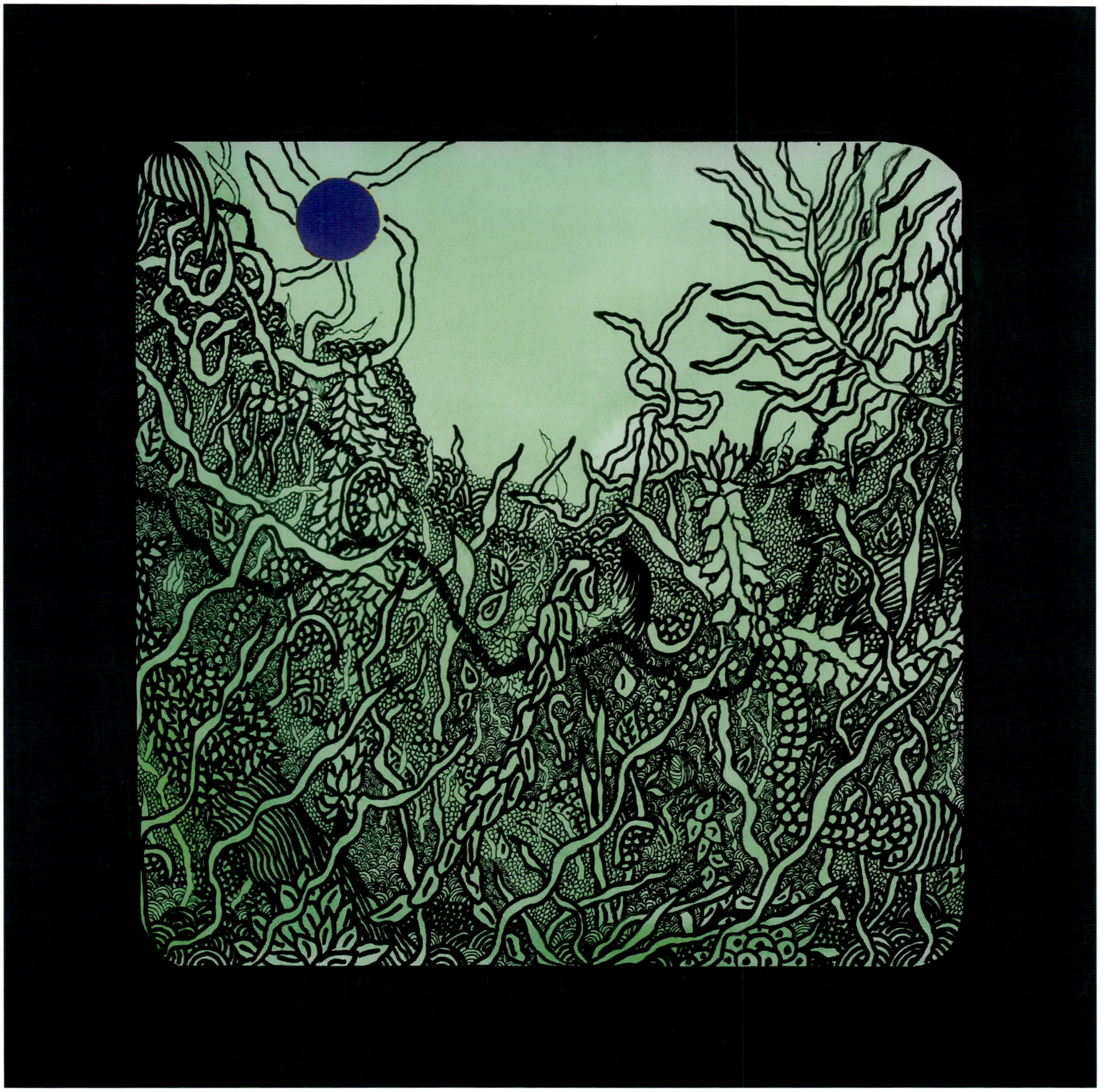

28 *The Barefoot Moon,* 2017, Acrylic on canvas, 24 x 24"

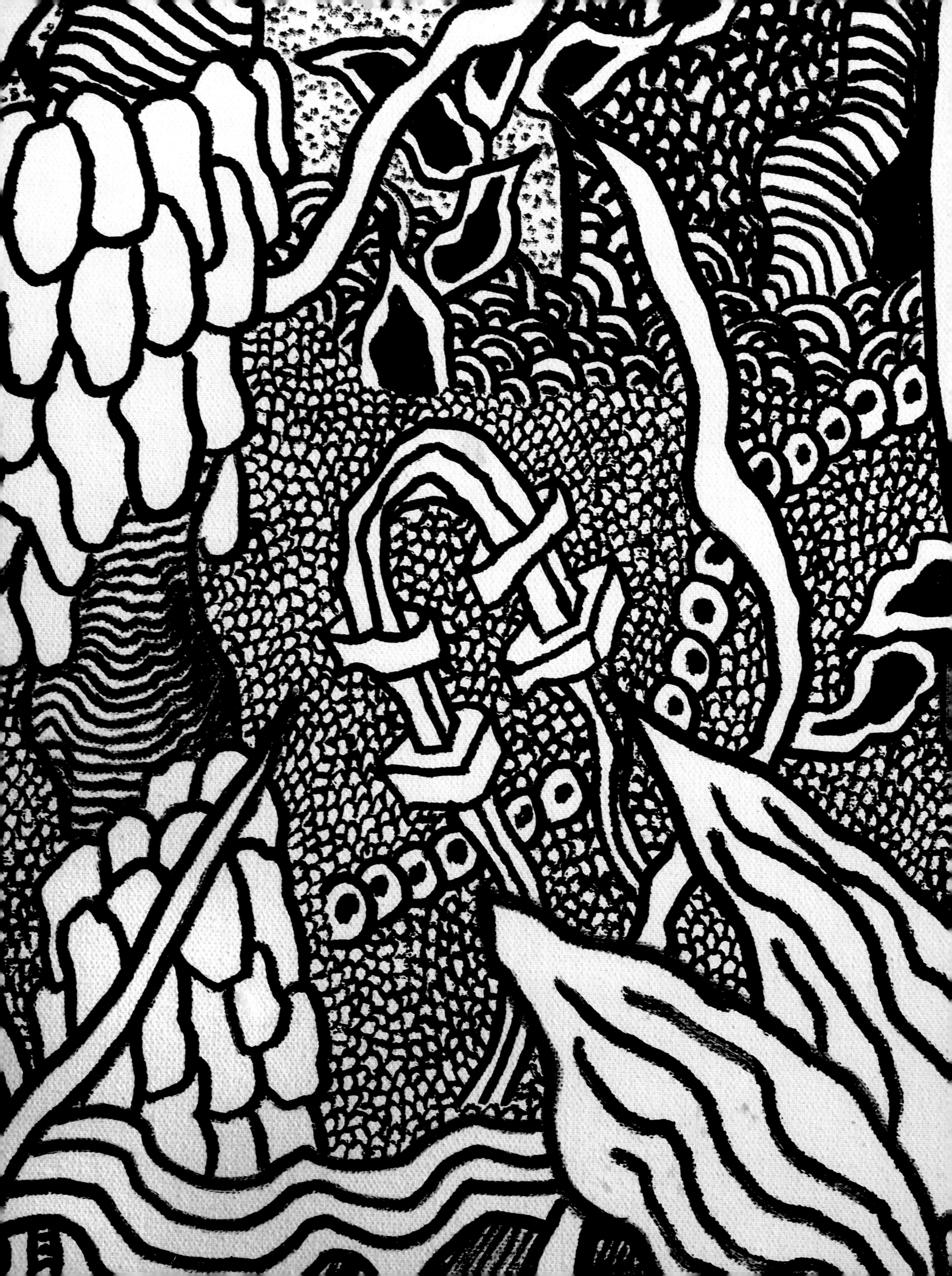

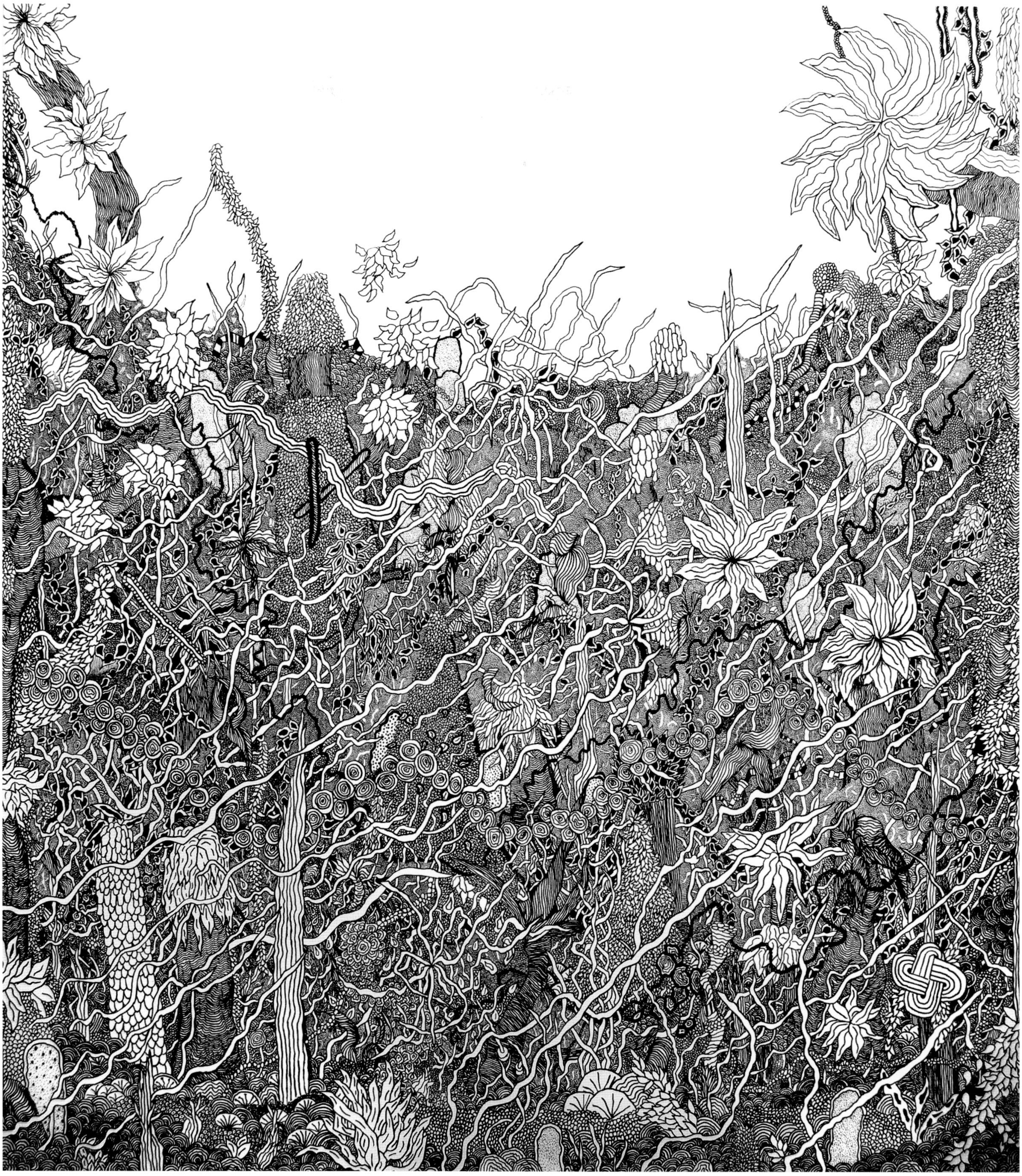

29 *Entwine the Heart,* 2018 (work in progress), Acrylic on canvas, 96 x 84"

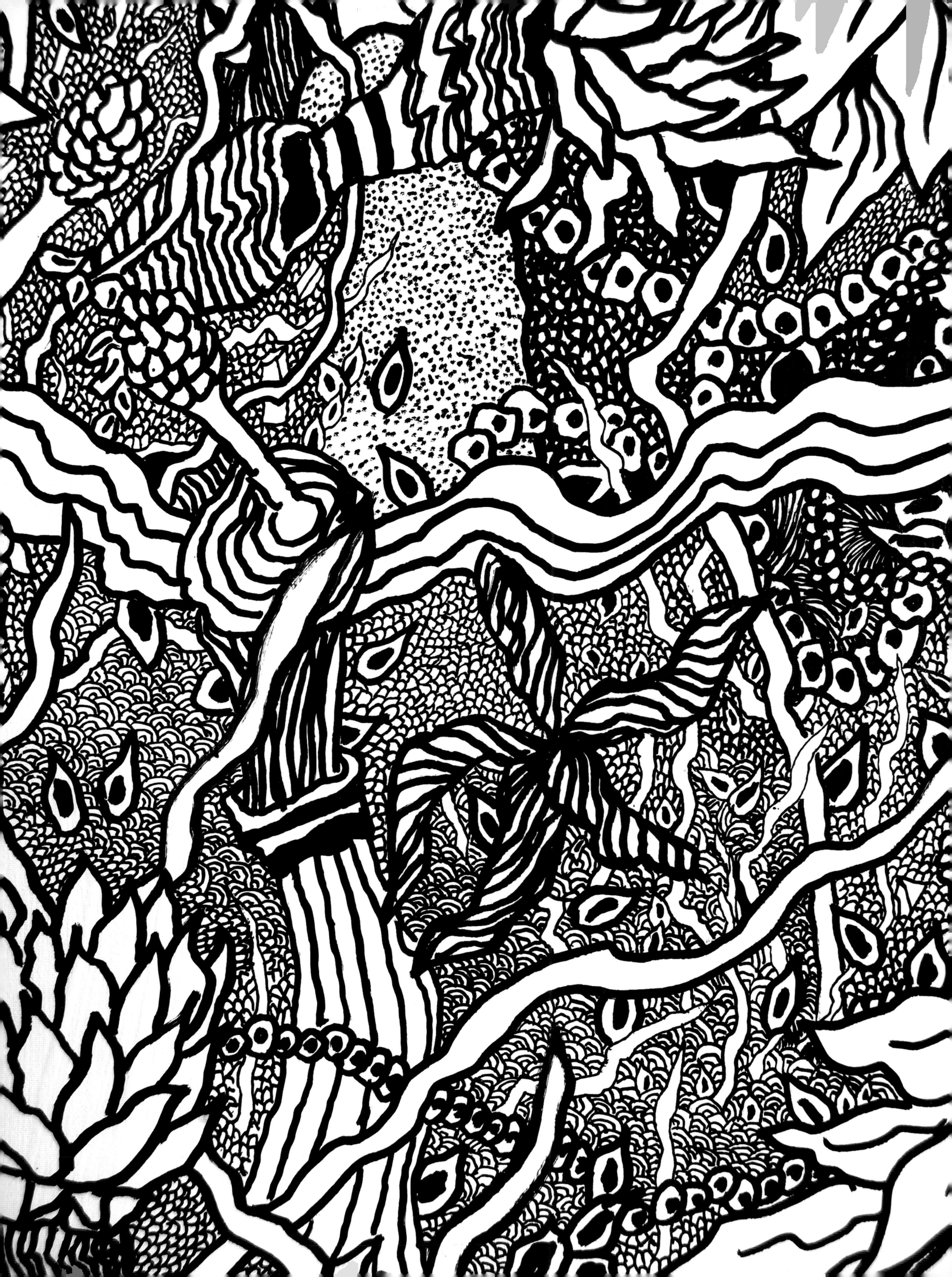

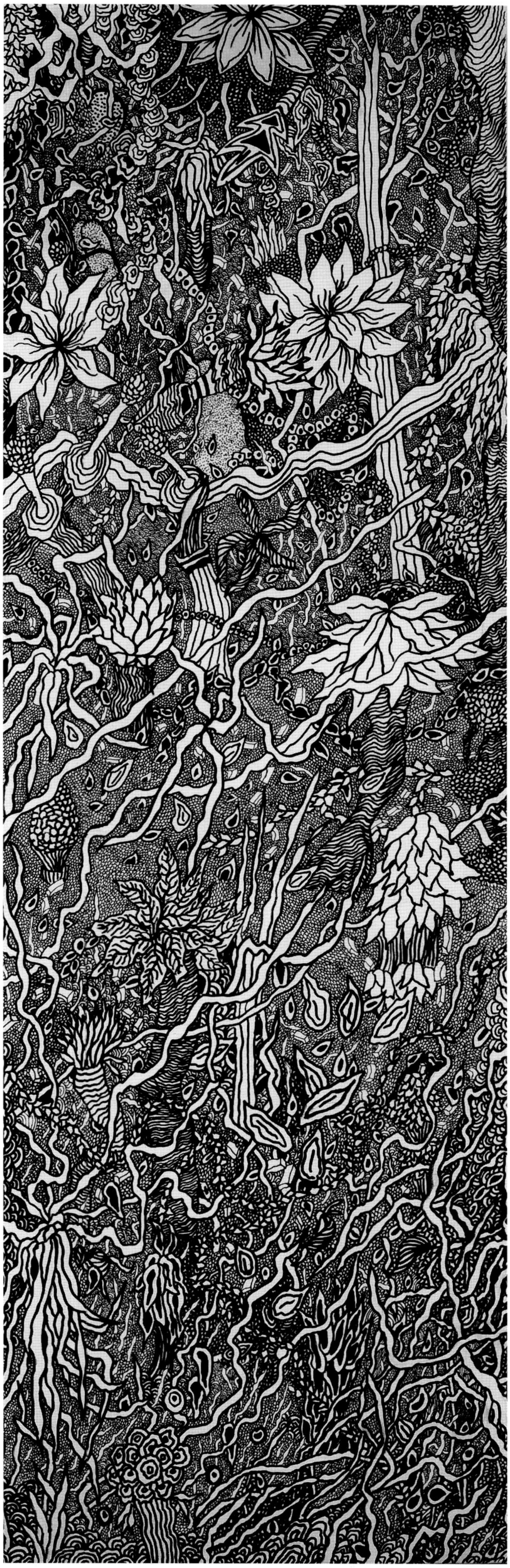

30 *All History is in This Moment,* 2018,
Acrylic on canvas, 60 x 20"

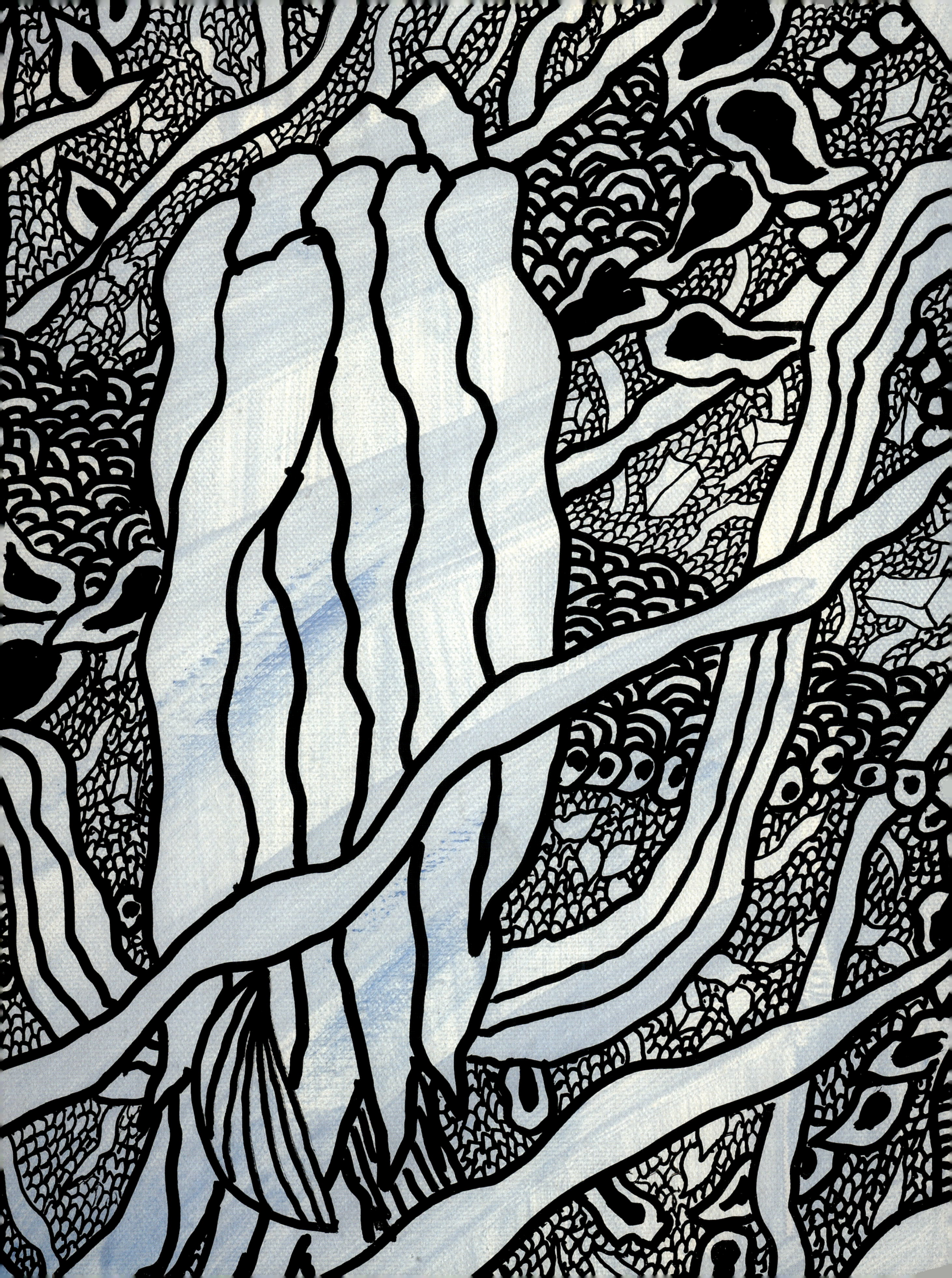

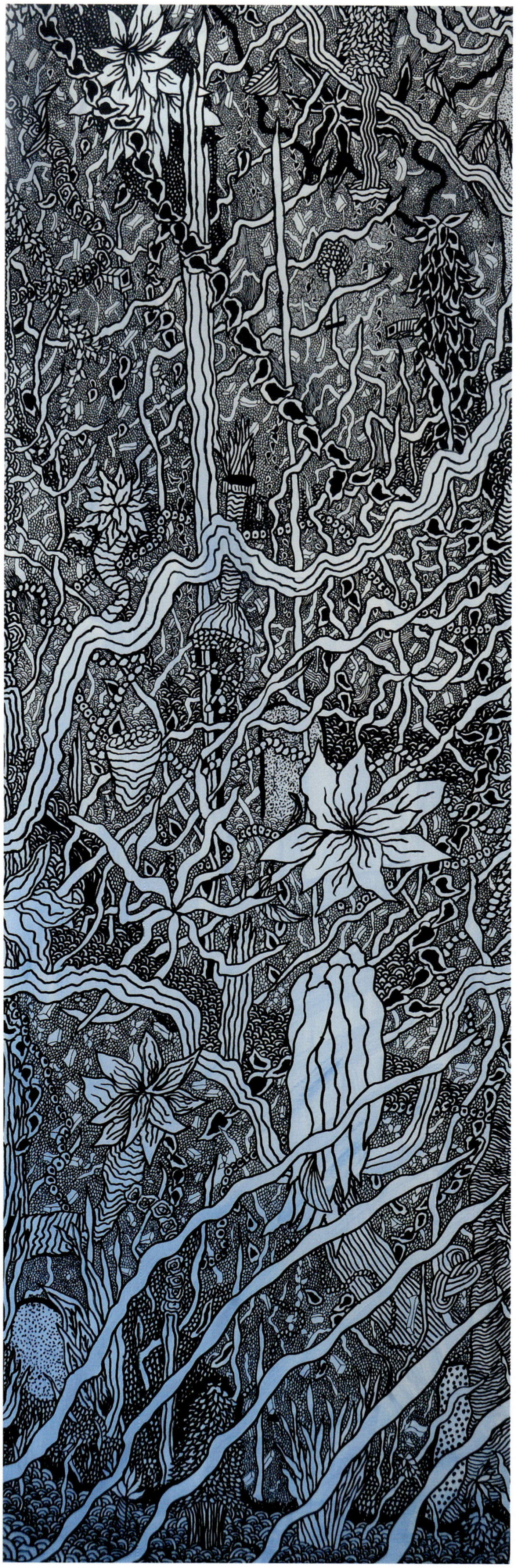

31 *Multiple Loves,* 2018, Acrylic on canvas, 60 x 20"

"...hand is not fighting my thoughts...
my hand just moves...
I'm still very conscious.
I love Paul Klee's quote...

A drawing
is
taking
a line
for a walk."

Works on Paper

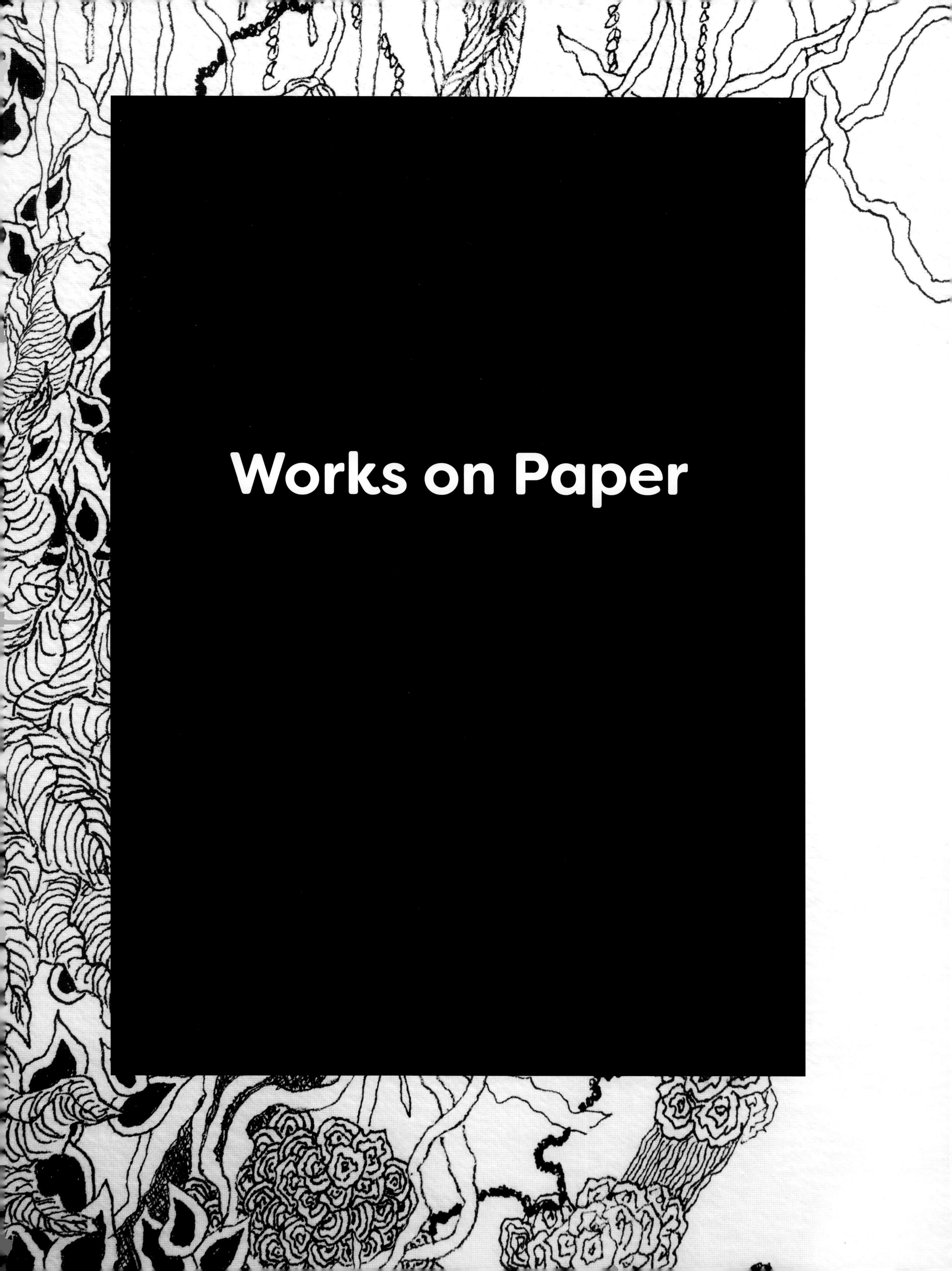

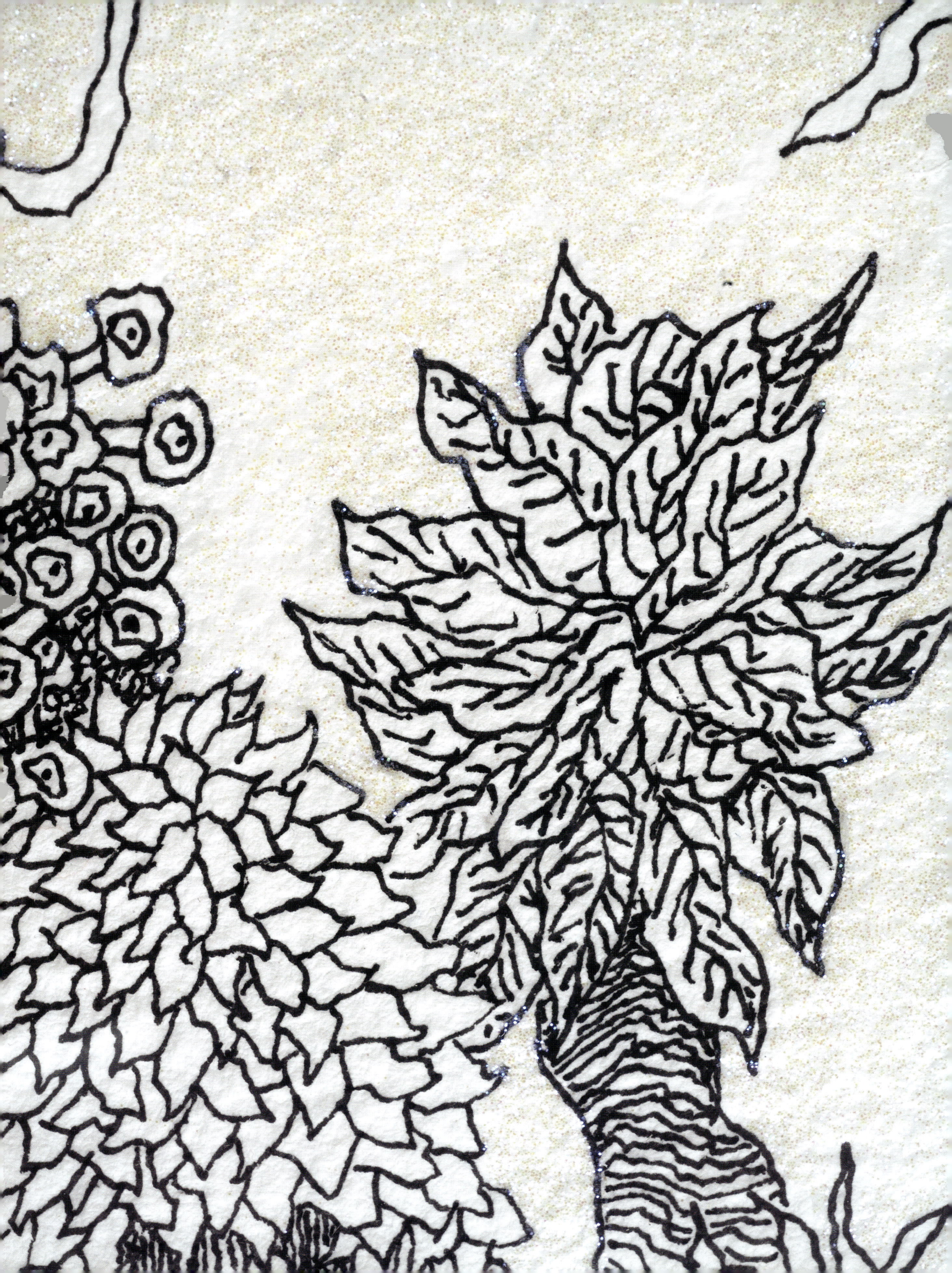

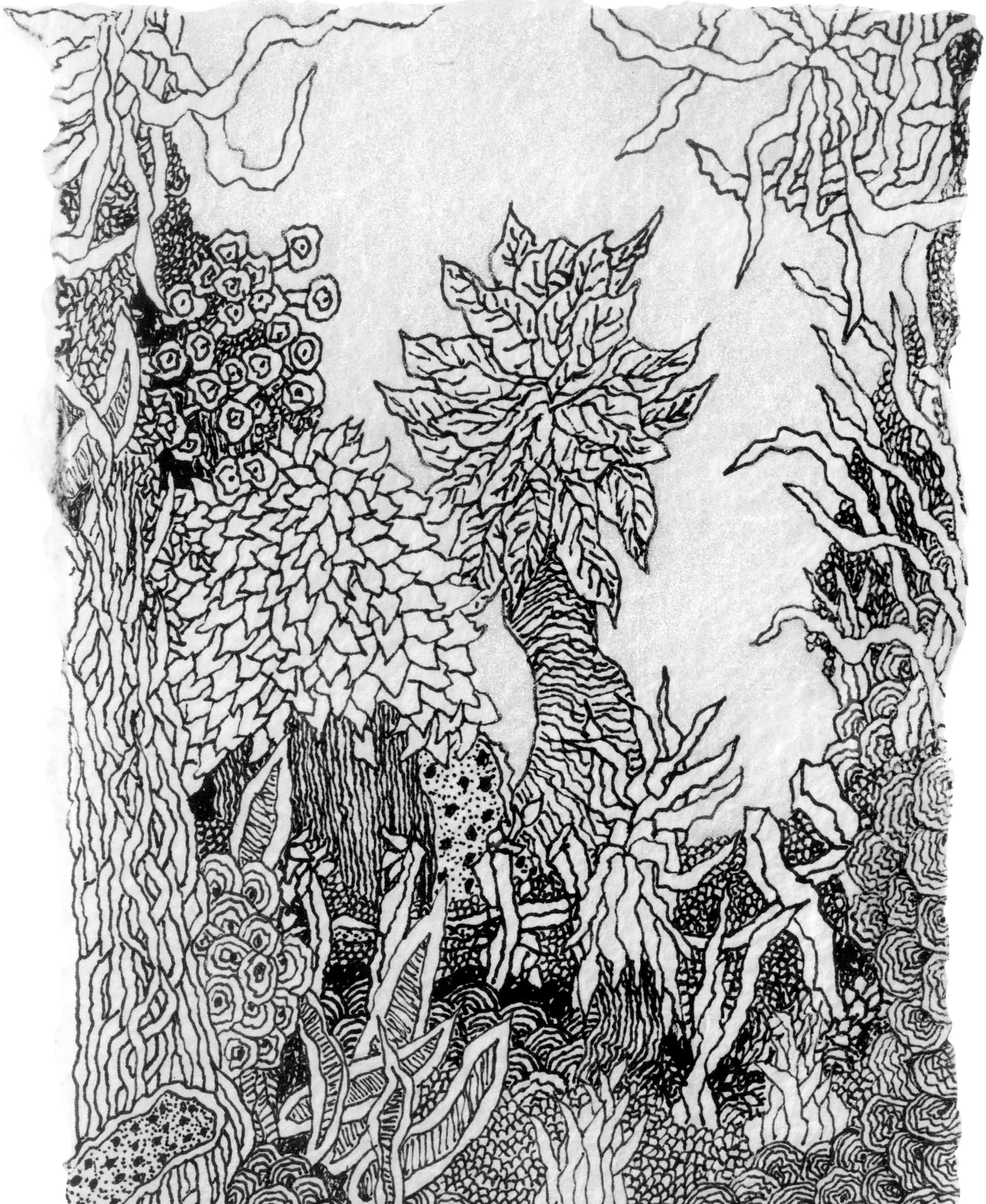

32 *Extravagant Eden 31,* 2016, Pen and ink on paper with polymer particles, 8 1/4 x 6 1/2"

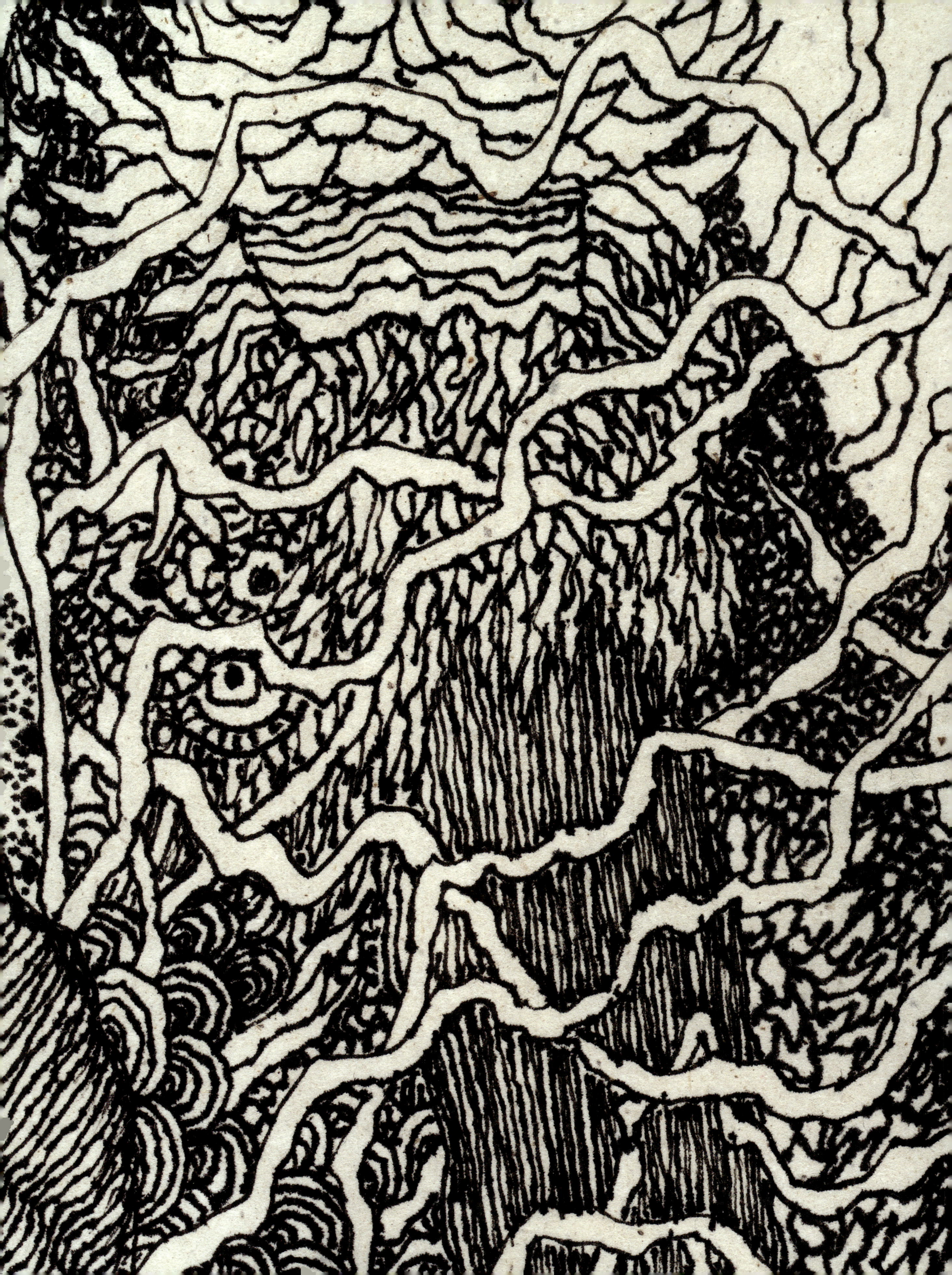

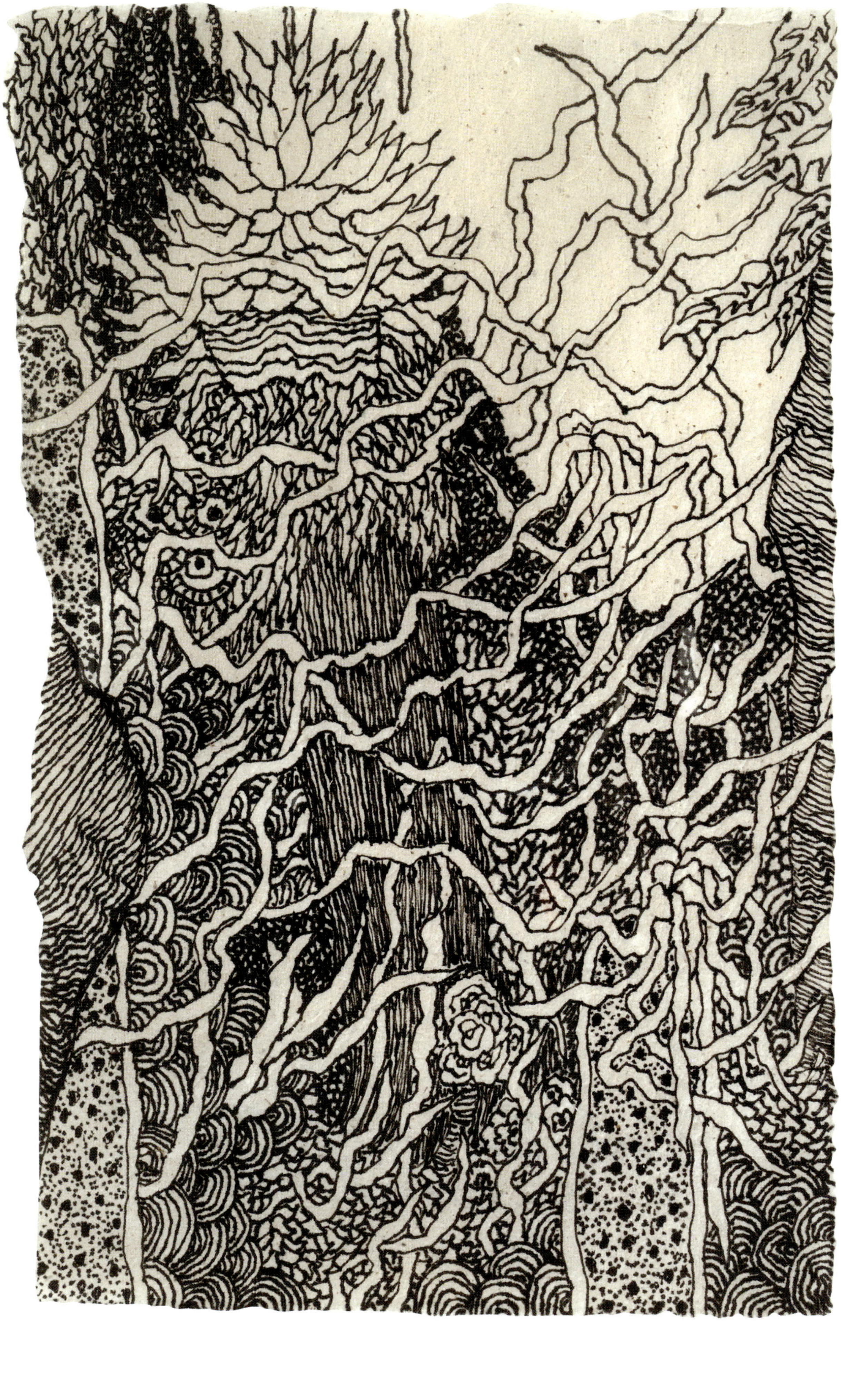

33 *Extravagant Eden 32,* 2016, Pen and ink on paper, 8 x 5"

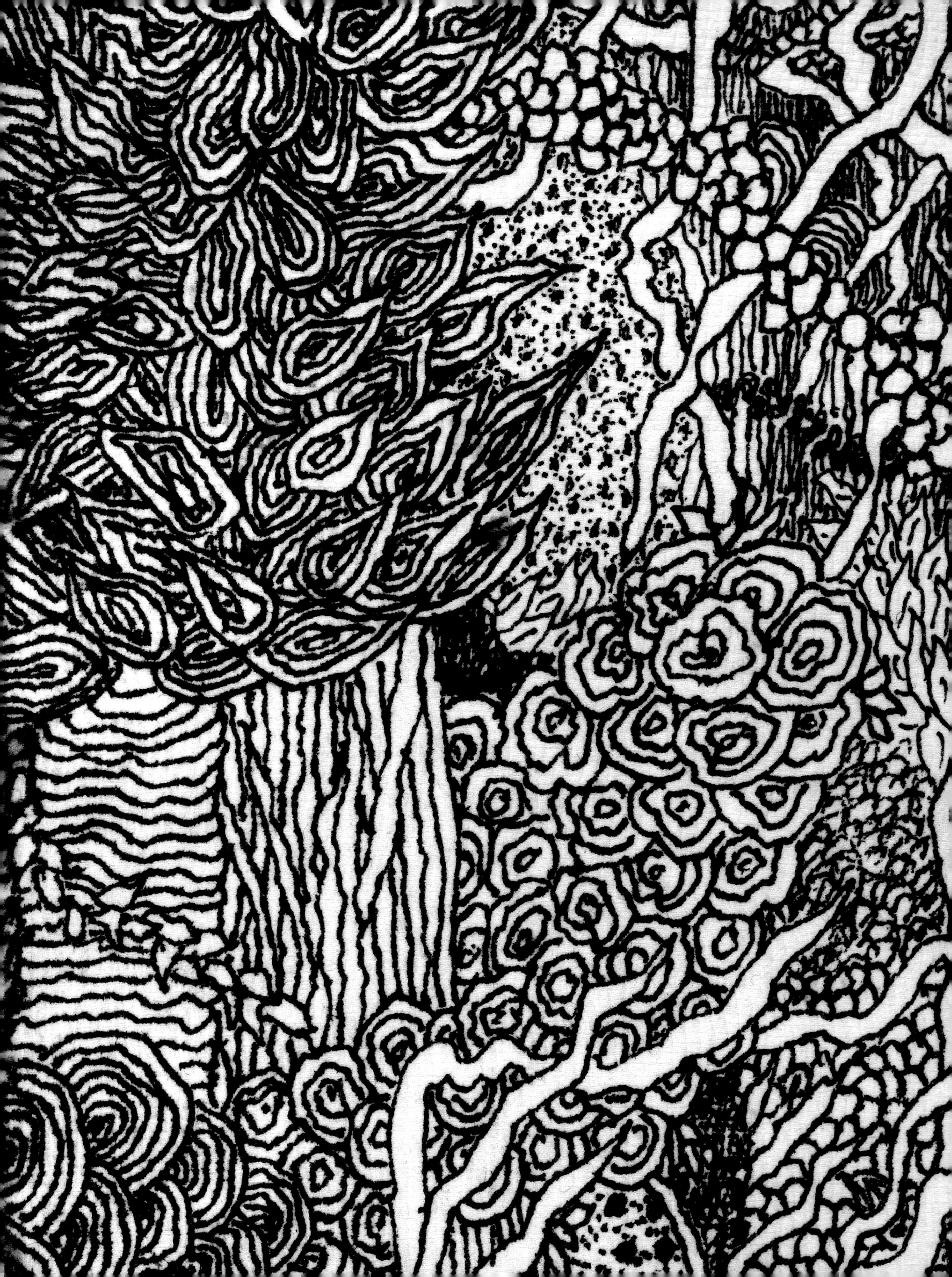

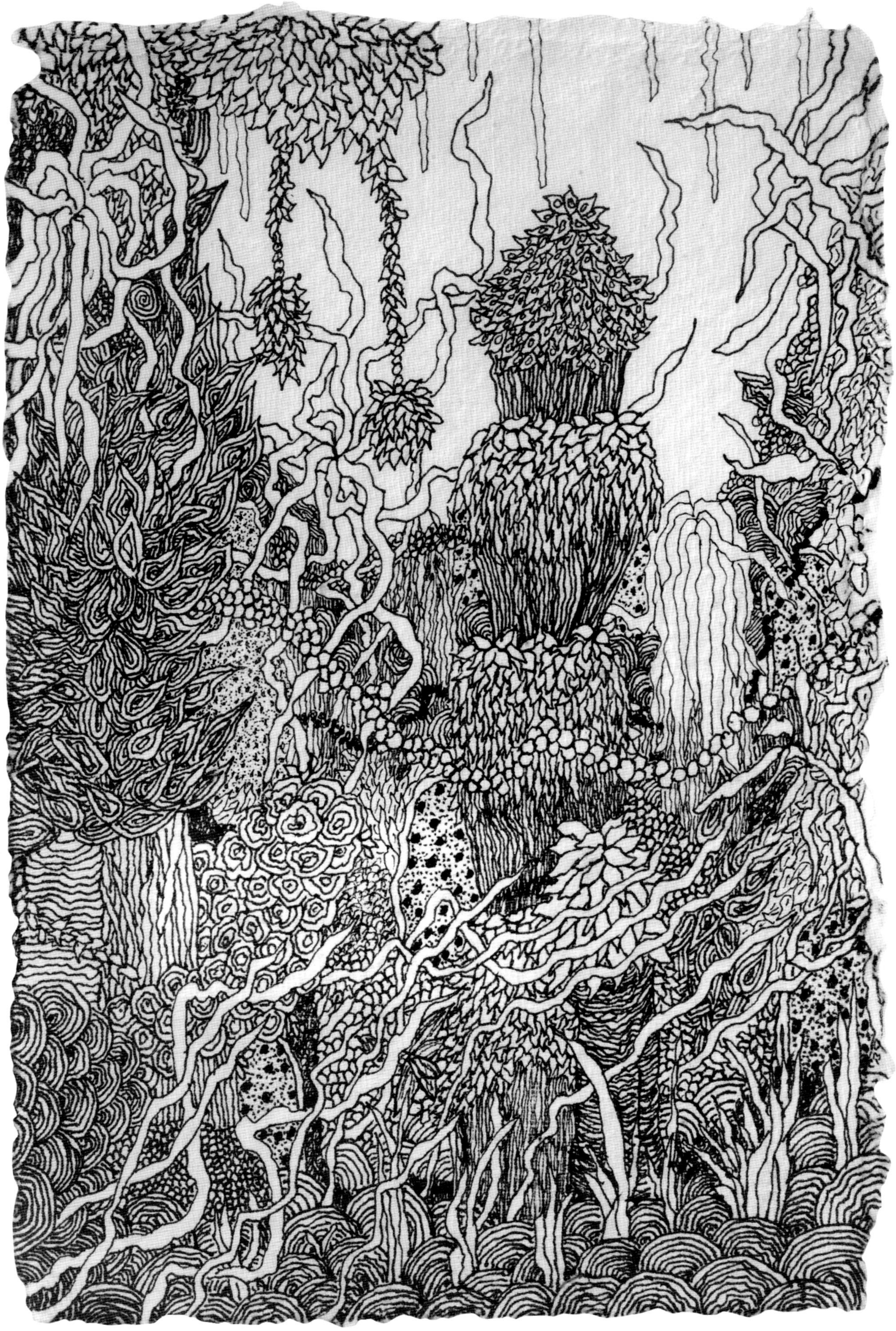

34 *Extravagant Eden 33,* 2016, Pen and ink on paper, 10 1/2 x 7"

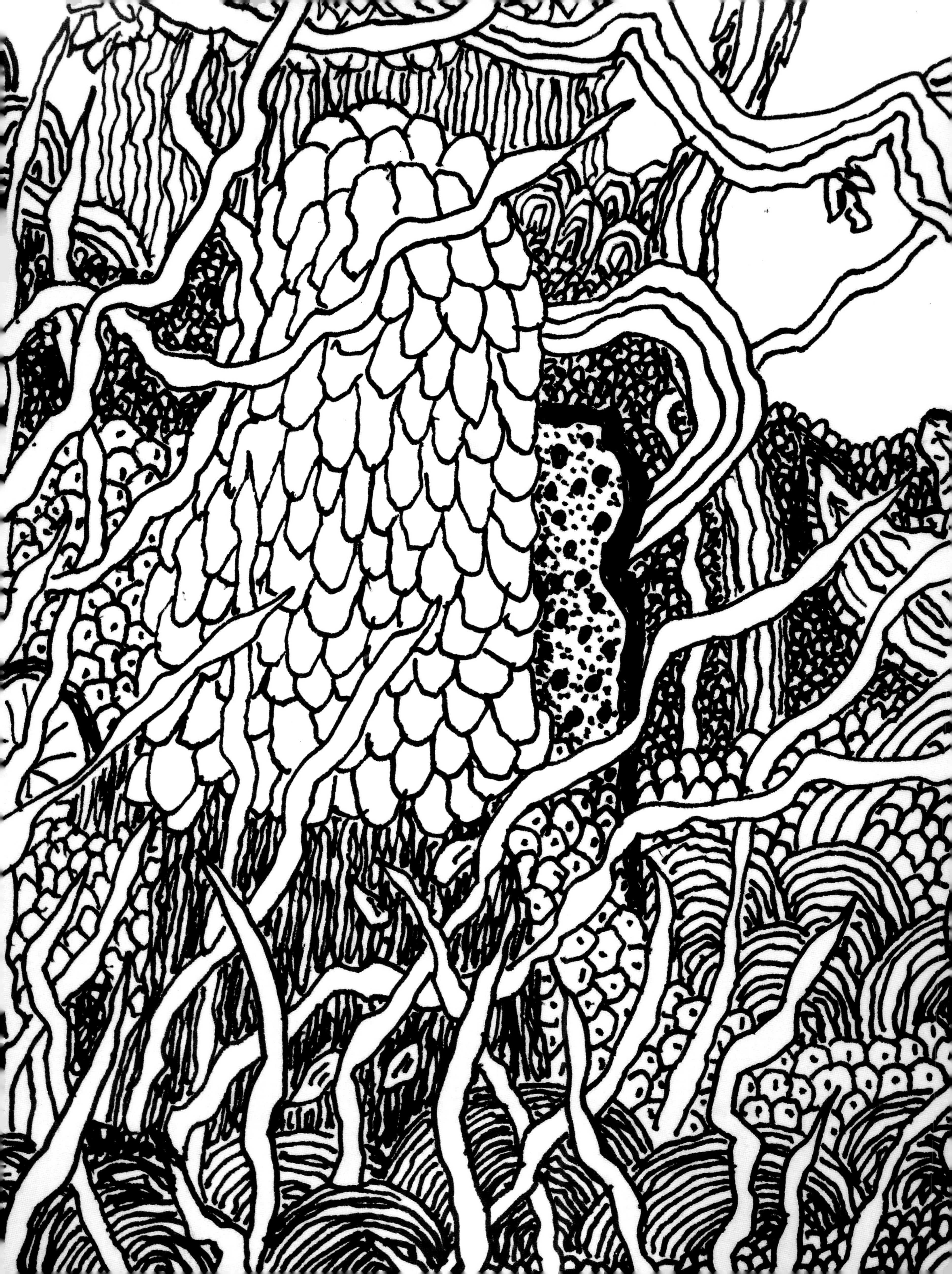

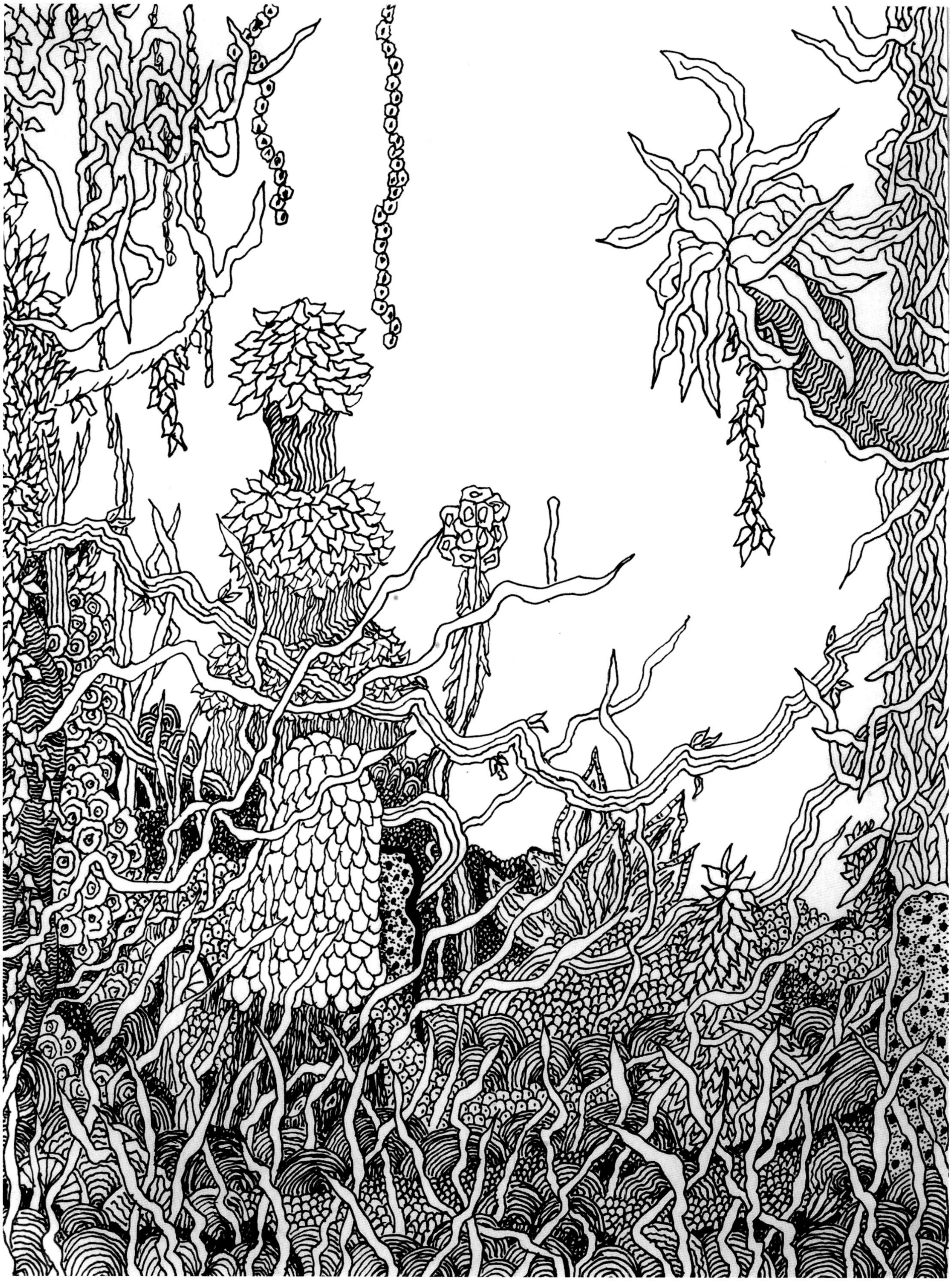

35 *Extravagant Eden 35,* 2017, Pen and ink on paper, 12 x 9"

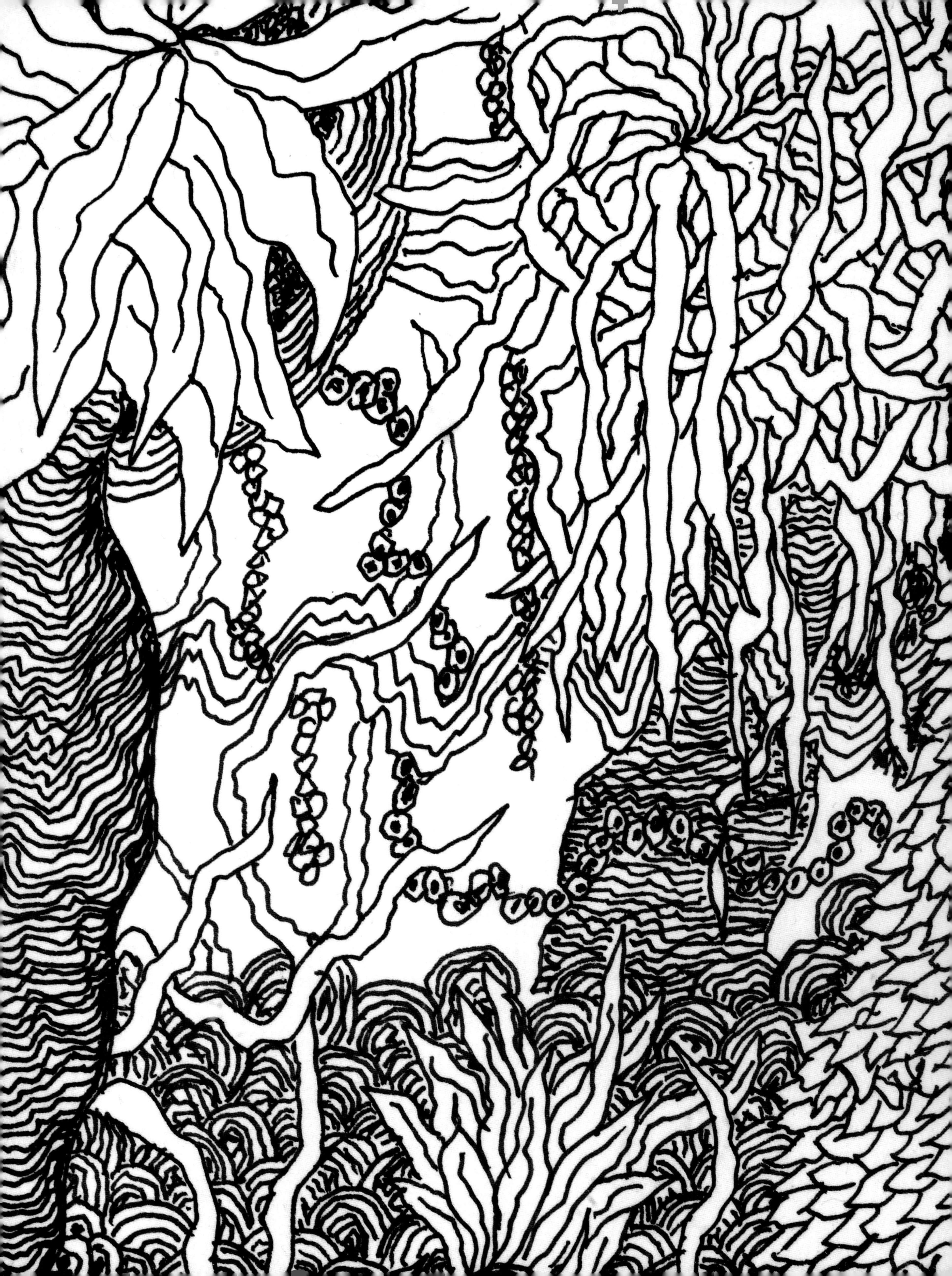

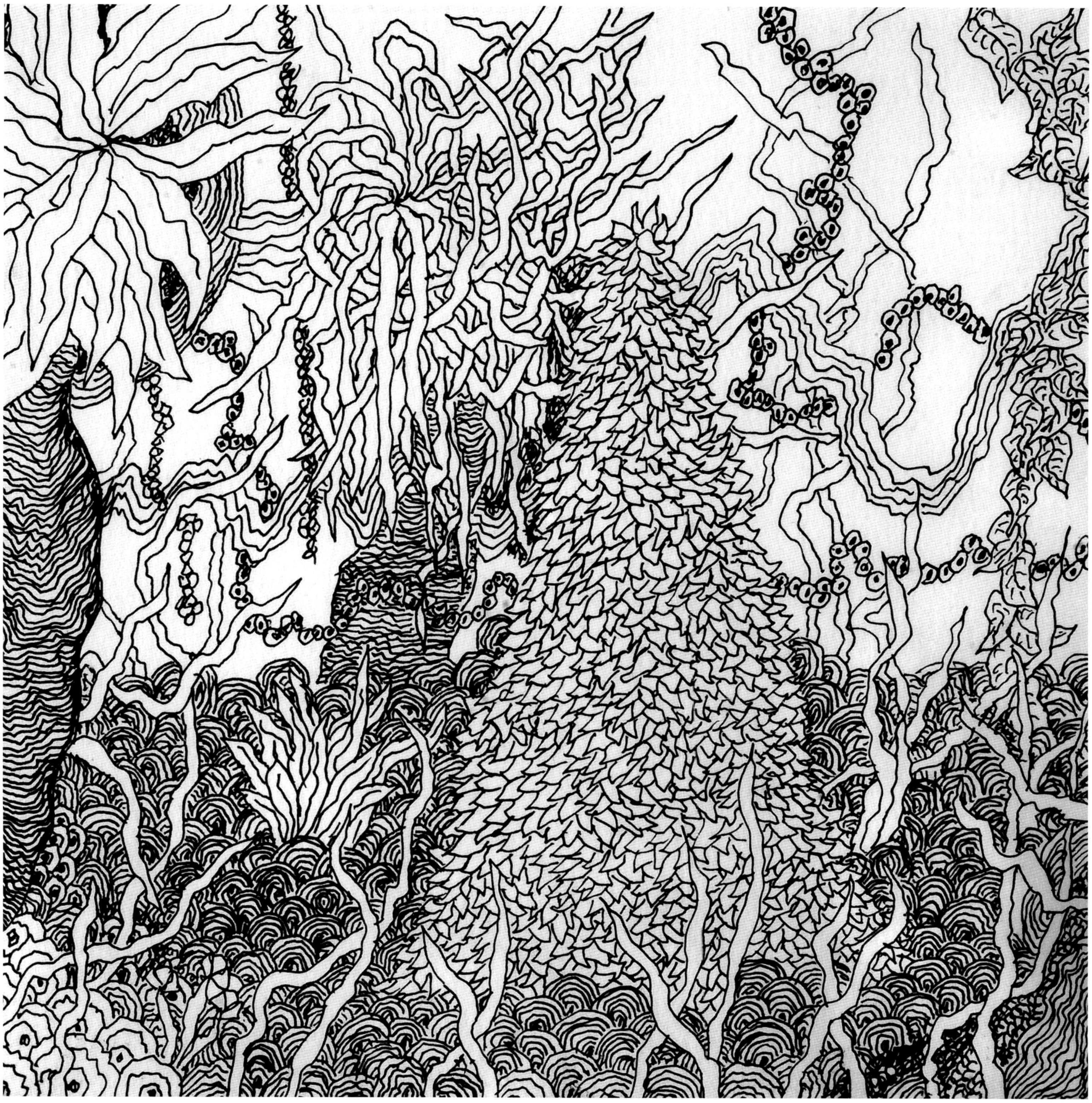

36 *Extravagant Eden 36,* 2017, Pen and ink on paper, 6 x 6"

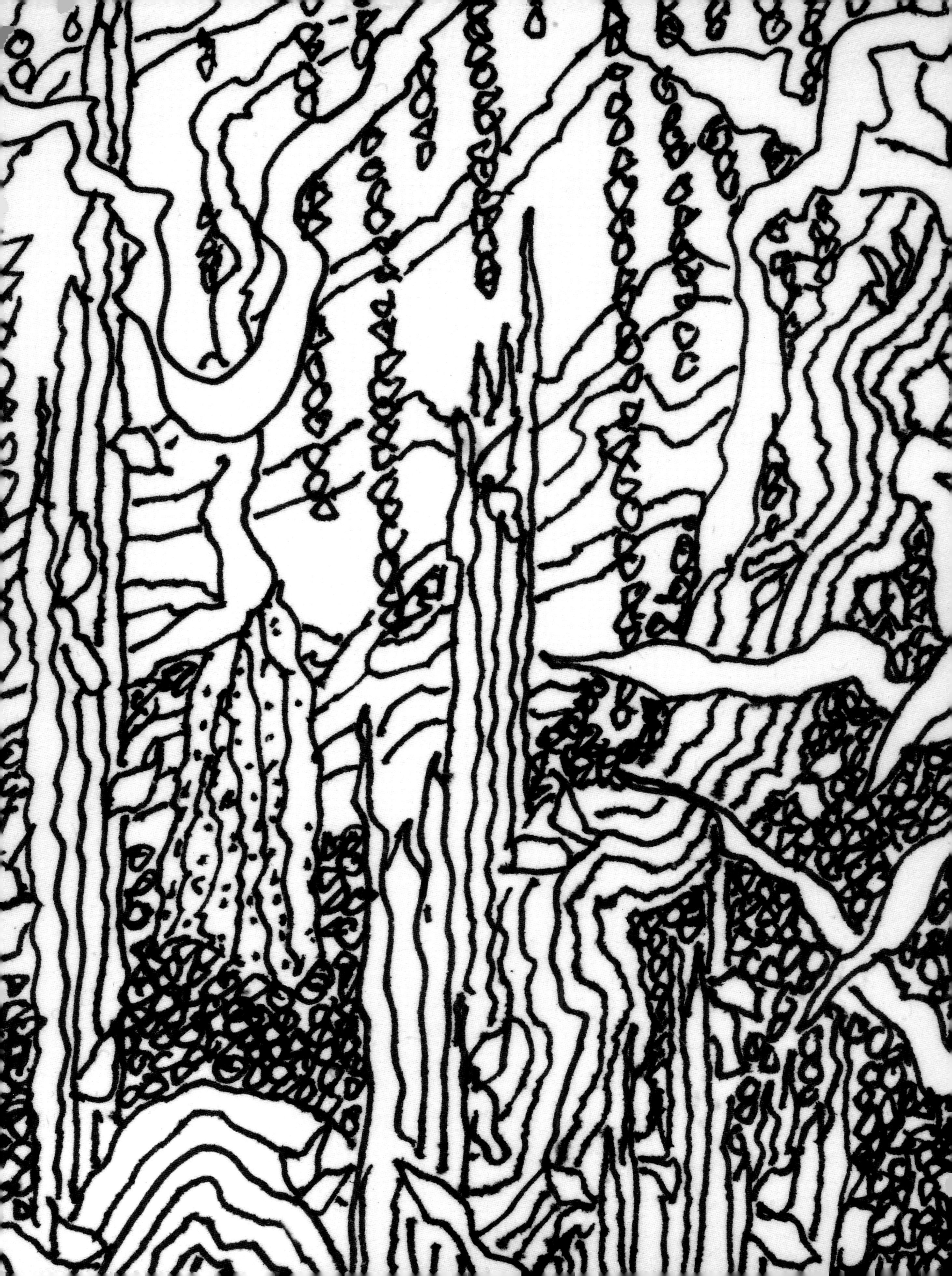

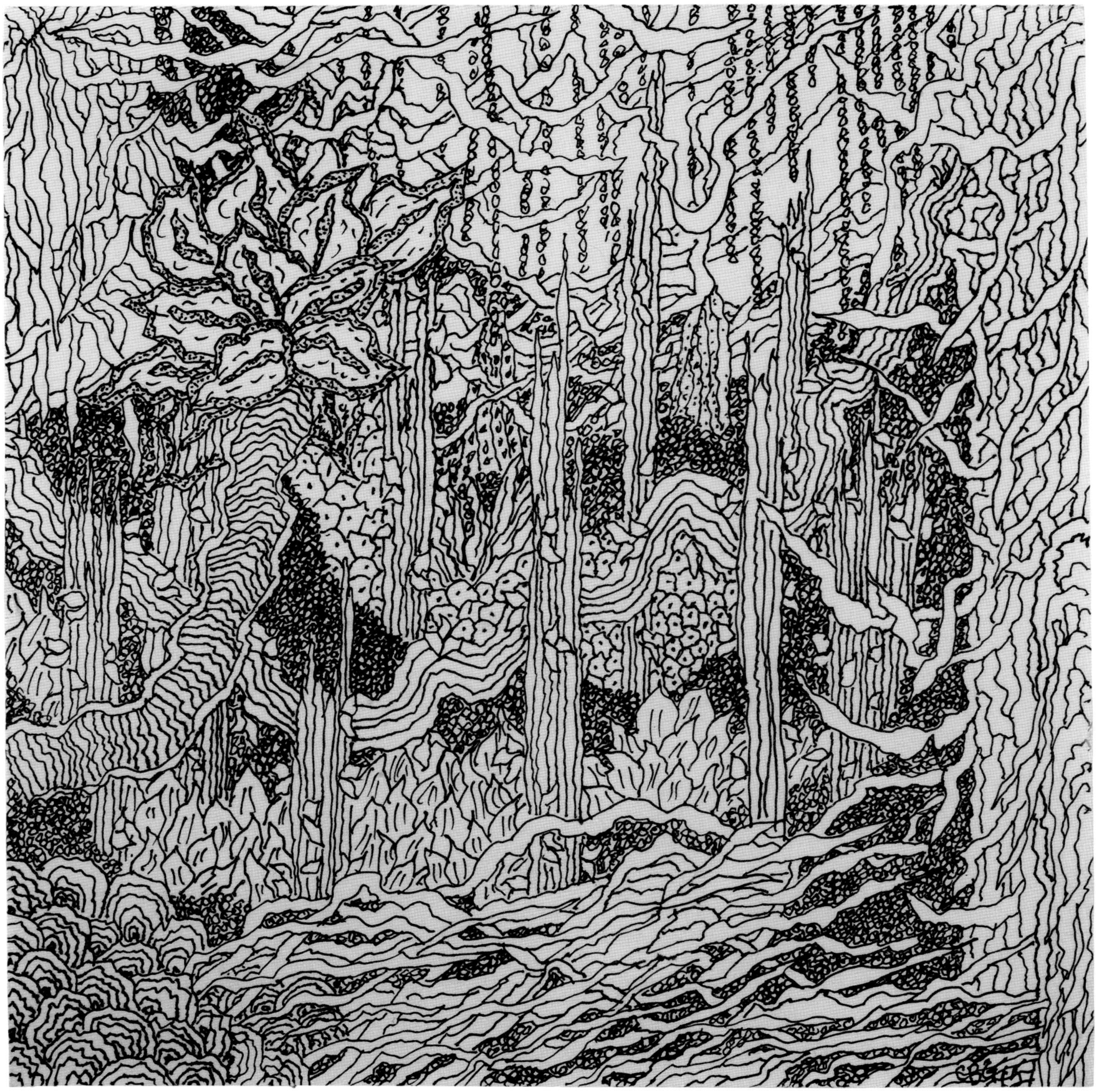

37 *Extravagant Eden 5,* 2015, Pen and ink on paper, 6 x 6"

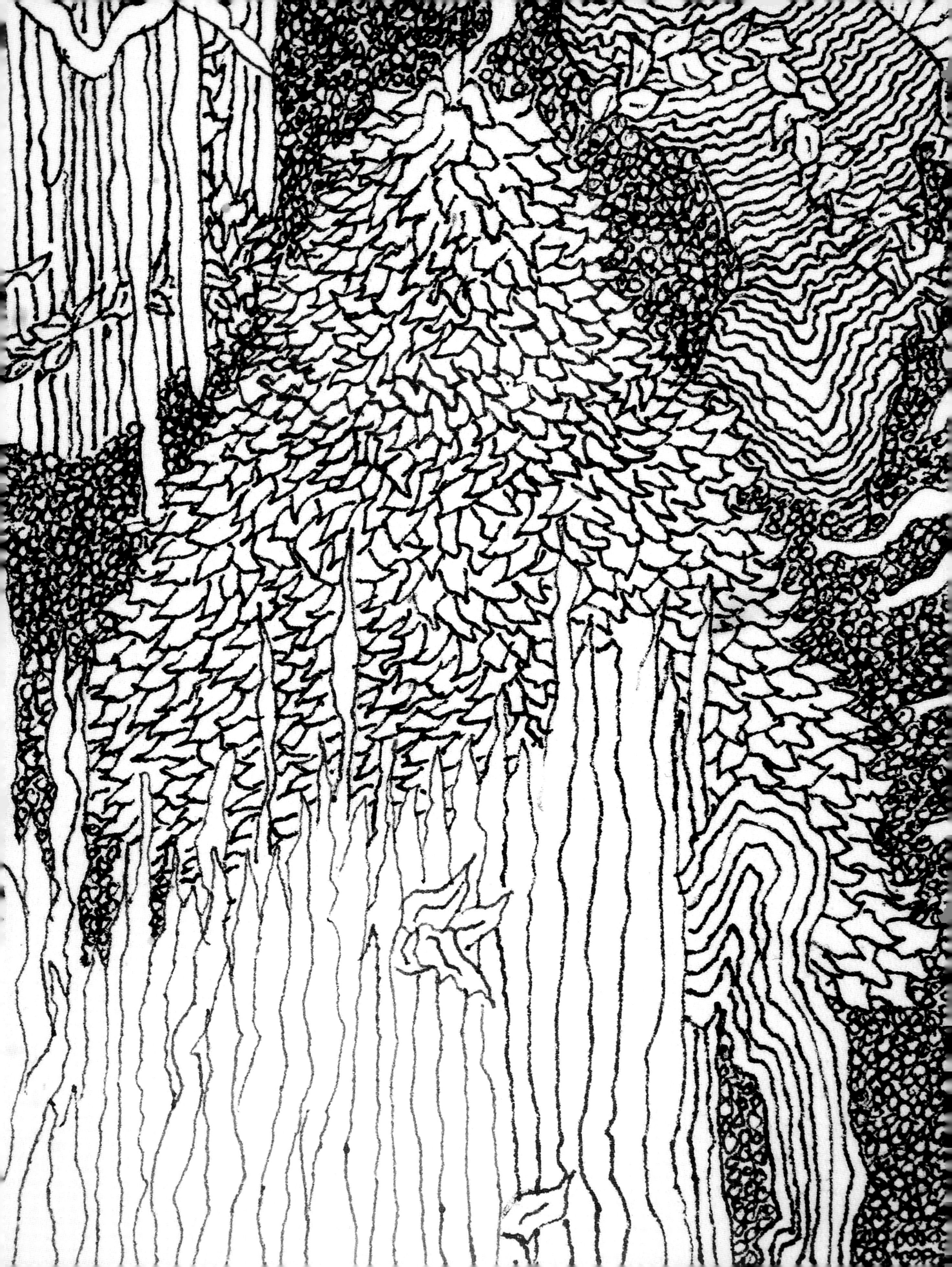

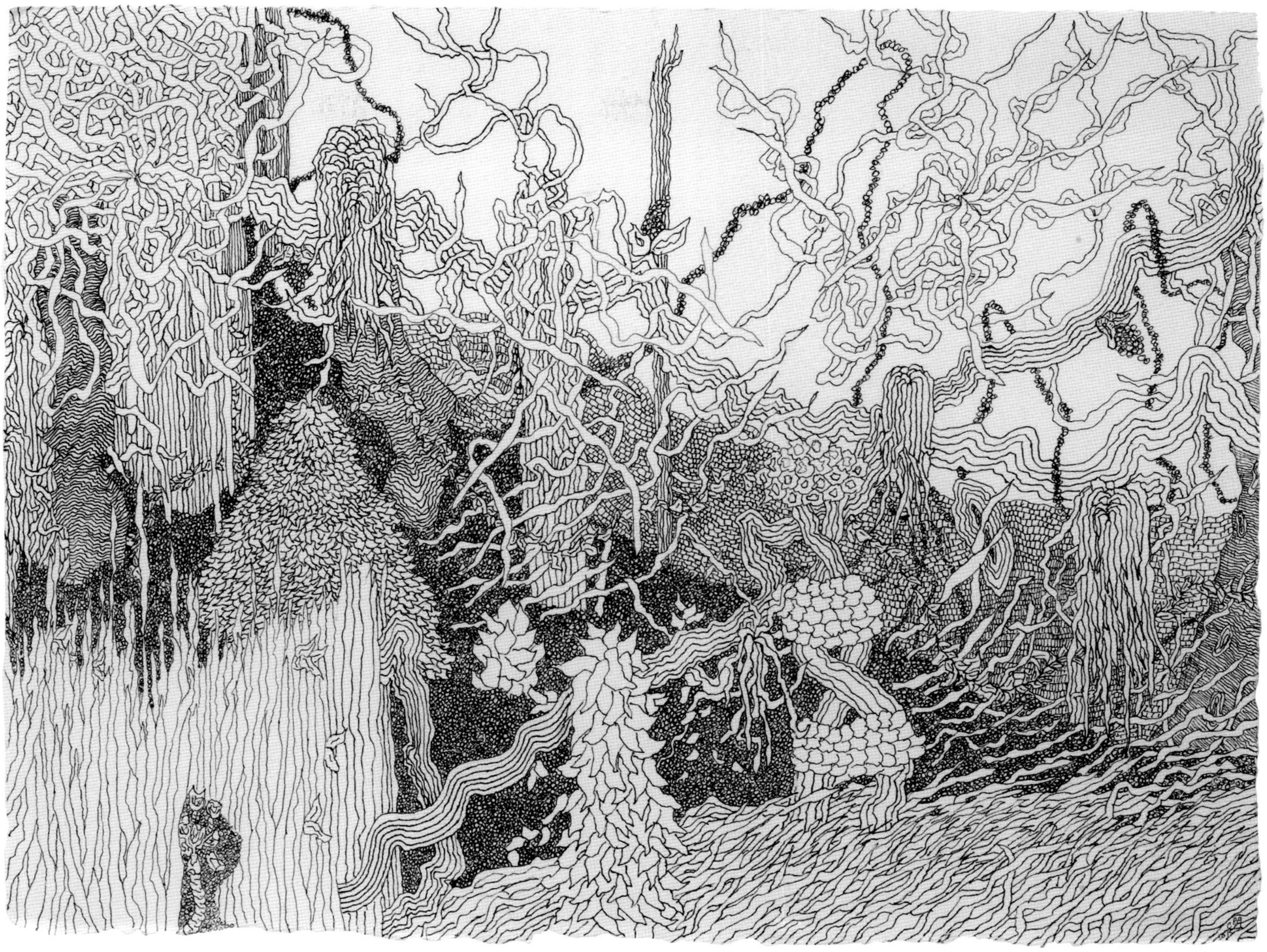

38 *Extravagant Eden 8,* 2015, Pen and ink on paper, 11 x 15"

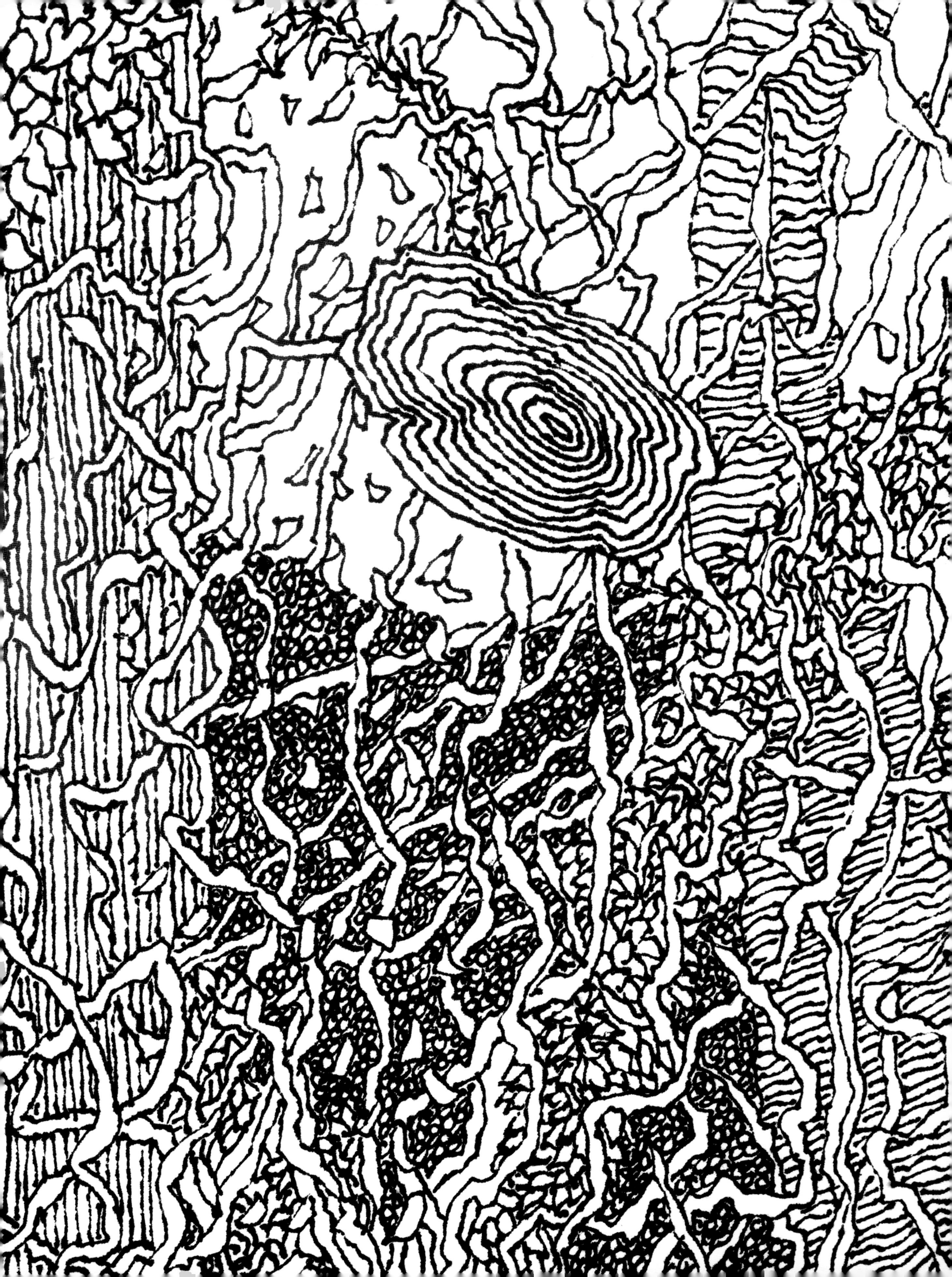

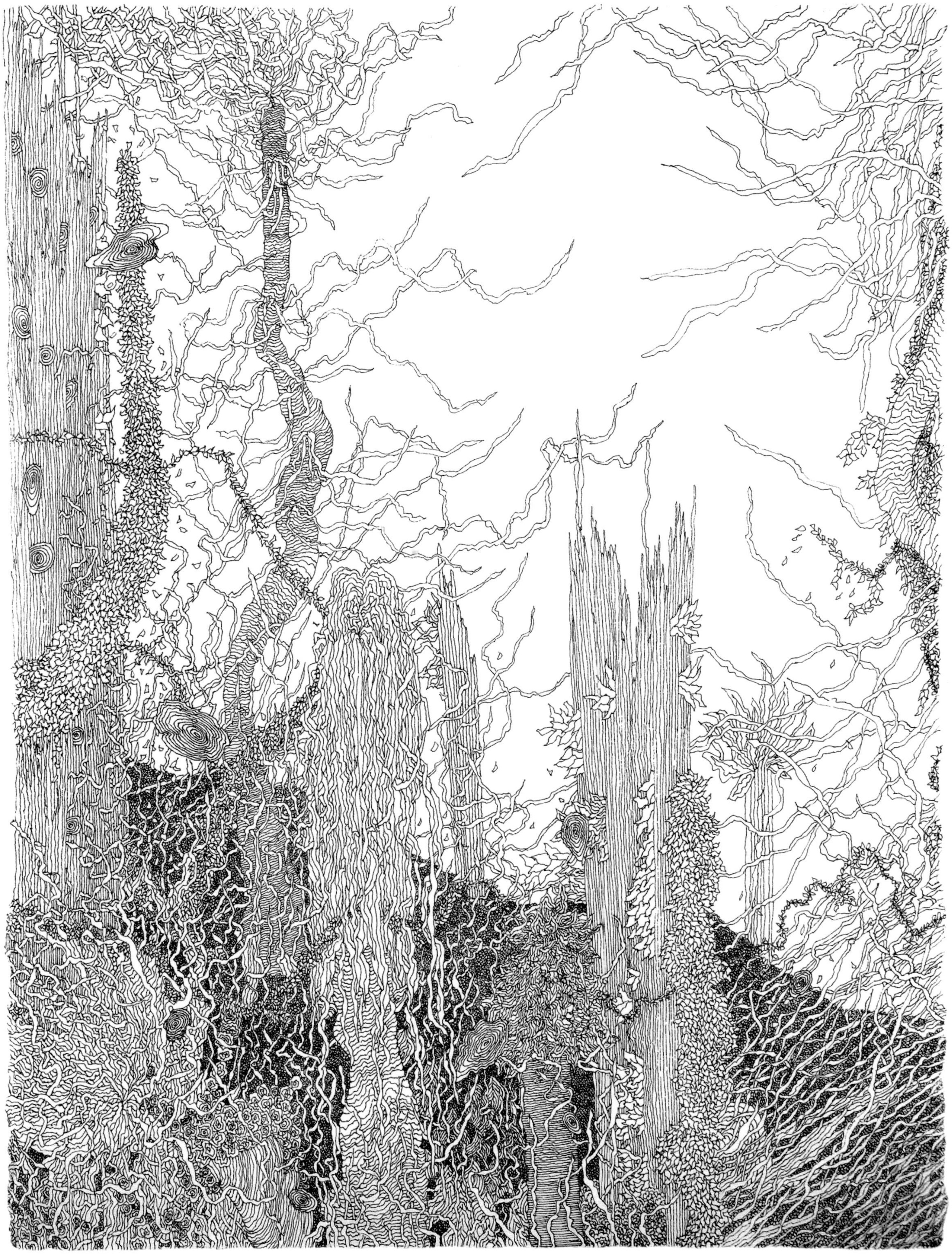

39 *PM 25,* Pen and ink on paper, 29 3/4 x 22 1/2"

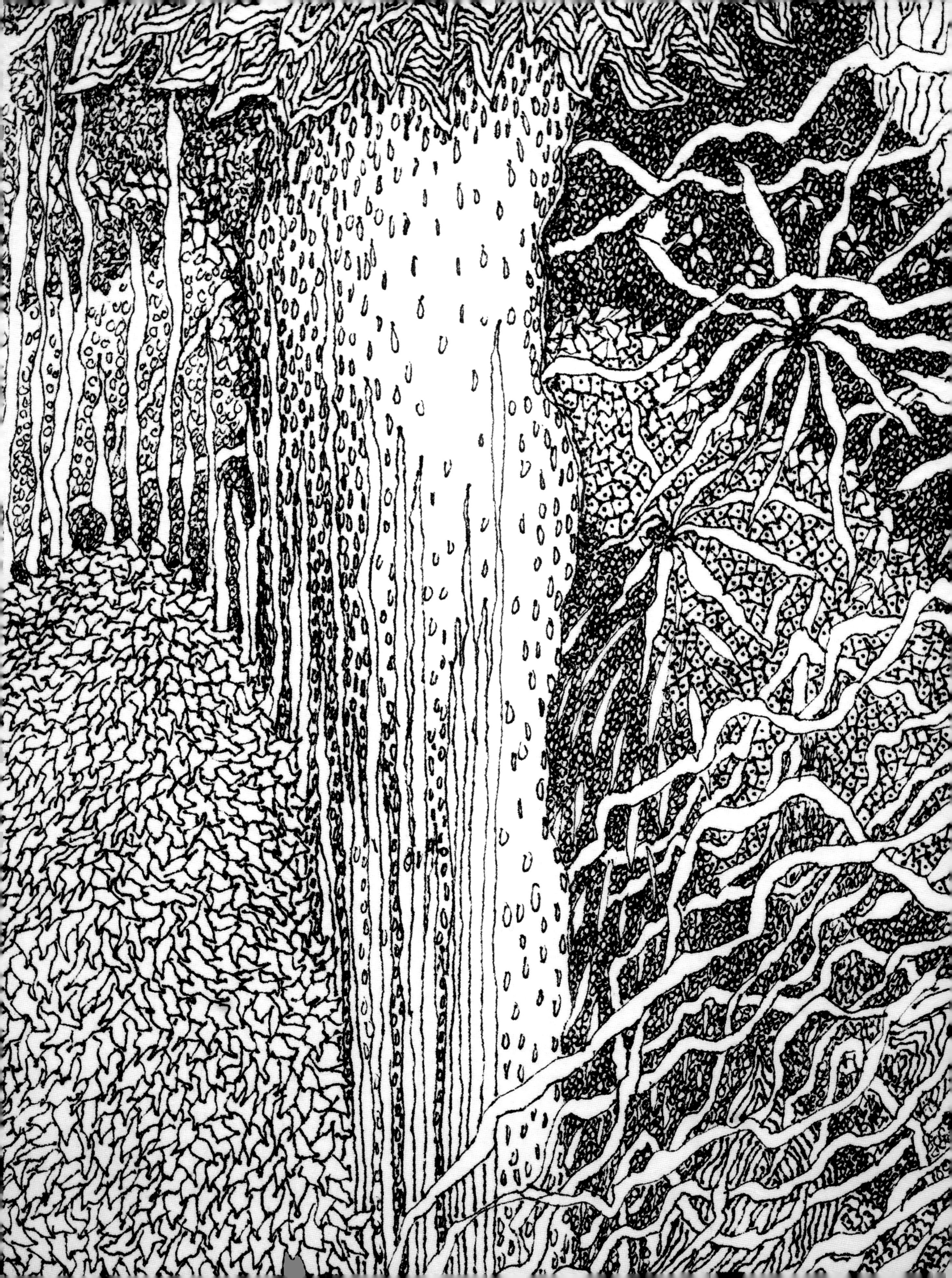

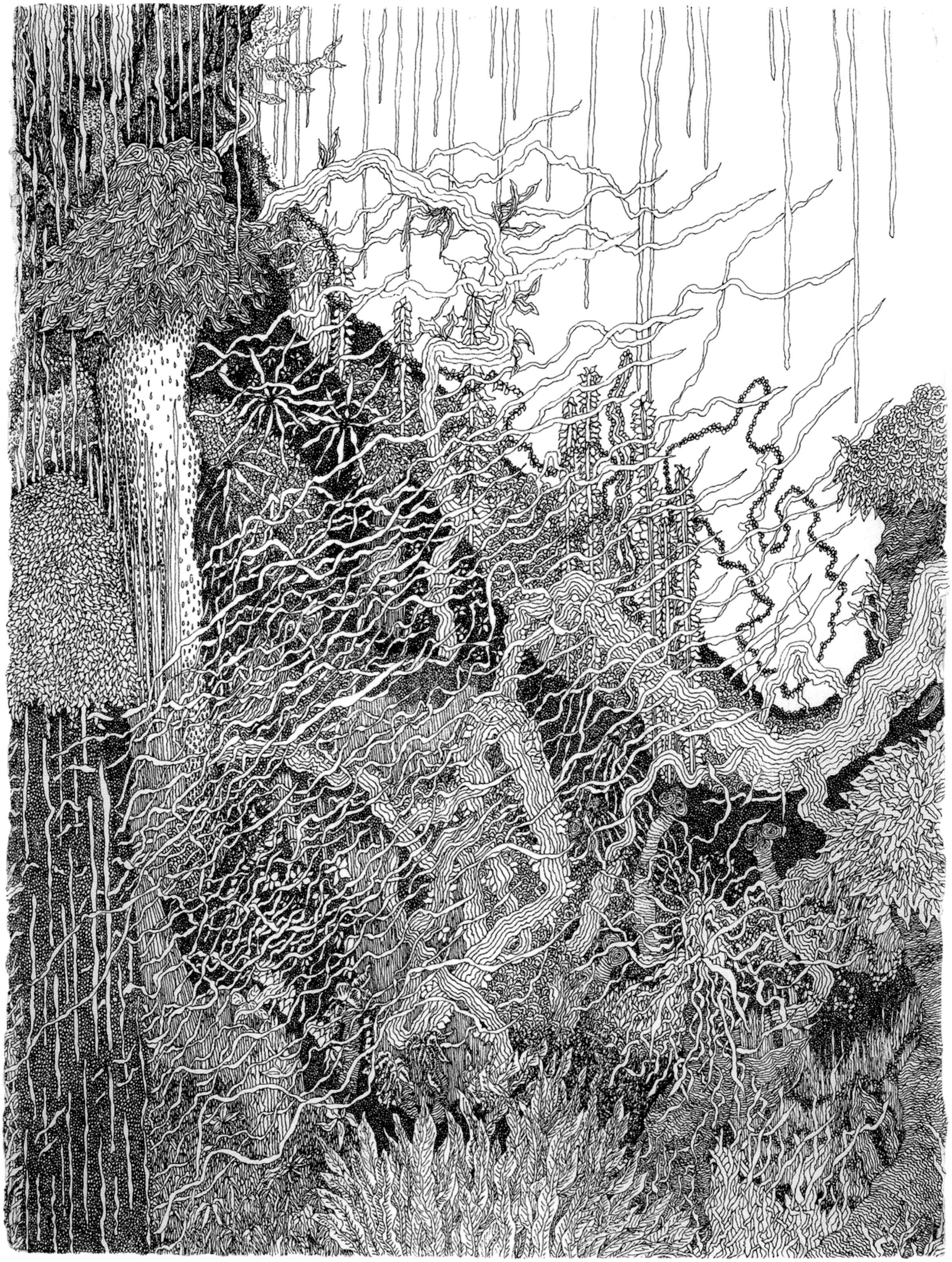

40 *PM 28,* Pen and ink on paper, 29 3/4 x 22 1/2"

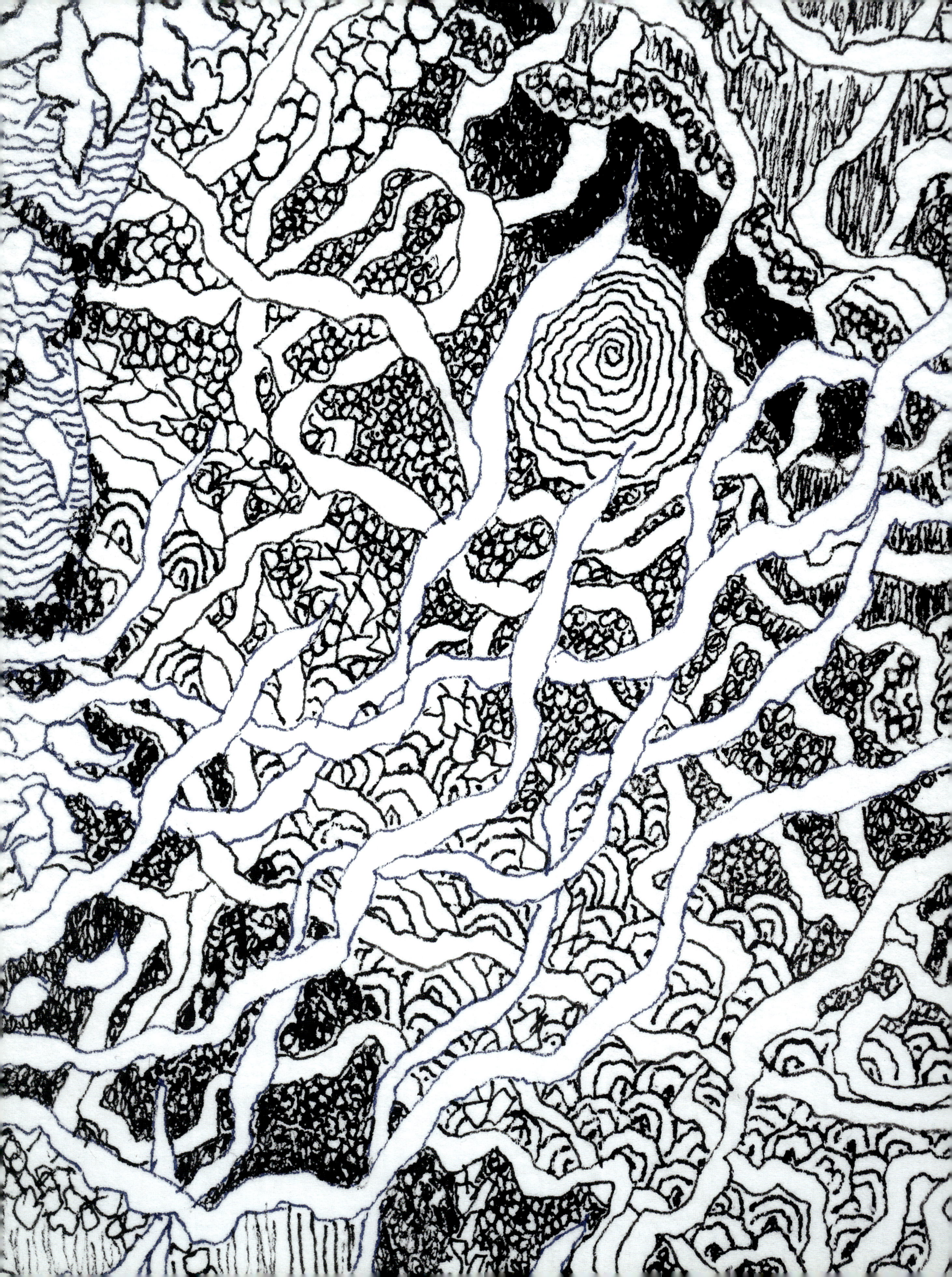

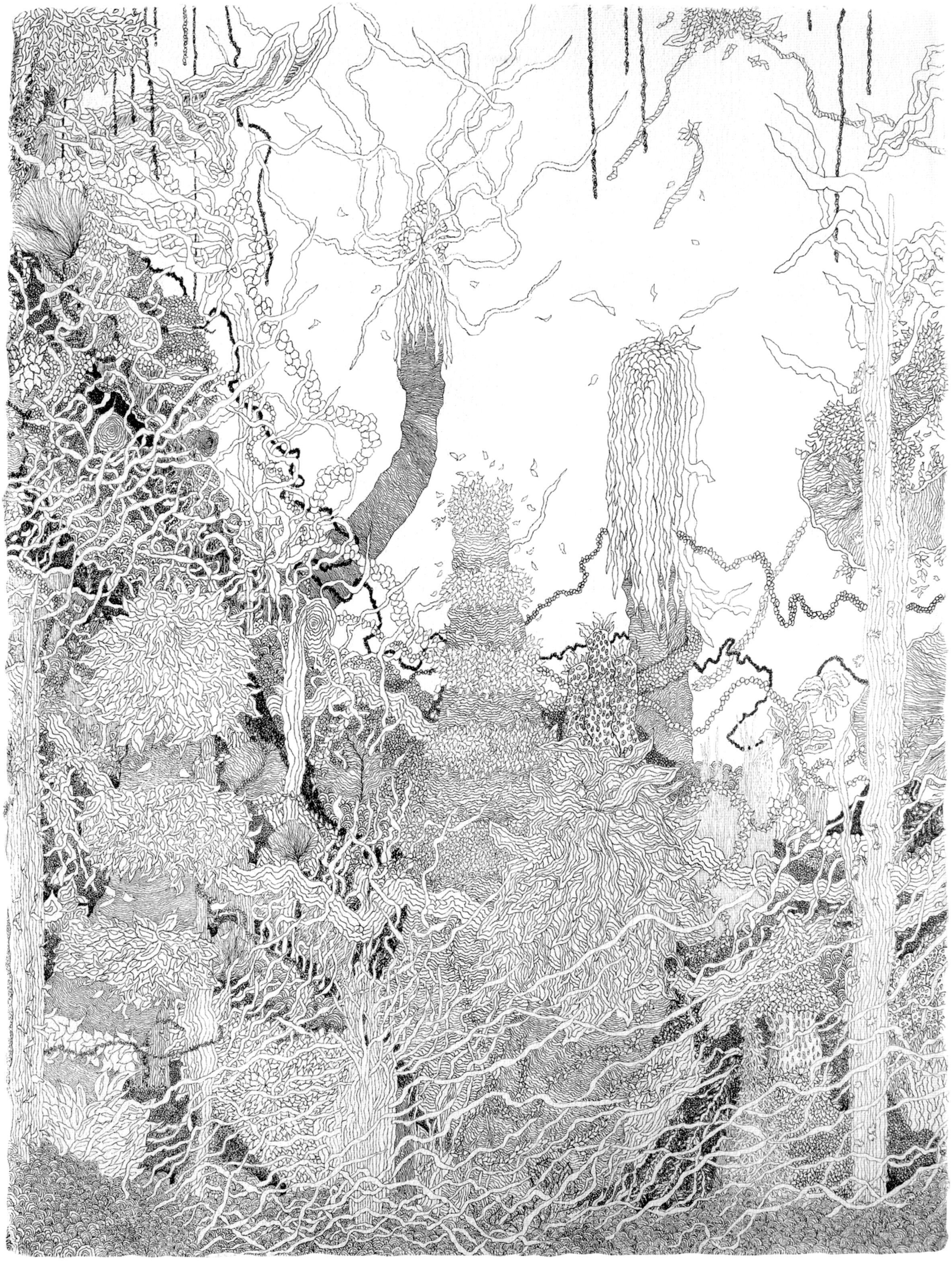

41 *PM 44,* 2015, Pen and ink on paper, 29 3/4 x 22 1/2"

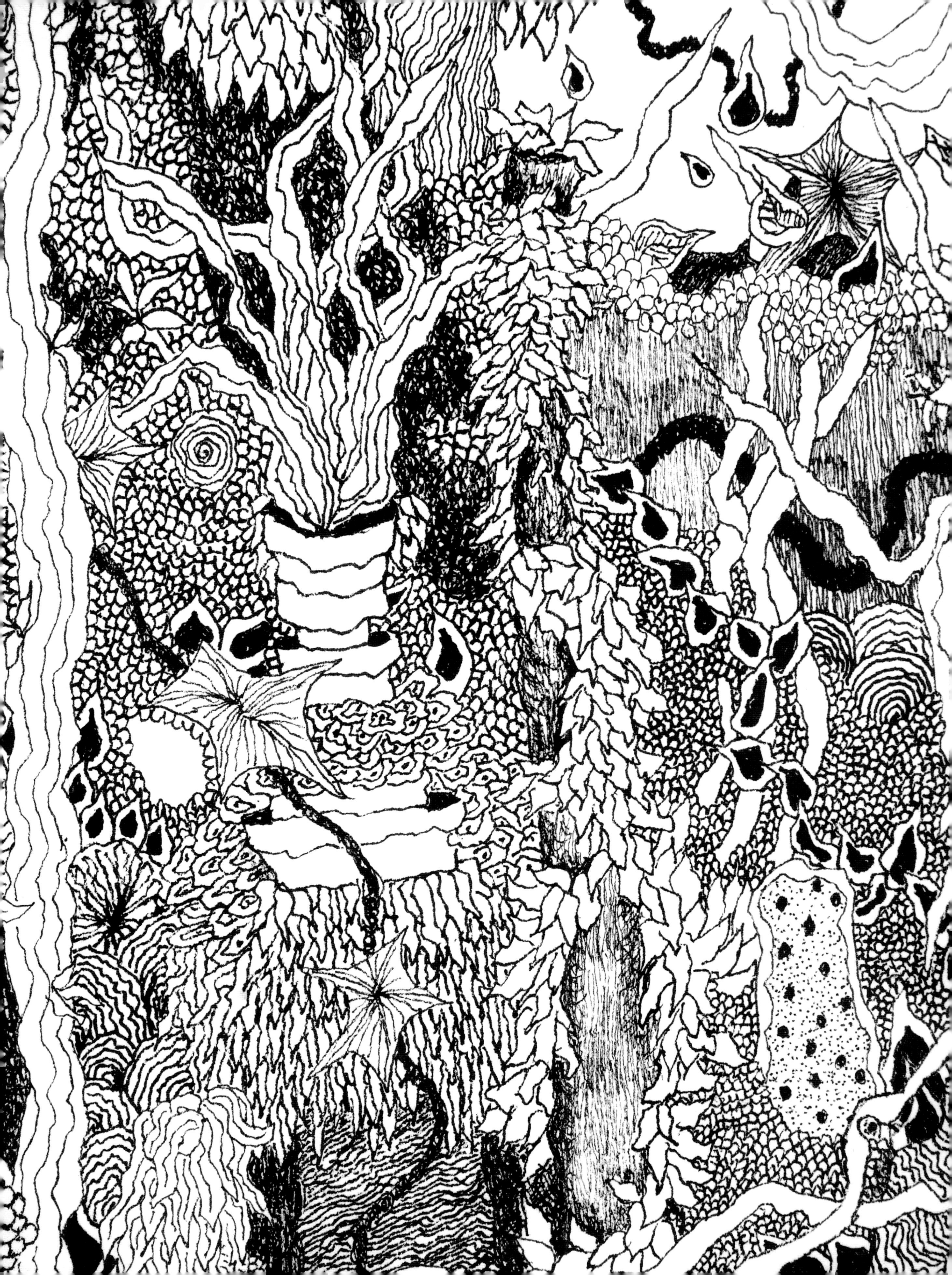

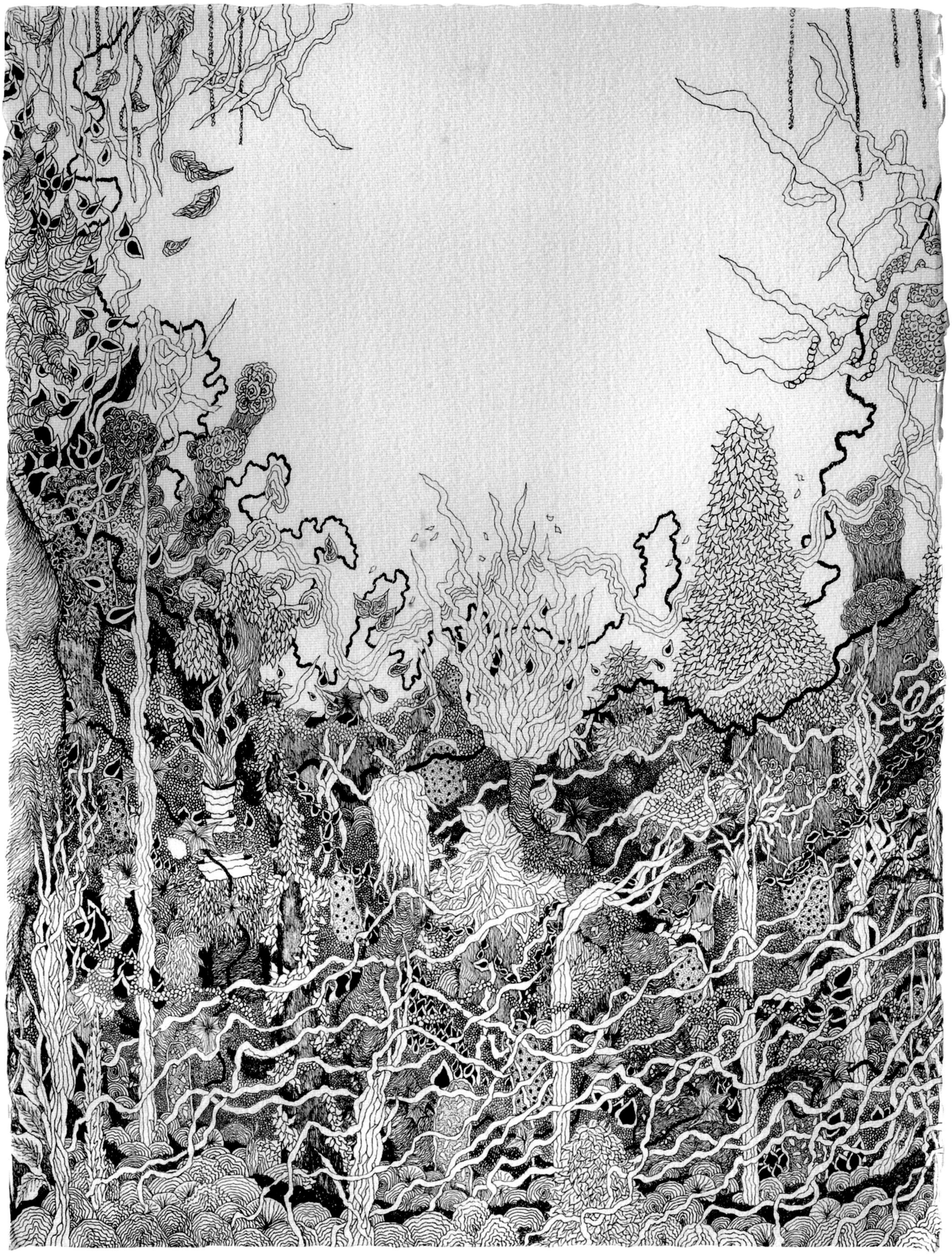

42 *PM 45*, 2016, Pen and ink on paper, 29 3/4 x 22 1/2"

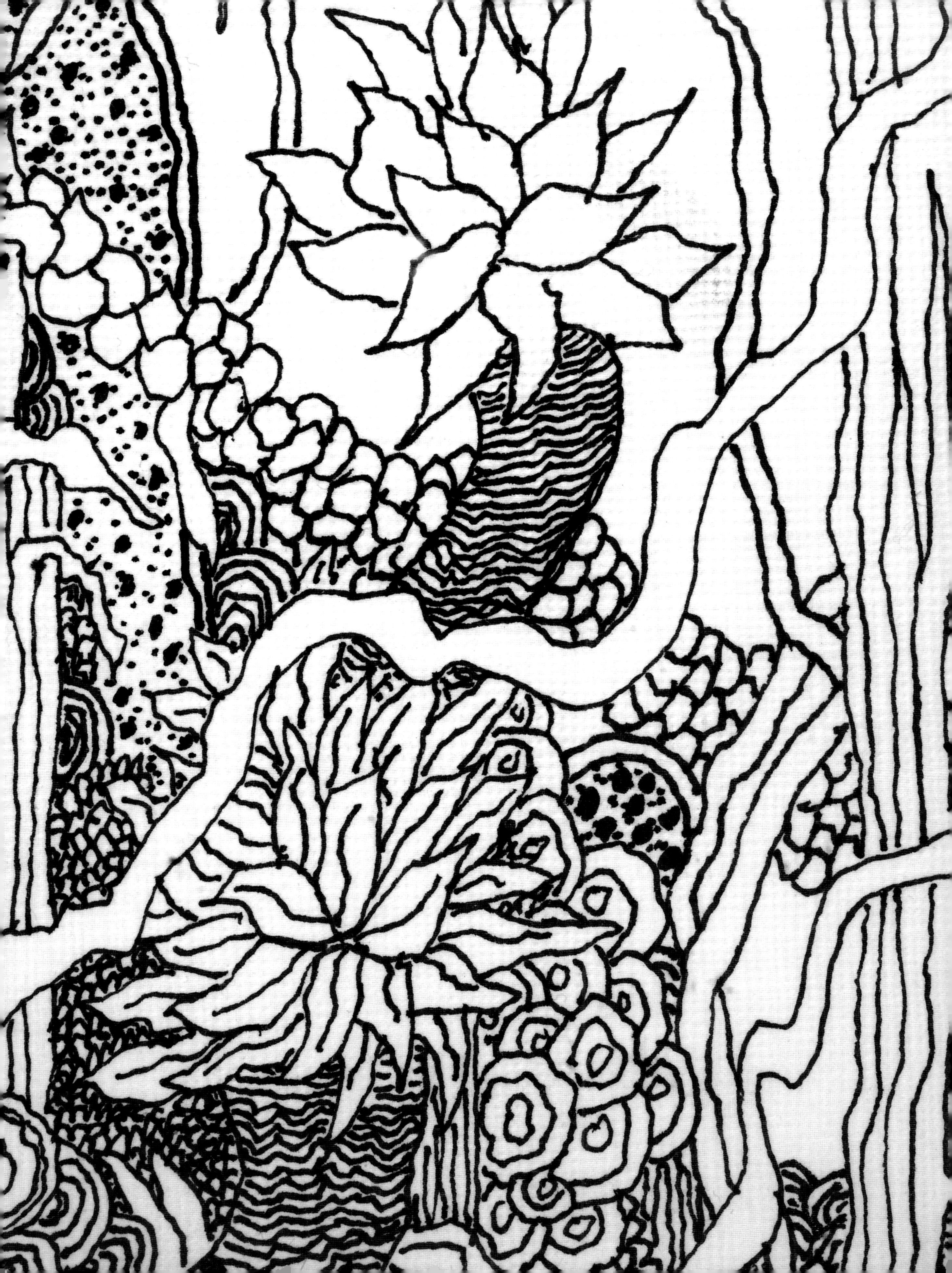

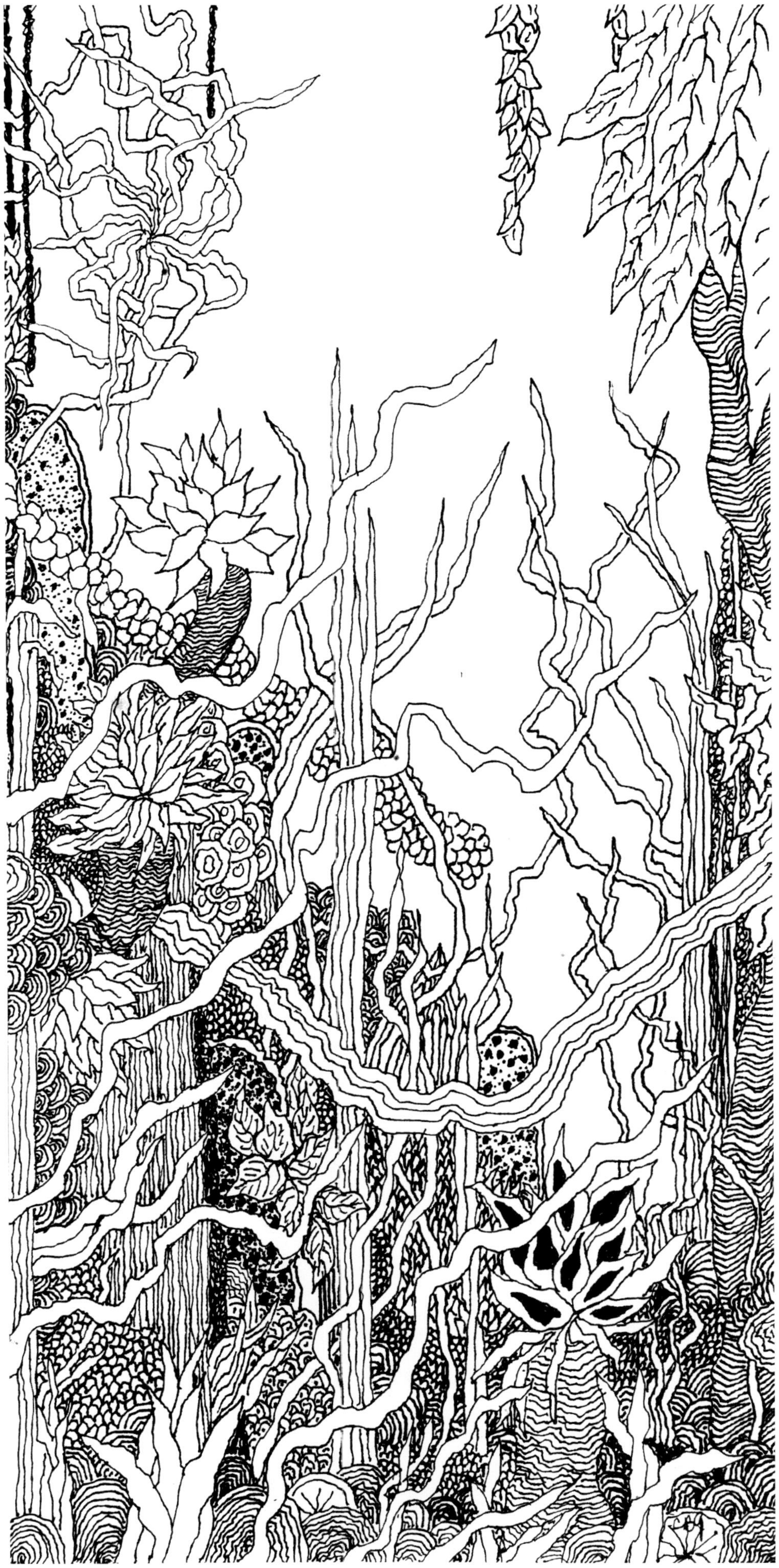

43 *Extravagant Eden 39*, 2017, Pen and ink on paper, 11 3/4 x 6"

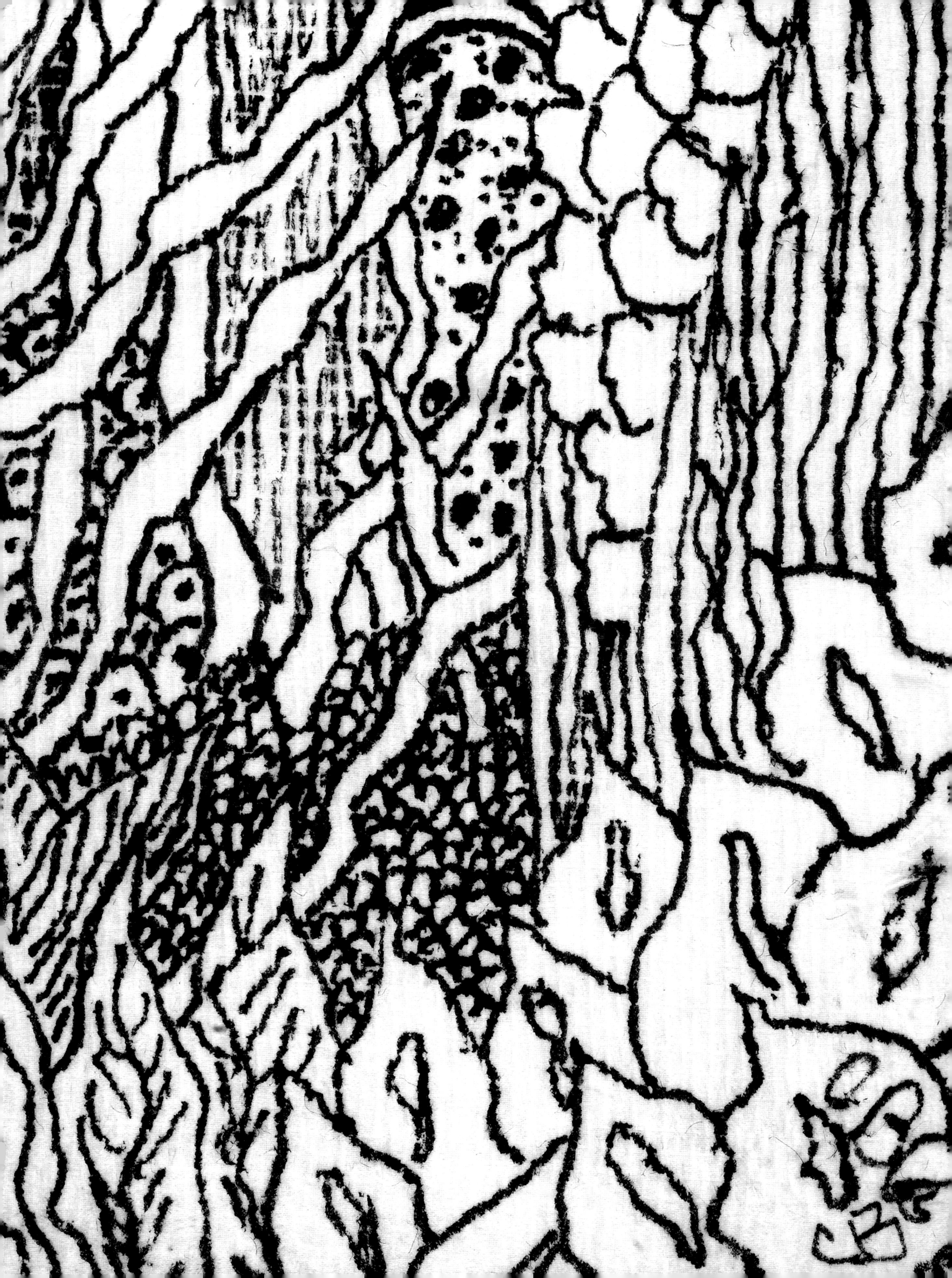

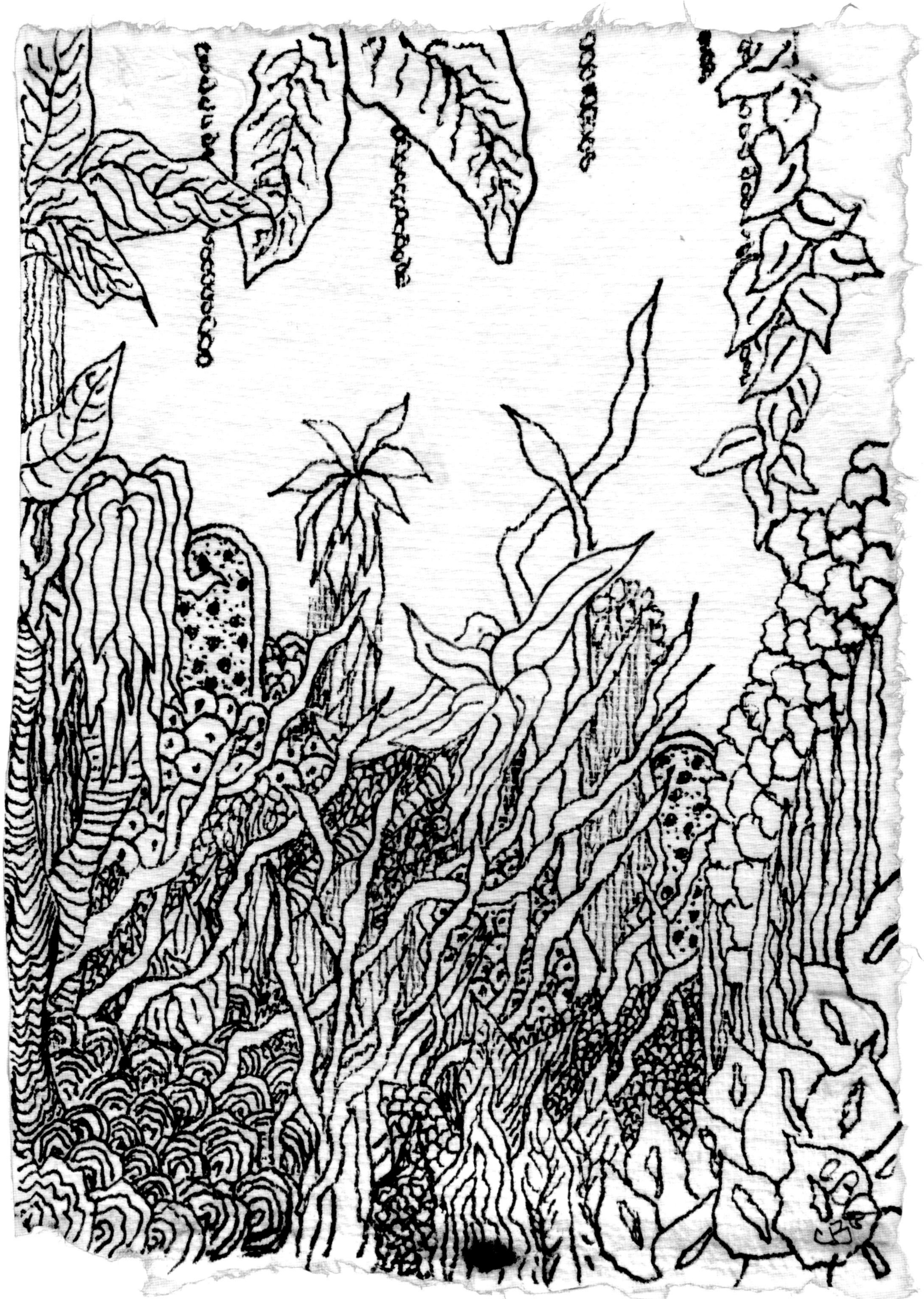

44 *Extravagant Eden 40*, 2017, Pen and ink on paper, 6 x 4 1/2"

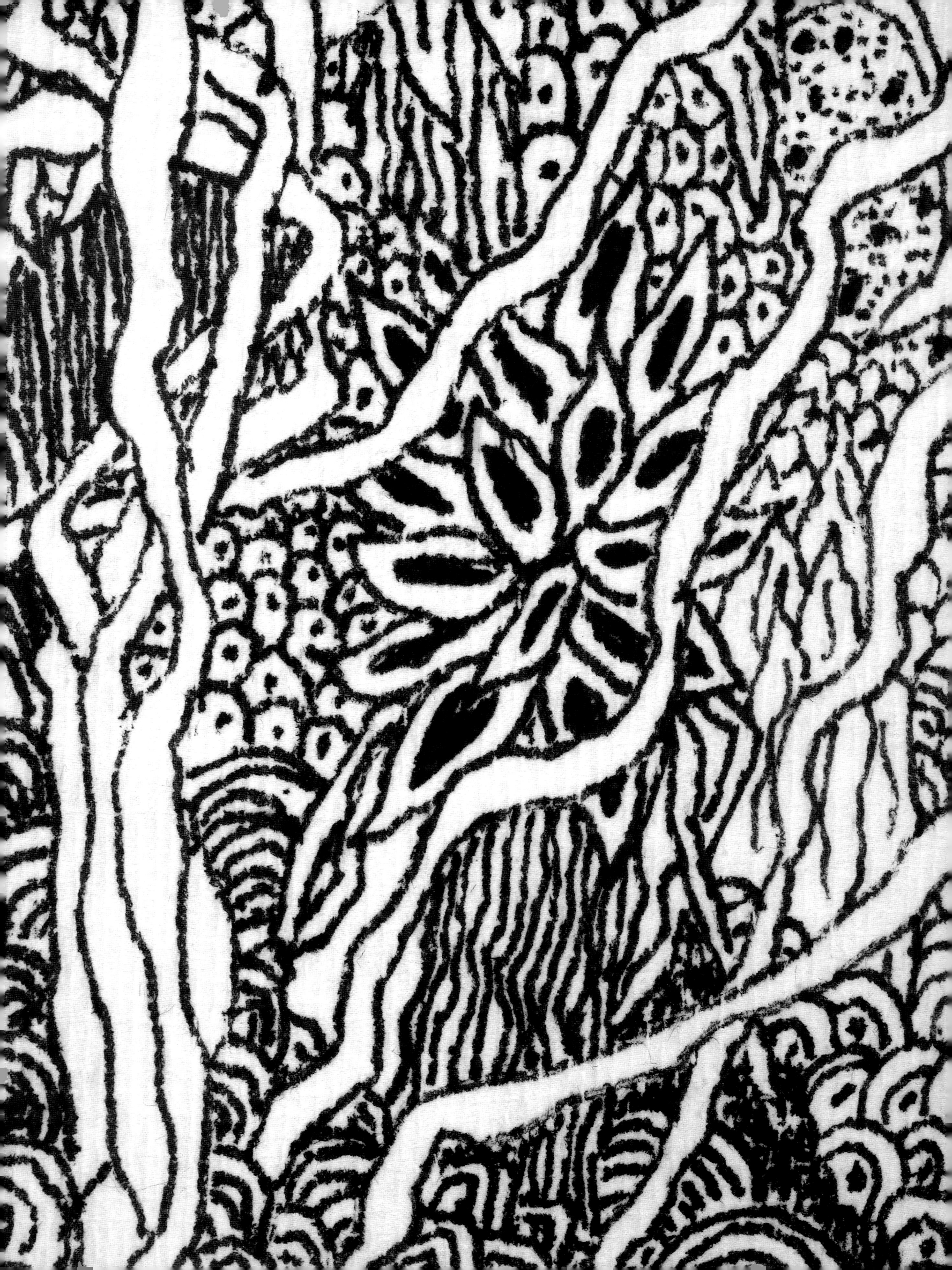

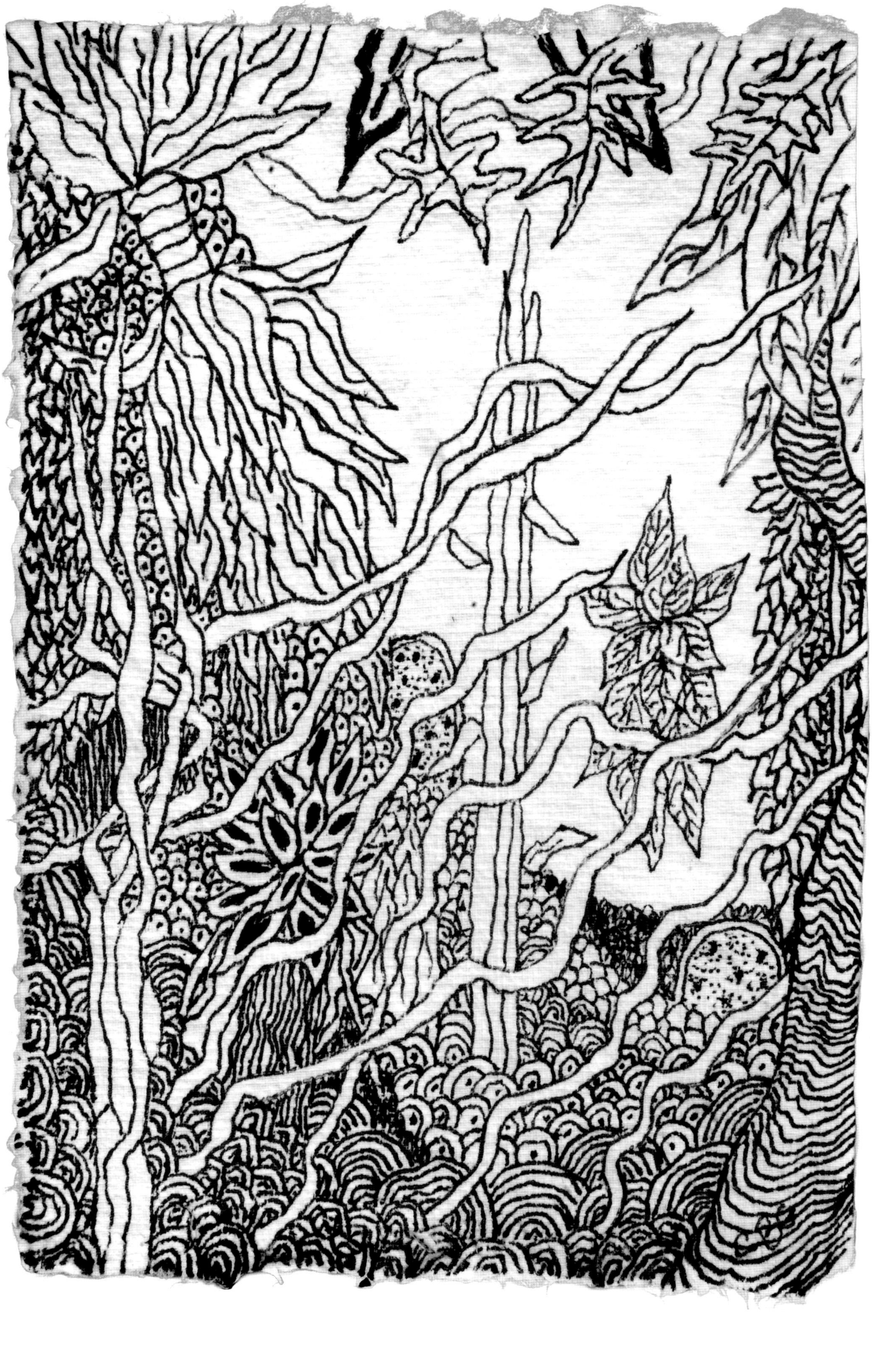

45 *Extravagant Eden 41,* 2017, Pen and ink on paper, 6 x 4"

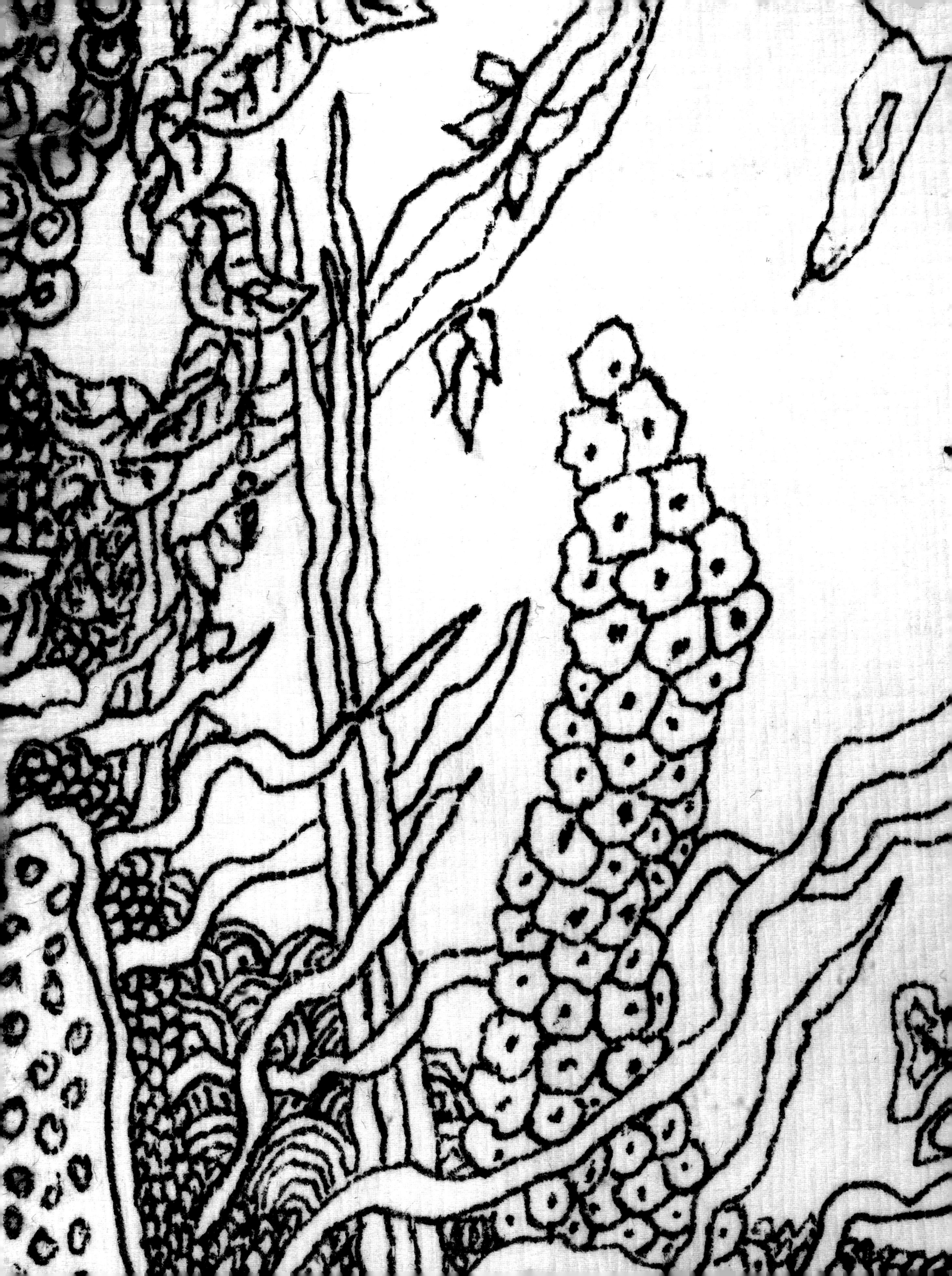

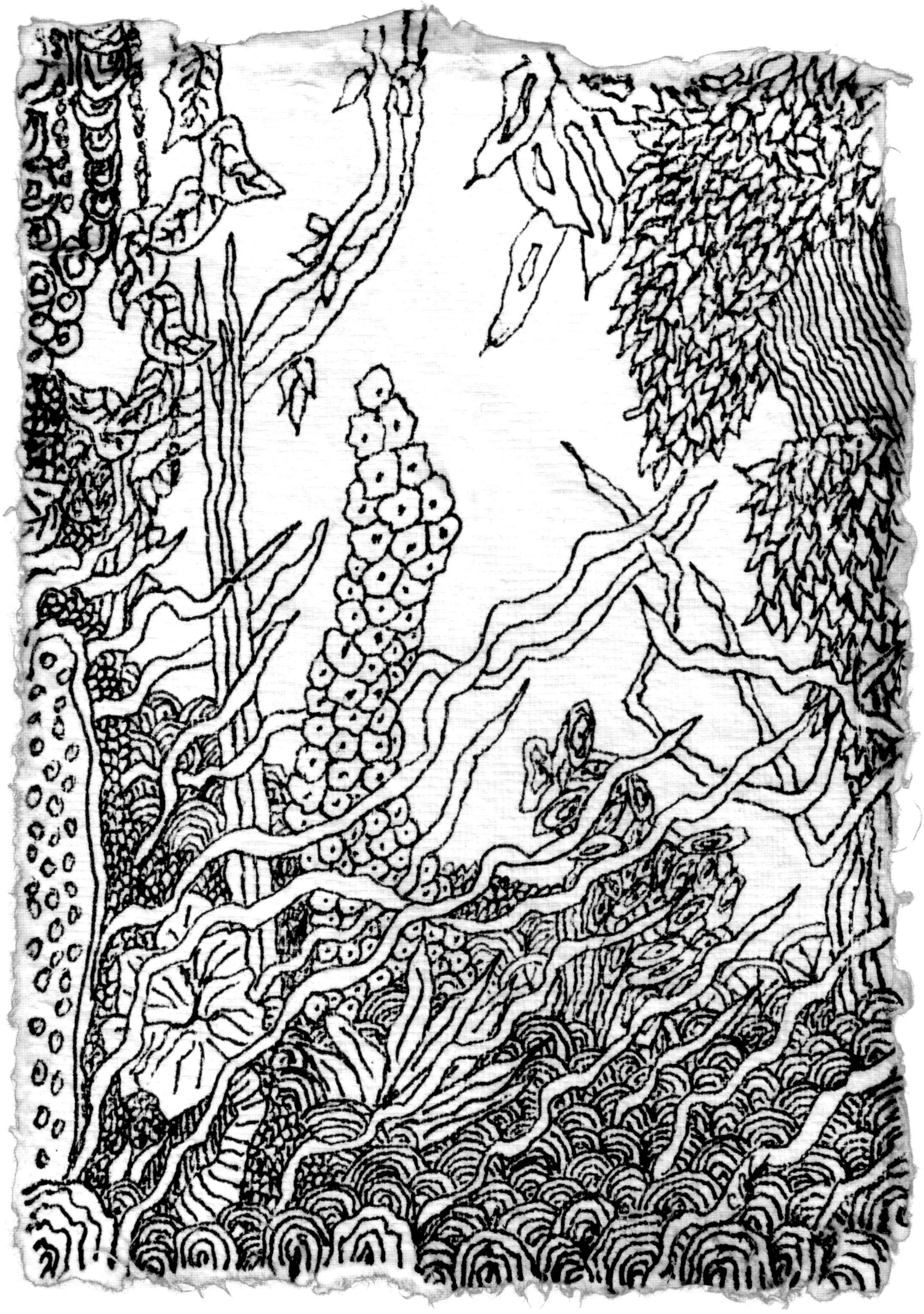

46 *Extravagant Eden 42,* 2017, Pen and ink on paper, 6 1/2 x 4 1/2"

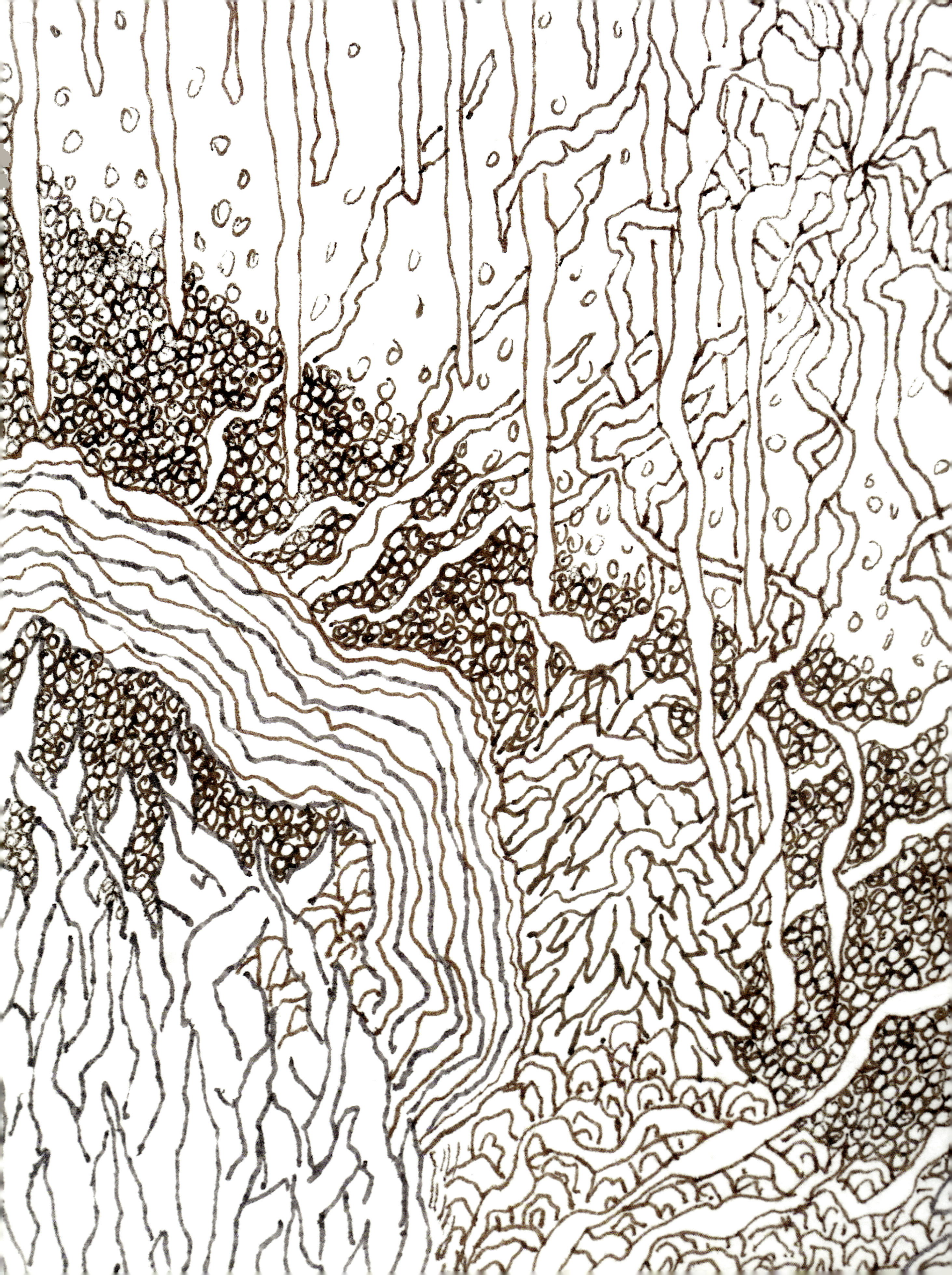

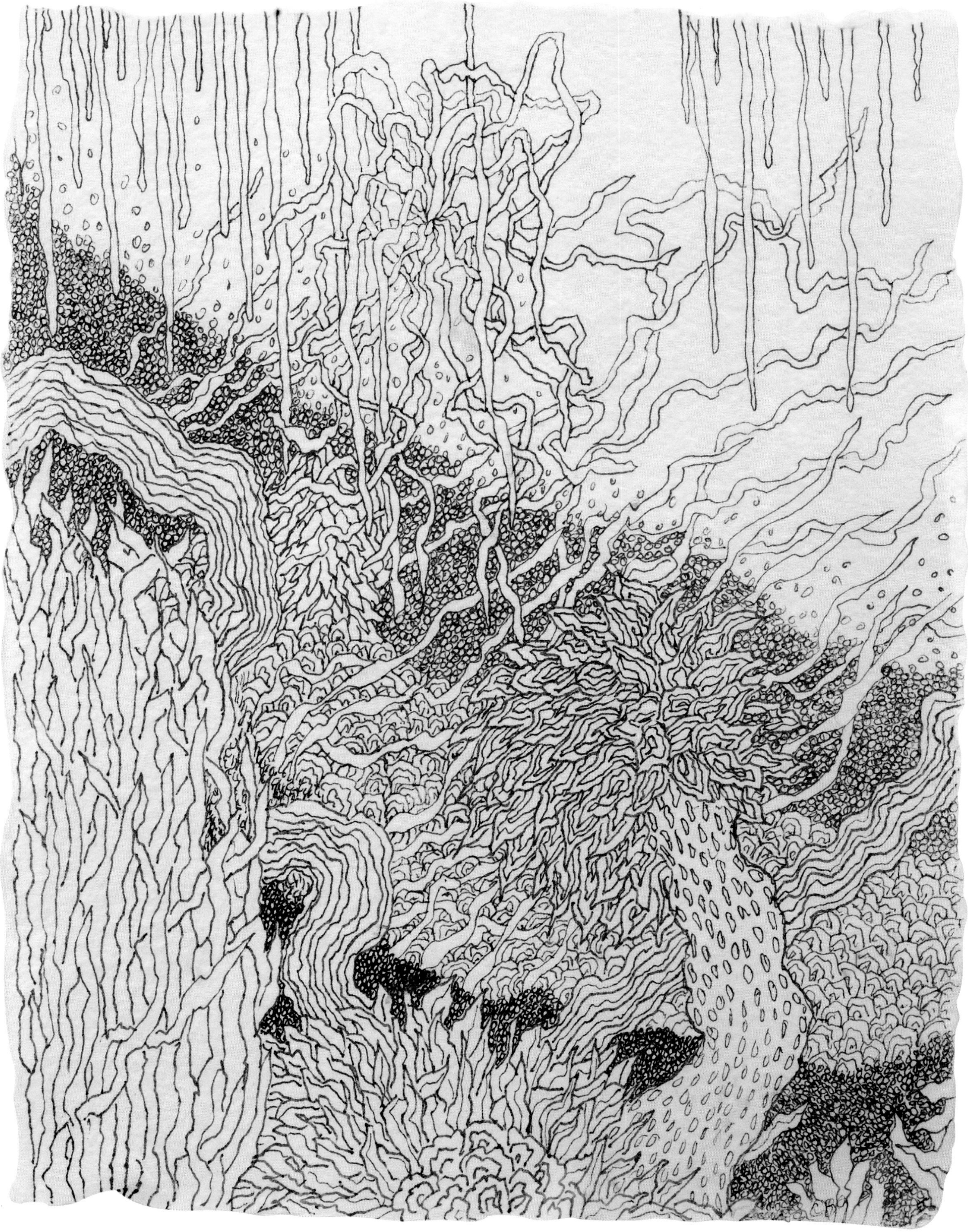

47 *Extravagant Eden 43,* 2017, Pen and ink on paper, 10 1/2 x 8 1/4"

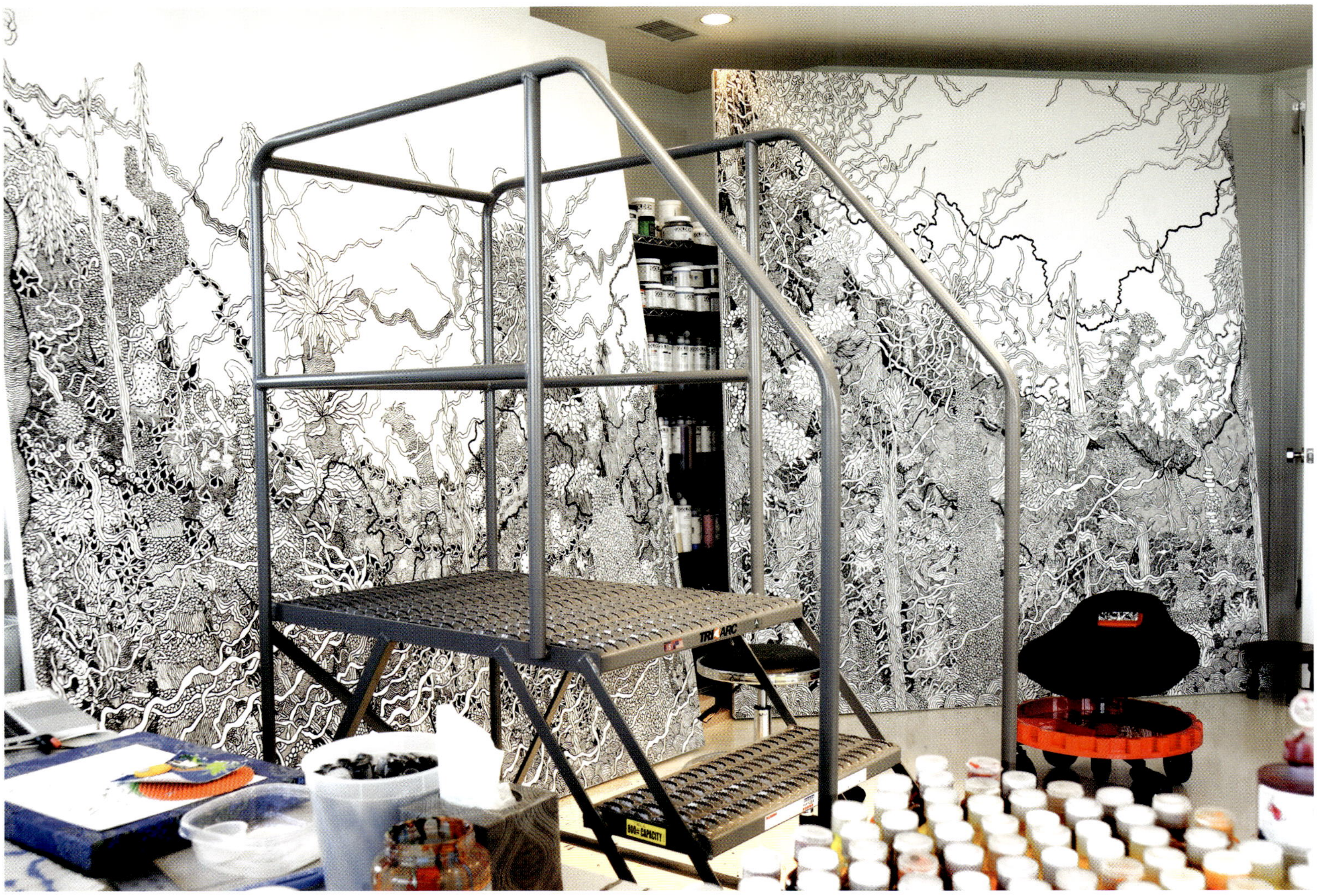

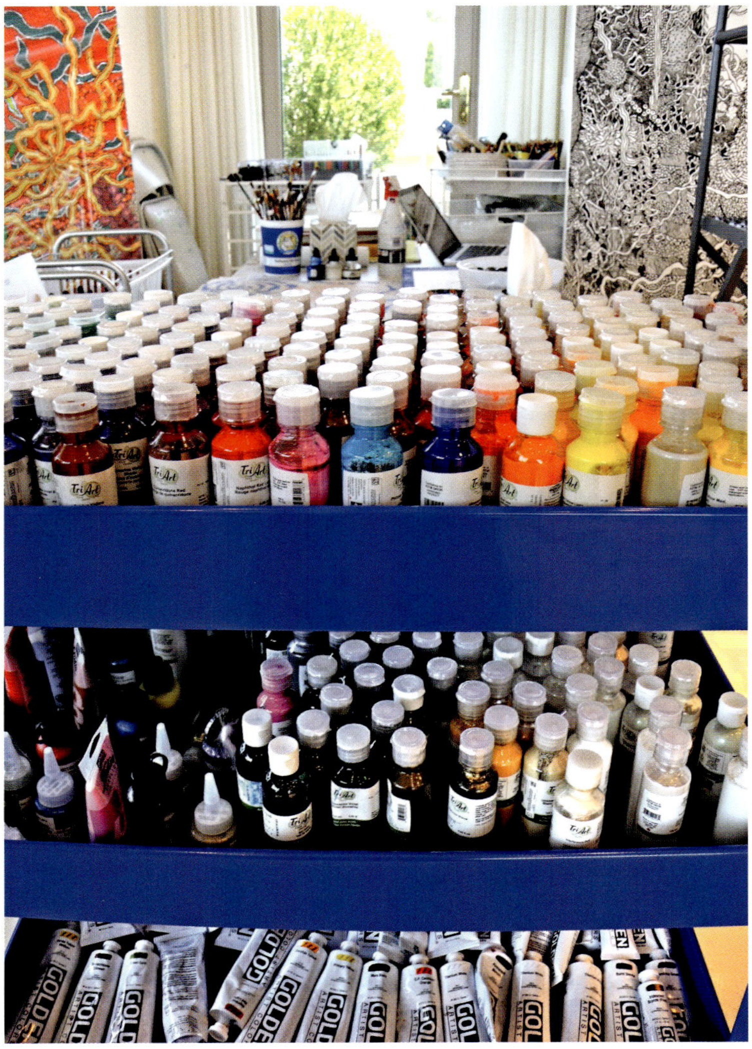

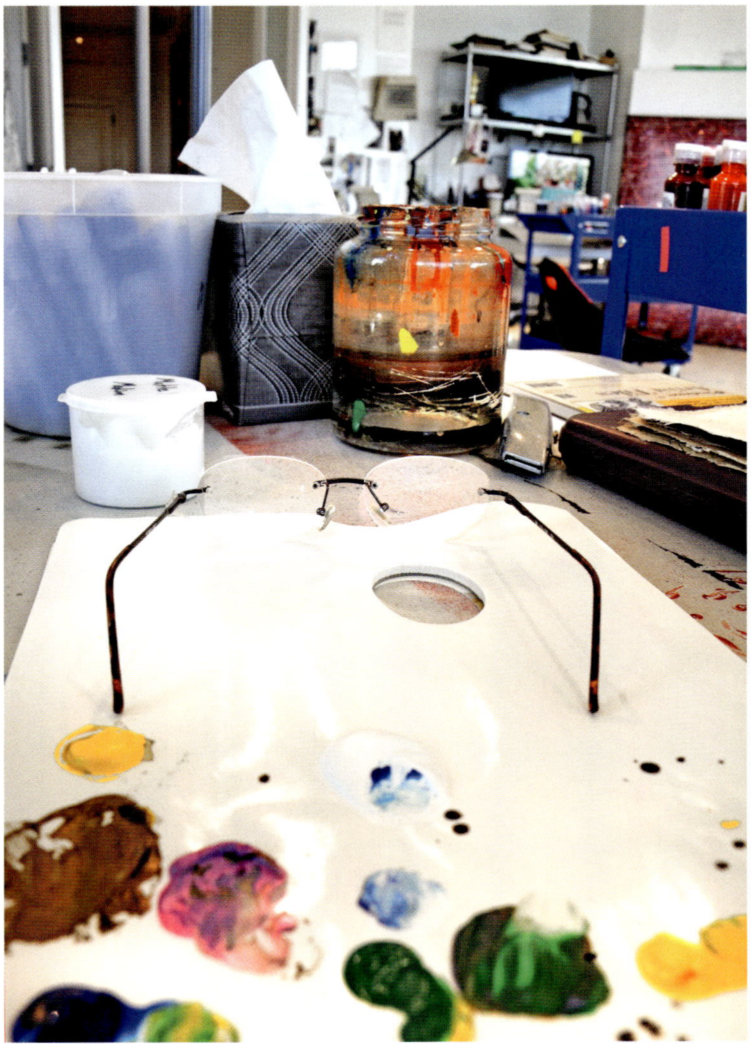

Artist's Biography

Carol Brown Goldberg was born in Baltimore, MD. She moved to the Washington, DC, metro area after graduating from the University of Maryland with a BA in American Studies. She received a second BA at the Corcoran School of Art, where she was honored with the Eugene M. Weisz award upon graduation. In 1989 and 1990, Goldberg produced and curated a 14-part lecture series, "Voices of Our Time," which explored the relationship between art and science. This interest in science has also led her to serve as a board member of the Johns Hopkins Lyme Disease Research Center. She has taught at American University and the University of Maryland, was Artist in Residence at Chautauqua Institute, is a recipient of the Maryland State Arts Award, and serves on the board of The Phillips Collection in Washington, DC, as well as on the Collector's Committee of the Reading Public Museum and the Contemporary Art Accessions Committee of the Baltimore Museum of Art.

In 2012 she was featured on the catalogue cover for Art Santa Fe. Also in 2012, she and neuroscientist Partha Mitra discussed "Creativity and the Brain" on a panel led by artist Fre Ilgen in Berlin, Germany. The same year, she produced the award-winning short film *The Color of Time*. In 2013 she was awarded third prize for a sculpture installation scheduled for the Parque de Levante in Murcia, Spain. From 2014 to 2016, her paintings and sculpture were on a touring exhibition that included the Vero Beach Museum of Art, the Foosaner Art Museum, South Dakota Art Museum, and Lake Charles Cultural Center. Other recent exhibition venues include the Frost Art Museum, The Phillips Collection, and Reading Public Museum. Forthcoming exhibitions in 2018 include the Katzen Arts Center at American University and the Washington County Museum of Fine Arts.

She has shown in the US and internationally in over 100 solo and group exhibitions, including solo traveling painting exhibitions throughout Spain and Mexico. Her work is included in many museums and private collections, including New Orleans Museum of Art and National Museum for Women in the Arts, as well as in permanent outdoor sculpture installations at Medina del Campo Sculpture Park in Spain, The Kreeger Museum, the Katzen Arts Center at American University, George Washington University, Montclair State University, Reading Public Museum, Chautauqua Institution, Johns Hopkins Hospital, and (forthcoming) at Martha's Table in Washington, DC. She is represented by Addison/Ripley Fine Art in Washington, DC.

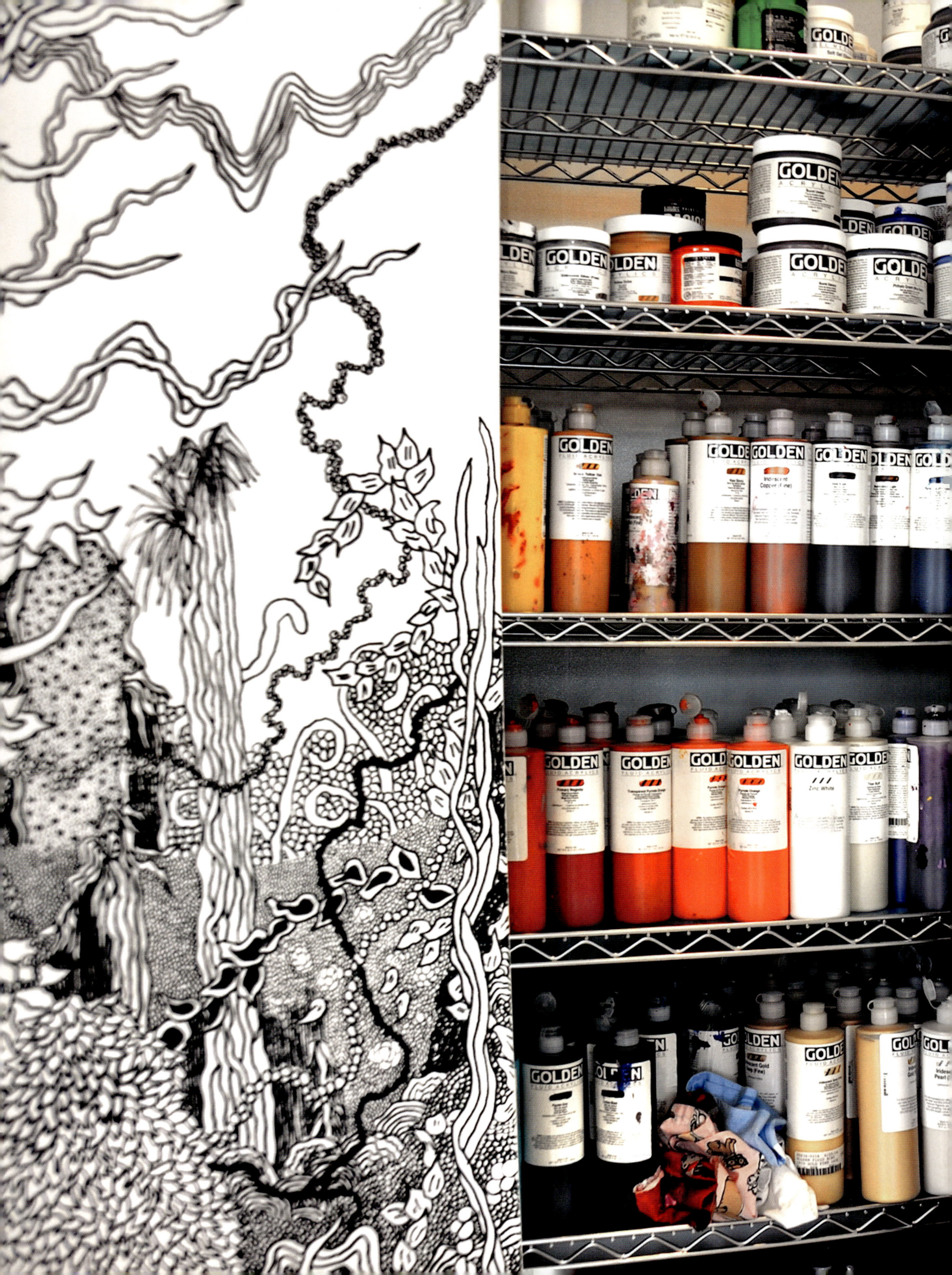

GOLDEN
ACRYLICS
GOLDEN
FLUID ACRYLICS
Iridescent Copper (Fine)
Zinc White

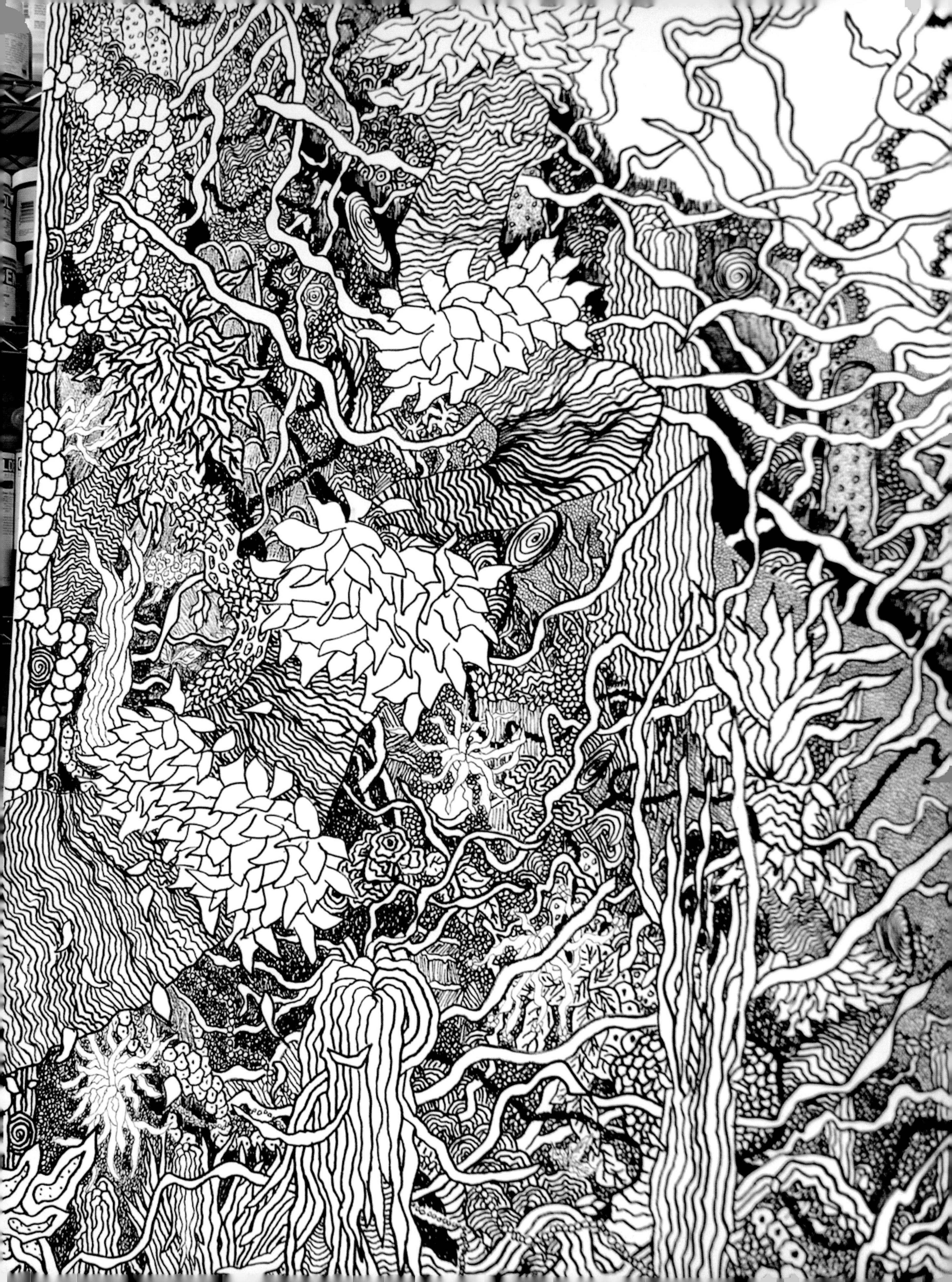

Artist's CV

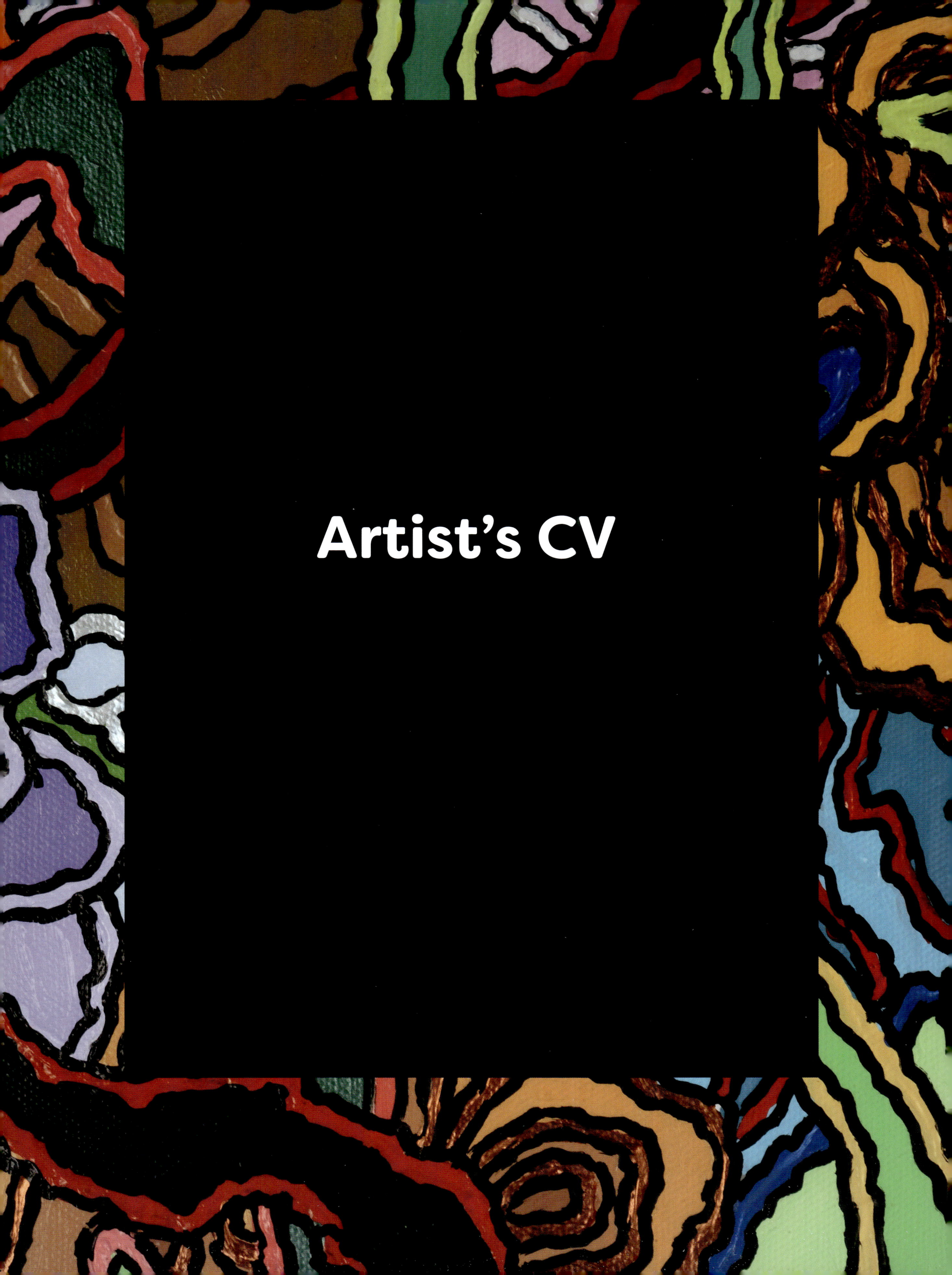

AWARDS AND HONORS

2016 Juror's Award, "Making Sense: See, Smell, Hear, Taste, Touch," McLean Project for the Arts; McLean, VA

2014 Short Film Festival, Hudson Valley, NY, *The Color of Time* film

2014 Short Film Festival, Warwick, NY, *The Color of Time* film

2014 Short Film Selection, YouTube, *The Color of Time* film

2013 Third Prize; International Sculpture Competition; Parque de Levante; Murcia, Spain

2013 FilmColumbia 2013; *The Color of Time* film

2012 Best Experimental Film; London Film Awards; *The Color of Time* film

2012 Award of Excellence, La Jolla Short Film Festival; Best Shorts Competition; *The Color of Time* film

2010 Maryland State Arts Council: Individual Artist Award; Baltimore, MD

1994 AMANA Award; "Concertina"; video

1987 Outdoor Sculpture Honorarium; City of Rockville; Rockville, MD

1987 Outdoor Sculpture Honorarium; Martin Luther King Park; Montgomery County, MD

1976 Eugene M. Weisz Memorial Award; Corcoran School of Art; Washington, DC

LECTURES AND PROJECTS

2017 "Tangled Nature Wall Mural," 22 x 6 ft wall mural involving collaboration with hundreds of students, faculty, and staff at Florida International University.

2016 "The Studio: A Place of Transformation," 38 ft photographic mural; Carol Brown Goldberg with Jack Rasmussen and Ramon Osuna; Katzen Arts Center at American University; Washington, DC

2016 "Coffee and Conversation," Carol Brown Goldberg with Jack Rasmussen and Christopher Addison; Addison/Ripley Fine Art; Washington, DC

2015 "A Day at the Kreeger Museum with Smithsonian Associates," Presentation; The Kreeger Museum; Washington, DC

2015 "One on One," Conversation with Klaus Ottmann; The Phillips Collection; Washington, DC

2015 "Carol Brown Goldberg: Recent Works," Artist Presentation; South Dakota Art Museum; Brookings, SD

2014 "Meet the Artist - Carol Brown Goldberg," Speaker Series Presentation; Cosmos Club; Washington, DC

2014 "The Artist: Genuine Creativity and Cultural Identity"; Discussion moderated by Dorothy Kosinski with Frellgen and Anil Revri; American University; Washington, DC

2013 *The Color of Time*, Film presentation, Chilmark Public Library, Chilmark, MA

2013 Curator; "Sigil," Addison/Ripley Fine Art; Washington, DC

2013 *The Color of Time; Memory and Art*, OLLI Speaker Series; American University; Washington, DC

2012 "The New Baroque Abstraction," Discussion with Donald Kuspit; The New York Studio School; New York, New York

2012 *The Color of Time*; Film Installation; American University; Washington, DC

2012 "Bring Your Brain"; Discussion moderated by Frellgen with Prof. Partha Mitra; Berlin, Germany

2011 Montclair State University Symposium; With Donald Kuspit, Glenn Harper, Don Kimes, and Lenore Miller, Montclair, NJ

2010 Donald Kuspit Lecture, "Mystical Physics: Carol Brown Goldberg"; Lebanon Valley College; Annville, PA

2009 Guest lecturer; The Hirshhorn Museum and Sculpture Garden; Washington, DC

2008 Conversation with the artist; George Washington University, Luther W. Brady Art Gallery; Adamar Gallery; West Palm Beach, FL

2008 Guest lecturer; Chilmark Public Library; Chilmark, MA

2007 "ART TALK"; Interview with Lila Snow; Montgomery County Cable; Kensington, MD

2007 "Artist Talk"; The Kreeger Museum; Washington, DC

2003-2001 Artist Residency: Chautauqua Institute; Chautauqua, NY

2001 VOICE OF AMERICA; Video Interview, "The Next Chapter"

2000 Visual Artist Workshop Leader; "Leadership Montgomery"; Olney, MD

2000 Cosmos Club: "Art in the 21st Century"; Lecture; Washington, DC

1999 Curator: Internat'l Visions Gallery; "Amnesty Internat'l Artists"; Washington, DC

1998 Panelist; "Artists with Staying Power"; Art Dealers Assoc.; Washington, DC

1998 Lecturer: "Painting in the 21st Century; Cosmos Club; Washington, DC

1996 Bosnia Human Rights: "Solar Night"

1996 The Johns Hopkins University: "Childlife Project" with Sam Gilliam and Grace Hartigan; Baltimore, MD

1995 Chair/Moderator; Southeastern College Art Conference; "science and poetry for art"; Georgetown University; Washington, DC

1995 Pyramid Atlantic, Workshop Resident; "Exploration"; Silver Spring, MD

1993 Maryland Art Place: Painting and Video: "Concertina"; Baltimore, MD

1990-1991 Producer and curator: 8-Lecture Series "Voices of our Time" Strathmore Hall Arts Center; Bethesda, MD

1990 Painting; Amnesty International; Amnesty International Human Rights Day for the 1990s

1987 Visiting Artist; Mountain Lake Workshop; Blacksburg, VA

1979 Aspen Music Festival; Theatrical Masks for Opera, Houdini; Aspen, CO

1976 Corcoran Gallery of Art; "Juried Exhibit"; Washington, DC

PUBLIC SCULPTURE INSTALLATIONS

2017 "RA 055," Painted Bronze, Reading Public Museum, Reading, PA

2017 "Dr. Mike," Painted Aluminum, American University, Ward Circle, Washington, DC

2016 "Red Disks," Painted Aluminum, Wilmer Eye Institute at Johns Hopkins Hospital, Baltimore, MD

2015 "Secret Totem," Painted Bronze, Montclair State University, Montclair, NJ

2015 "Circles in Space," Painted Aluminum, Chautauqua Institute, Chautuaqua, NY

2012 "EdW," Painted Bronze, George Washington University, Washington, DC

2011 "RA 054," Bronze, The Kreeger Museum, Washington, DC

2011 "RA 055," Painted Bronze, American University, Ward Circle, Washington, DC, 2011-2017

2009 "Blue Circles," Painted Aluminum, Medina del Campo Sculpture Park, Medina del Campo, Spain

SELECTED SOLO EXHIBITIONS

2018 Forthcoming: "Entanglement," Katzen Arts Center at American University; Washington, DC

2018 Forthcoming: "Carol Brown Goldberg: Recent Works," Washington County Museum of Fine Arts; Hagerstown, MD

2017 "Tangled Nature," Frost Art Museum; Miami, FL

2016 "Extravagant Edens", Addison Ripley Fine Art; Washington, DC

2016 "Carol Brown Goldberg: Recent Works", Lake Charles Cultural Center, Lake Charles, LA

2015 "Carol Brown Goldberg", A Gallery; Oak Bluffs, MA

2015 "One on One: Carol Brown Goldberg/ Henri Matisse", The Phillips Collection: curator, Klaus Ottmann; Washington, DC

2015 "Carol Brown Goldberg: Recent Works", South Dakota Art Museum; Brookings, SD

2015 "Carol Brown Goldberg: The Color of Time", Denise Bibro Fine Art, New York, NY

2014 "Carol Brown Goldberg: Recent Works", Vero Beach Museum of Art; Vero Beach, FL

2014 "Carol Brown Goldberg: Recent Sculpture", Foosaner Art Museum; Melbourne, FL

2014 "Carol Brown Goldberg: Sculpture"; Cosmos Club; Washington, DC

2013 "The Circle of Time"; Reading Public Museum; Reading, PA

2013 "Color in Space"; David Richard Gallery; Sante Fe, NM

2012 Addison/Ripley Fine Art; Washington, DC

2012 Art Santa Fe; Osuna Art; Santa Fe, NM

2012 Katzen Art Center at American University; Washington, DC

2012 "Flow and Fluctuation"; American Center for Physics; College Park, MD

2012 "Abstract Realities"; The Gabarron Foundation, New York, NY

2012 "Sculpture and Works on Paper"; Luther Brady Gallery, George Washington University; Washington, DC

2011 Addison/Ripley Fine Art; Washington, DC

2011 "Painting and Sculpture"; George Segal Gallery, Montclair State University; Montclair, NJ

2010 Fundación Sebastian A.C.; Mexico City, Mexico

2010 The Suzanne H. Arnold Gallery; Lebanon Valley College; Annville, PA

2010 Galería Emma Molina; Monterrey, Mexico

2009 Centro de las Artes CONARTE Museum; Monterrey, Mexico

2009 Osuna Gallery; Washington, DC

2009 Casa de Vacas, Buen Retiro Park; Madrid, Spain

2009 Sala de Exposiciones Molinos de Río; Murcia, Spain

2008 The Gabarrón Foundation Museum; Valladolid, Spain

2008 The National Arts Club (Gramercy Park); New York, NY

2007 Osuna Gallery; Washington, DC

2007 American University, Katzen Arts Center; Washington, DC

2007 Chilmark Library; Chilmark, MA

2007 Osuna Art; Washington, DC

2006 Pyramid Atlantic Gallery; Silver Spring, MD

2005 Art Santa Fe; Osuna Art; Santa Fe, NM

2005 Osuna Art; Washington, DC

2004 Cosmos Club; Washington, DC

2003 The John and Esther Clay Fine Arts Gallery; Cheyenne, WY

2002 The Daryl Reich Rubenstein Gallery; Sidwell Friends School; Washington, D.C.

2002 Chautauqua Institute; Chautauqua, NY

2002 Anton Gallery; Washington, DC

2000 Cosmos Club; Washington, DC

1996 Compass Bank; Chilmark, MA

1995 APA; Washington, DC

1995 Troyer Fitzpatrick Lassman Gallery; Washington, DC

1995 "Art Santa Fe"; Osuna Gallery; Santa Fe, NM

1993 "Concertina" (Multi-Media); Maryland Art Place, Baltimore, MD

1992 Osuna Gallery; Washington, DC

1990 Amnesty International; Peat Marwick Main & Company; Washington, DC

1990 Osuna Gallery; Washington, DC

1989 Osuna Gallery; Washington, DC

1988 Osuna Gallery; Washington, DC

1987 Osuna Gallery; Washington, DC

1987 Virginia Polytechnic Institute; Squires Gallery; Blacksburg, VA

1986 Strathmore Hall Arts Center; Rockville, MD

1986 Osuna Gallery; Washington, DC

1985 The G. Sander Gallery; Daytona Beach, FL

1983 FIAC Grand Palais; Osuna Gallery; Paris, France

1982 Washington Hebrew Congregation; Washington, DC

1982 Osuna Gallery; Washington, DC

SELECTED MUSEUM COLLECTIONS

South Dakota Art Museum; Brookings, SD

Vero Beach Museum of Art; Vero Beach, FL

ArtBank; Washington, DC

Reading Public Museum; Reading, PA

Academy Art Museum; Easton, MD

The Kreeger Museum; Washington, DC

National Institutes of Health; Bethesda, MD

New Orleans Museum of Art; New Orleans, Louisiana

DC Commission on the Arts and Humanities; Art Bank 2006, 2009; Washington, DC

The Gabarrón Foundation Museum; Valladolid, Spain

The Suzanne H. Arnold Gallery; Lebanon Valley College; Annville, PA

National Museum of Women in the Arts; Washington, DC

Museum of Arts and Sciences; Daytona Beach, FL

Deland Museum of Art; Deland, FL

Foosaner Art Museum (formerly Brevard Art Center and Museum); Melbourne, FL

Museum of the University of Central Florida; Orlando, FL

The Artery Group; Bethesda, MD

The Charles E. Smith Companies; Arlington, VA

Regional Center for Infants and Children; Rockville, MD

New England Contemporary Art Museum; Brooklyn, CT

The Frances Lehman Loeb Art Center; Vassar College; Poughkeepsie, NY

Peat Marwick Main & Company; Washington, DC

Federal Home Loan Mortgage Corporation; Vienna, VA

The Ruth and Marvin Sackner Archives; Miami Beach, FL

Amnesty International; Washington, DC

The George Washington University; Washington, DC

University of Maryland; College Park, MD

Howrey and Simon; Washington, DC

Fannie Mae Organization; Washington, DC

American University; Washington, DC

Art in Embassy Program

SELECTED GROUP EXHIBITIONS

2017 "Being Sentient/Sentient Being," 18th Annual Wills Creek Exhibition at Allegany Arts Council; juror, Aneta Georgievksa-Shine; Cumberland, MD

2017 "Drawn From: 15 Years of Exhibitions at the Luther W. Brady Art Gallery," The Luther W. Brady Art Gallery at George Washington University; Washington, DC

2016 "MAP 35th Anniversary Exhibition," Maryland Art Place, Baltimore, MD

2016 "Making Sense: See, Smell, Hear, Taste, Touch," McLean Project for the Arts; juror, Nora Atkinson; McLean, VA

2015-2016 "Micro-Monuments," Presented by the Washington Sculptors Group, Salzlandmuseum; Schönebeck, Germany and the Center for Hellenic Studies; Washington, DC

2015 "Transformer 12th Annual Silent Auction," Katzen Arts Center at American University; Washington, DC

2015 "Rain or Shine: Art in Nature, Nature in Art," The Luther W. Brady Art Gallery at George Washington University; Washington, DC

2015 "Cosmos at the Cosmos," The Cosmos Club; curator, Lenore Miller; Washington, DC

2015 "Alchemical Vessels," Smith Center for Healing and the Arts; Washington, DC

2014 "Sculpture Now 2014 - 30th Anniversary, Washington Sculptors Group"; American University Museum at the Katzen Arts Center; curator, Jack Rasmussen; Washington, DC

2014 "Survival," Cosmos Club, Washington, DC

2014 "Washington Color Abstraction," The Gabarron Foundation; curator, Donald Kuspit; New York, NY

2013 "Fall for the Arts," The Katzen Arts Center at American University; Washington, DC

2013 "Washington Art Matters," The Katzen Arts Center at American University; Washington, DC

2013 "Alchemical Vessels," Smith Center for Healing and the Arts; Washington, DC

2012 "Signals," DC Arts Center; curator: J.W. Mahoney; Washington, DC

2012 "Fall for the Arts," The Katzen Arts Center at American University; Washington, DC

2012 "Select 2012," Washington Project for the Arts; Washington, DC

2011 National Museum of Women in the Arts; Washington, DC

2011 "Catalyst"; Washington Project for the Arts, American University; curator: J.W. Mahoney; Washington, DC

2010 Juried "Call for Artists Show"; BlackRock Center for the Arts, Germantown, MD

2010 "Gaps"; Greater Reston Art Center; curator: Vesela Sretenovic, Reston, VA

2010 "Cream"; Washington Project for the Arts; curator: Mera Rubbell, The American University; Washington, DC

2008 "Personal Geometry"; Emerson Gallery; Mclean, VA

2007 "Washington Women in the Arts: A Selection"; Osuna Gallery; Washington, DC

2006 "On the Verge"; American Center for Physics; College Park, MD

2006 "Pulse 2006"; Hillyer Art Space; Washington, DC

2005 "Faces of the Fallen"; Women's Military Museum; Arlington, VA

2004 Chautauqua Institute; Chautauqua, NY

2003 Chautauqua Institute; Chautauqua, NY

2002 Chautauqua Institute; Chautauqua, NY

2002 "Math=Art"; Frostburg College; Frostburg, MD

2001/2002 Anton Gallery; Washington, DC

2000 American University; Vaughn Associate; New York, NY

1999 "International Visions"; Artists for Amnesty International; Washington, DC

1999 Emerson Gallery; McLean, VA

1997 "Flowers"; Osuna Gallery; Washington, DC

1997 Auction; Corcoran Gallery of Art; Washington, DC

1997 Maryland Art Place; Baltimore, MD

1995 "Three Visions"; Washington Project for the Arts; Washington, DC

1995 "Artist to Artist"; Rock Creek Gallery; Washington, DC

1995 AFTA: Embassy of Federal Republic of Germany; Washington, DC

1995 "Collaboration at its Best"; George Mason University; Fairfax, VA

1995 "Portraits"; The George Washington University; Washington, DC

1995 "Prints 1995"; Baltimore Museum of Art; Baltimore, MD

1984-1994 Auction; Washington Project for the Arts; Washington, DC

1994 A New Nature"; Emerson Gallery; McLean, VA

1993 "Cryptics"; School 33; Baltimore, MD

1993 "NNDG"; Emerson Gallery; McLean, VA

1992 St. John's College; Collegeville, MN

1992 "Alumni"; Corcoran Gallery of Art; Washington, DC

1992 "WPA Show"; Corcoran Gallery of Art; Washington, DC

1991 "The Critic's Choice"; Watkins Gallery, The American University; Washington, DC

1991 "Collector's Favorites"; RAP; Rockville, MD

1991 "Washington Print Show"; Brody Gallery/ Gallery K; Washington, DC

1990 "Moscow/Washington, DC Exchange"; Moscow, USSR

1990 "Art Against AIDS"; Washington Projects Arts; Washington, DC

1990 "Metaphoric Messages"; Strathmore Hall Arts Center; Rockville, MD

1990 Rockville Arts Place; Rockville, MD

1989 "Select Auction"; Washington Projects Arts; Washington, DC

1988 "Four Sculptors"; Washington Square; Washington, DC

1987 "Sculpture"; Georgetown-Omni Hotel; Washington, DC

1987 "Paintings and Sculptures"; Osuna Gallery; Washington, DC

1987 "Figurative Show"; Washington Square; Washington, DC

1986 Driscoll Gallery; Denver, CO

1986 "Art and Function"; Painted sculpture; Washington Square; Washington, DC

1986 "Select Sculpture"; G. Sander Fine Art Gallery; Daytona Beach, FL

1986 "Disquieting Figure"; Osuna Gallery; Washington, DC

1986 "Garden of Earthly Delights"; Gallery Ten; Washington, DC

1985 "Artists' Self Portrait"; Jane Haslem Gallery; Washington, DC

1985 "The Washington Show"; Corcoran Gallery of Art; Washington, DC

1984 "Washington Galleries"; Strathmore Hall Arts Center; Washington, DC

1982 "Summer Exhibit"; Osuna Gallery; Washington, DC

1981 "Hanover Place"; Osuna Gallery; Washington, DC

1981 "OPTIONS '81"; Washington Project for the Arts; Washington, DC

1977 "Summertime"; Pyramid Gallery; Washington, DC

1976 "Summer Exhibit"; Pyramid Gallery; Washington, DC

SELECTED ESSAYS AND REVIEWS

Reading Eagle, "Reading Public Museum brings sculpture outside," Ron Devlin; October 14, 2017

Vineyard Gazette, "Finding Herself Through Art, Guided by Intuition," August 3, 2017

ArtfixDaily, "Frost Museum Explores the Metaphysical Relationship Between the Arts, Science and Nature," April 18, 2017

eGlobal Travel Media, "Tangled Up in Supernatural Realms," April 10, 2017

Art Daily, "Nature, science, and art intertwine at the Patricia & Phillip Frost Art Museum FIU," April 8, 2017

SciArt Magazine, "REVIEW: Tangled Nature at the Frost Art Museum," Betty Milonas; March 28, 2017

FIU News, "Frost super-murals a collaboration of hundreds," Gisela Valencia; March 20, 2017

The Washington Post, "In the galleries: 'Micro-Monuments' that take on a global perspective," Mark Jenkins; September 24, 2016

The Washington Post, "In the galleries: Carol Brown Goldberg," Mark Jenkins; April 1, 2016

Feature: *DC Modern Luxury*, "Paradise Found," by Holly Mazar-Fox, March 2016

Interview: *Open Prairie*, "Carol Brown Goldberg: A Personal Journey;" Leda Cempellin, 2015

Interview: *Juliet Art Magazine*, "Carol Brown Goldberg: A Personal Journey;" Leda Cempellin, October – November, 2015

Montclair State University, "New Sculpture on Campus by Artist Carol Brown Goldberg;" August 17, 2015

The Washington Post, "In the galleries: Carol Brown Goldberg," Mark Jenkins; August 14, 2015

MV Times; "An Arresting Display at A Gallery," Gwyn MacAllister; August 12, 2015

MV Times; "Chilmark," Valerie Sonnenthal; February 12, 2015

SpaceCoastDaily.com, "Carol Brown Goldberg Sculptures Coming To Foosaner," Adam Lowenstein, September 14, 2014

The Washington Post; "Sculpture gives a nod to nature," Mark Jenkins; November 30, 2014

VeroNews; "Two shows feature works of Carol Brown Goldberg," Ellen Fischer; September 11, 2014

"Artist? The Hypothesis of Bodiness," by Fre Ilgen; 2014

Reading Eagle; "'The Circle of Time' expands abstraction," Ron Schira; December 1, 2013

Vineyard Gazette; "Chilmark," Janie Slater; November 8, 2013

Arts & Ideas Magazine; "Artist Profile; Carol Brown Goldberg," Summer 2013

"Washington Art Matters: Art and Life in the Capital 1940-1990," by Jean Lawlor Cohen, Sidney Lawrence, Elizabeth Tebow; 2013

The Huffington Post; "Haiku Reviews: From Atmospheric Abstractions To Semi-Operas," Peter Frank; June 12, 2013

The Washington Post; "Coded messages, big and bold," Michael O'Sullivan; June 7, 2013

Where Magazine; "The D.C. Eight," Jean Lawlor Cohen; May 2013

The Washington Post; "Space and light, right on the dot," Mark Jenkins; January 4, 2013

The Washington Post; "Critic Review for Carol Brown Goldberg," Michael O'Sullivan; December 21, 2012

The Washington Post; "Museum keeps things fresh this fall," Michael O'Sullivan; November 23, 2012

The Washington Post; "'Signals' shows there's plenty going on in the Washington art scene," Mark Jenkins; November 9, 2012

The Washington Post; "Gallery Opening of the Week," Michael O'Sullivan; October 12, 2012

GW Today; "Artist Creates Outdoor Sculpture for University;" Julia Parmley; September 14, 2012

Catalogue Cover; "Art Sante Fe," July 2012

The Washington Post; "Carol Brown Goldberg," Mark Jenkins; April 2012

Essay: in "Carol Brown Goldberg; Sculpture and Works on Paper," Meanders by Christopher Addison, The George Washington University, 2012

The Washington Post; "A Viewpoint; Women Making Sculpture," Michael O'Sullivan; November 2011

Washingtonian; "Take a Look at That!" Kathleen Bridges, October 2011

The Montclair Patch; "The Cosmic Everyday: Carol Brown Goldberg – Painting and Sculpture," Carol Selman, October 2011

"Essay: in Carol Brown Goldberg; Painting and Sculpture." The Transpersonal and the Personal" by Donald Kuspit, George Segal Gallery, 2011

"Interview: in Carol Brown Goldberg Painting and Sculpture. Thinking With Things with Glenn Harper," George Segal Gallery, 2011

La Crónica de Hoy; "Mi pintura busca plasmar la evolución del tiempo: Carol Brown;" *Juan Carlos Talavera*; February 27, 2010 (Culturas)

The Washington Post; "Churning through D.C.'s studios to find the 'Cream'"; Jessica Dawson; December 18, 2009 (Style C1)

Valley News; "Physics Inspires the Paintings of the Renowned Artist Carol Brown Goldberg; Show Opens in January"; December 16, 2009

El Norte; "Integran en expo luz, ciencia y color"; November 18, 2009

El Norte; "Une arte y ciencia," Abraham Vázquez; October 29, 2009 (VIDA 13)

El Norte; "El caos y la belleza," Guadalupe Loaeza; October 10, 2009

ABC; "Una opción por lo Bello," María Candela; August 8, 2009

Que.es; "La Casa de Vacas se abre a los colores y círculos cósmicos de Carol Brown Goldberg"; August 4, 2009

The Gazette; "Science, Spirit Combine in Works by Carol Brown Goldberg," Claudia Rousseau; July 1, 2009

La Opinión; "Carol Brown muestra en Murcia su passion por la física y el Universo," A. Guardiola; June 18, 2009 (46)

Elfaro; "Carol Brown reivindica la física del arte abstracto con su polícroma 'Obra Reciente,'" María

Astilleros; June 18, 2009 (Cultura 28)

La Verdad; "Carol Brown llena Los Molinos del Rió de miles de cristales pulverizados;" June 18, 2009 (54)

El Mundo, Valladolid; "Carol Brown exhibe su abstración geométrica y luminiscente en la Fundación

Gabarrón;" October 8, 2008, no. 6.869

El Día de Valladolid; "Geometría abstracta del orden y el caos," Daniel G. Rojo; October 8, 2008, no. 3.017

El Norte de Castilla; "Orden musical," María Aurora Viloria; October 8, 2008, 152:59.018

ABC, Premios Gabarrón; "Brown Goldberg: La nueva abstracción," H. Díaz; October 10, 2008

Shift: At The Frontiers Of Consciousness; Institute of Noetic Sciences; "Endpoint," September – November, 2008

Art in America; "Report from Washington DC: To a Different Drum," J.W. Mahoney; May 2008 (94-98)

Carol Brown Goldberg. "The Shape of Time by Barbara Rose," 2007

Carol Brown Goldberg. "Afterword" by Jack Rasmussen, 2007

Carol Brown Goldberg. "Reinventing Aura: Carol Brown Goldberg's Abstract Paintings by Donald Kuspit," 2007

The Washington Post; "Sunday Source Pick of the Week"; September 3, 2006

Essay: "Painting as Meditation" by Barbara Rose, 2005

Wingspan; Cheyenne, Wyoming; Sept. 22, 2003-"Abstract Artist to Show 9-11 Thoughts"

Montgomery County Gazette; March 10, 2000-Bernice August- "Portrait of an Artist Writing from the Heart" by Nancy Slonum Aronie, Hyperion Press, New York, February, 1998

George Washington Magazine; Winter 1996; Paul Claussen; "George Washington and the Mystery of the Fifty Missing Shares"

City Paper; August 18, 1995-Martha McWilliams; "George Washington... Past and Present"

The Washington Post Weekend; June 30, 1995, Hank Burchard; "Washington Crossing the Spectrum"

University of Maryland; Undergraduate Program, Summer 1994; Maryland Artists Collection

Baltimore Alternative; October, 1993, Cecelia Meisner; "Patterns of Harmony and Anguish"

Baltimore Sun Newspaper; October 9, 1993, John Dorsey

Baltimore Magazine; September/ October, 1993- "At the Galleries"

The Baltimore Sun; May 12, 1993, John Dorsey

The Baltimore City Paper; May 4, 1993, Mike Giuliano, "Cracking the Codes"

Art in America; July, 1992, J.W. Mahoney - "Carol Goldberg"

The Washington Review; April/May, 1992, Mokha Laget, "New Works on Paper"

The Washington Post; February 8, 1992, Michael Welzenbach

The Washington Post; October 6, 1990, Michael Welzenbach

The New Art Examiner Magazine; March, 1990, Jane Addams Allen

The Washington Times; January 4, 1990, Alice Thorson; "Exhibits Redefine Washington's Art Identity"

The Chevy Chase Gazette; December 14, 1989, Ruth Palombo; "Artist Blends Physics with Chaos-Pastel Paintings"

Eyewash; December 1989, Ellen Gordon Gordon, "Carol Goldberg"

The Washington Post, December 2, 1989, Michael Welzenbach, "Goldberg at Osuna"

The Washington Post Magazine; December 15, 1988, Jura Koncius; Taking a Bough; "Artists Deck Their Halls"

Museum and Arts Magazine; September, October, 1988, A.J. Loftin

New Art Examiner; June, 1988, M. Laget

New Art Examiner; Art Review, Paul Bowman, 1987

Tokyo, Japan's La Seine, August 1987, "Three Women of Washington, DC"

Roanoke Times & World News; April 19, 1987, Ann Weinstein

Virginia Tech Collegiate Times; April 14, 1987, Andy Cohell and Terrie Gabriel

Hill Rag; March 4-18, 1987, Cover

Washington Review; Dec/Jan, 1986-1987, Roz Kuehn, Art & Function

Hill Rag; July 2-15, Cover

New Art Examiner; Summer, 1986, J. W. Mahoney, Washington, DC, "Carol Goldberg"

The Montgomery Journal, June 6, 1986, Linda Waters

The Washington Post; May 17, 1986, Jo Ann Lewis, "Goldberg's Winter Wonderland"

The Washington Times; May 8, 1986, Michael Welzenbach, "Goldberg's Cutout Celebrate Joy of Color"

The Washington Post Magazine; December 8, 1985, Paul Feinberg, "Artist's Fantasies"

The Washington Times; June 20, 1985, Michael Welzenbach

Volusia Magazine; June 2, 1985, Cover

Daytona Beach Journal; May 28, 1985, Sharon O'Neill

The Washington Post Magazine; February 8, 1985, Joan Nathan

New Art Examiner; October, 1984

The Washington Post; September, 1983, Chuck Lonconi

The Washington Post; April 29, 1982, Jo Ann Lewis

The Washington Star; April 20, 1982, Ben Forgey; "Dynamite Show of 'OPTIONS' at Washington Project for the Arts"

The Washington Post; July 16, 1976, Jo Ann Lewis

TEACHING

2009	Adjunct Professor of Art; University of Maryland; College Park, MD
2005-1998	Adjunct Professor of Art; American University; Washington, DC
2002-1998	Chatauqua Institution; Chautaqua, NY

EDUCATION

1976	BFA, Corcoran School of Art, Washington, DC
1964	Graduate studies; University of Maryland, College Park, MD
1962	Bachelor of Arts; University of Maryland, College Park, MD

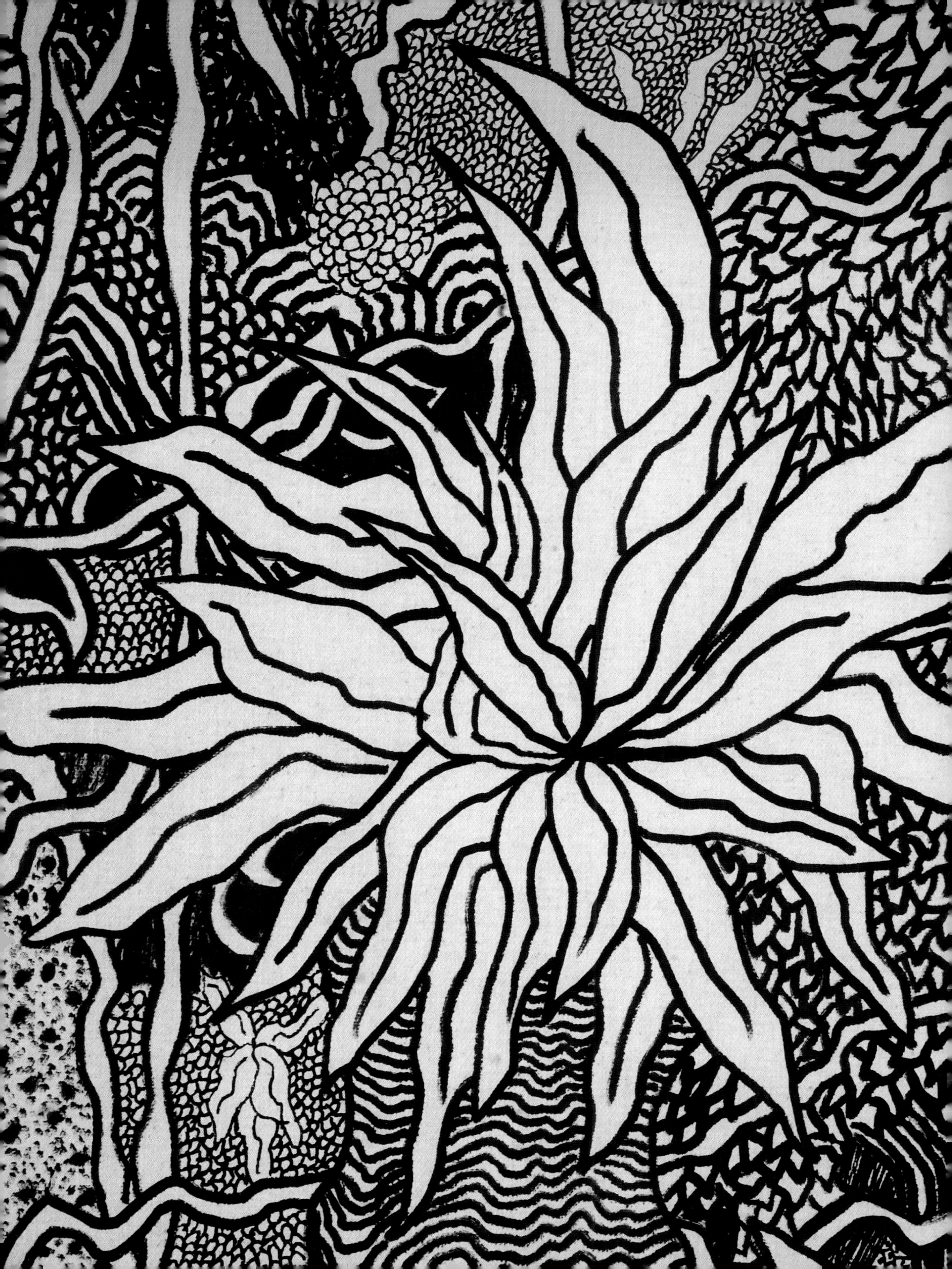

Special Thanks

Jordana Pomeroy
Klaudio Rodriguez
Christopher Addison
Romy Silverstein
Ramon Osuna
Tanya Augostinos
David Furchgott
Greg Staley
Frank Adams
Chandi Kelley
Chas Colburn
Robert M. Mattison
Jack Rasmussen
Dorothy Kosinski
Klaus Ottmann

Extra special thanks to
Hank Goldberg
whose love and support
is ever present.

In memory of
Trish Vradenberg.

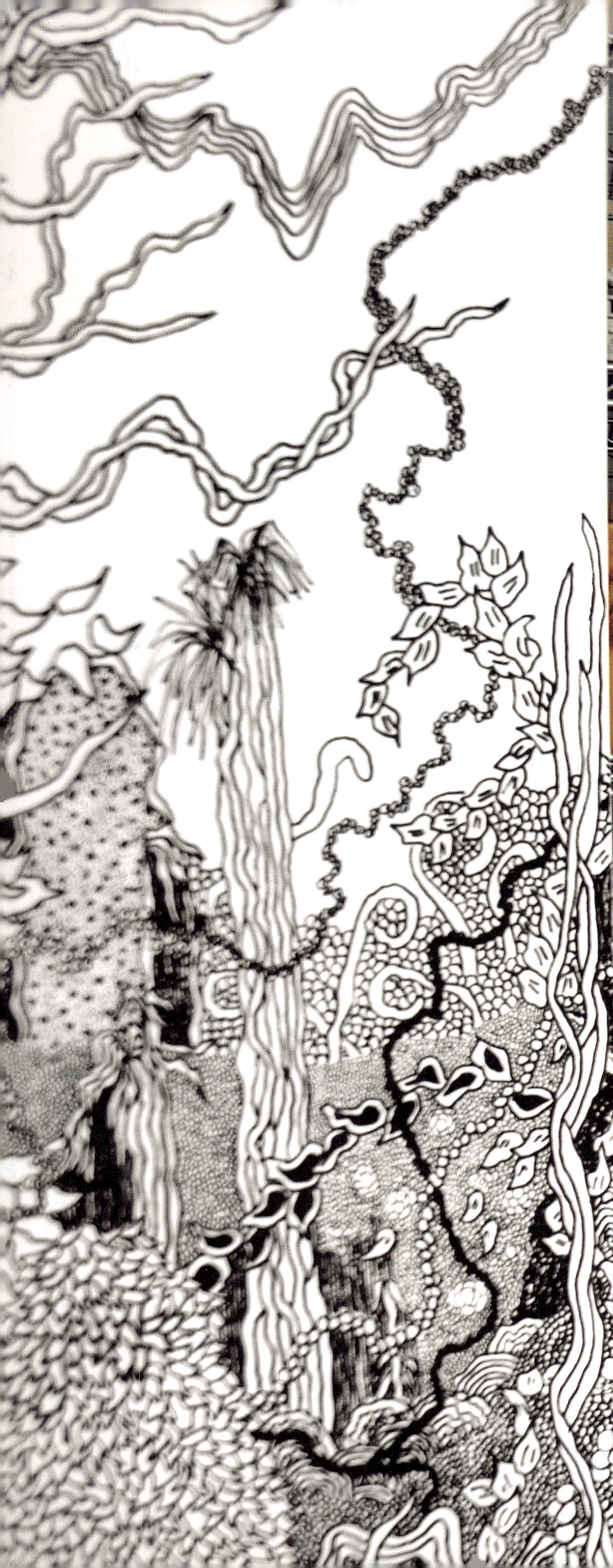

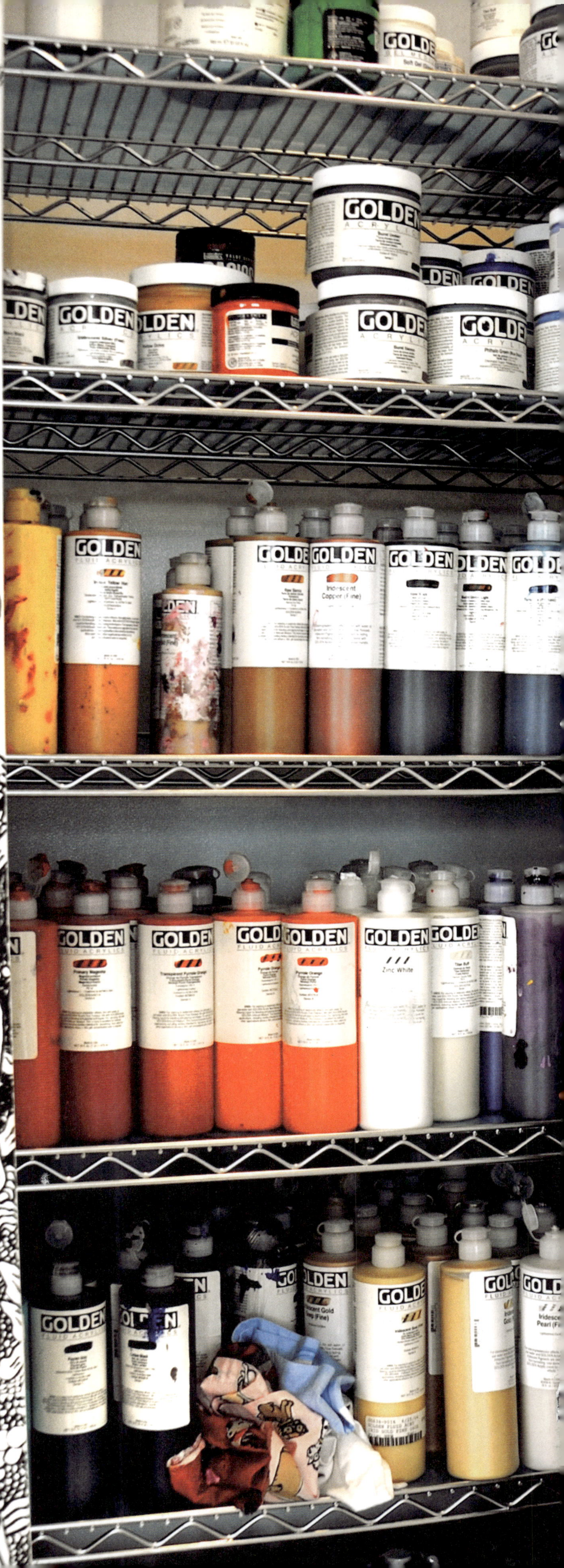
GOLDEN
Zinc White